Responsible Management of Information Systems

Bernd Carsten Stahl
De Montfort University, UK

IDEA GROUP PUBLISHING
Hershey • London • Melbourne • Singapore

Acquisitions Editor:	Mehdi Khosrow-Pour
Senior Managing Editor:	Jan Travers
Managing Editor:	Amanda Appicello
Development Editor:	Michele Rossi
Copy Editor:	Maria Boyer
Typesetter:	Sara Reed
Cover Design:	Lisa Tosheff
Printed at:	Yurchak Printing Inc.

Published in the United States of America by
Idea Group Publishing (an imprint of Idea Group Inc.)
701 E. Chocolate Avenue
Hershey PA 17033
Tel: 717-533-8845
Fax: 717-533-8661
E-mail: cust@idea-group.com
Web site: http://www.idea-group.com

and in the United Kingdom by
Idea Group Publishing (an imprint of Idea Group Inc.)
3 Henrietta Street
Covent Garden
London WC2E 8LU
Tel: 44 20 7240 0856
Fax: 44 20 7379 3313
Web site: http://www.eurospan.co.uk

Library of Congress Cataloging-in-Publication Data

Stahl, Bernd, 1968-
 Responsible management of information systems / Bernd Stahl.
   p. cm.
Includes bibliographical references.
 ISBN 1-59140-172-0 (hardcover) — ISBN 1-59140-282-4 (softcover)–
 ISBN 1-59140-173-9 (ebook)
 1. Information technology—Management. 2. Information
technology—Moral and ethical aspects. 3. Information resources
management—Moral and ethical aspects. 4. Business ethics. 5. Social
responsibility of business. I. Title.
 HD30.2.S77 2004
 658.4'028—dc21
                         2003008877

British Cataloguing in Publication Data
A Cataloguing in Publication record for this book is available from the British Library.

All work contributed to this book is new, previously-unpublished material. The views expressed in this book are those of the authors, but not necessarily of the publisher.

Responsible Management of Information Systems

Table of Contents

Chapter IV.
The Theory of Responsibility and Information Systems 44

Chapter V.
Reflective Responsibility 117

Preface

In order to survive and prosper, almost every business in our global economy has to make use of new and evolving information technologies. This starts with the local baker who needs a telephone to be able to contact his suppliers or customers, and ends with the international virtual Internet business that exists solely in virtual reality. The use of information technology affects many aspects of our private and business life. It leads to changes in routines, new ways of understanding our environment, new distributions of power, money, and influence. The changes are sufficiently severe to warrant speaking of a new technological revolution. Like every other revolution this one will produce winners and losers, proponents and opponents. Whatever else one may think of this development, it is hard to deny that it is ethically relevant. Old forms of morality seem to lose their validity while new ways of communicating and living together emerge.

The strongest motor of these developments seems to be the economic system. Especially the impact of economic interests on the Internet is an indication of this. The Internet, introduced by the U.S. military and subsequently used mainly for scientific exchange of data has, in the last few years become a major application for all sorts of businesses. This has met the resistance of many old users of the Net, but the economic interests appear to outweigh these by far. The theoretical advantages of the Internet for businesses, the decrease of transaction costs, the incredible market reach, the unknown possibilities of communicating and interacting with all sorts of business partners have propelled the Internet and its related technologies to the top space in the interest of businesses. A sign of the economy's enthusiasm for the Internet was the dot.com bubble. Even after the bubble burst, however, the economic promises of new information technologies seem stunning.

Economic interest in the new technologies will most probably not change in the near future, and it is a safe bet that the economy will increase its drive towards new technologies. It is just as safe a bet that this will aggravate existing moral problems and at the same time create new ones. The purpose of this book is therefore to analyse the ethical and moral questions that new technologies and especially their use in businesses and the economy produce. As the central concept of this discussion, this book will use the notion of responsibility. Responsibility is a term especially suited for the job of discussing ethical questions in business and technology. There are several structural similarities between the three terms responsibility, business, and technology. Also, the acceptance of responsibility in business as well as in technological settings allows analyses that might otherwise be resented by the affected persons. Managers and technical personnel often react negatively to moral claims because they do not feel that their work is subject to ethical scrutiny. On the other hand, every manager and every technician will agree that he or she has responsibilities.

We will therefore start this book by defining the concepts of information systems and business information technology. The term "information systems" is used in the academic world to denote the intersection of ICT and social entities, usually companies or other formal organisations. Information systems research tends to focus on the social impact of technology or the influence the social has on the use of technology. Academic information systems departments are often located in schools of business which is a good indicator that they are well-positioned to address the different aspects of the social, the ethical, and the technical that are at the heart of this book. The connection between these aspects can most easily be made by analysing the underlying concepts of business, information, and technology, which are combined in information systems.

Following this initial introduction to the subject area, we will then proceed to give an introduction to normative problems by contrasting the terms 'ethics' and 'morality' in the light of different philosophical traditions. On the basis of the understanding of normative questions developed in this chapter, we will then investigate why responsibility is a concept that seems to offer solutions to ethical and moral problems of business information technology.

A subsequent deeper analysis of the concept of responsibility will show, however, that there are severe problems with the application of responsibility to concrete questions in information systems. Based on this analysis we will then develop a reflective notion of responsibility that emphasises the communicational character of the ascription that constitutes responsibility. It also takes seriously the openness, teleology, and consequentialism of responsibility and asks what is responsible about the use of the concept of responsibility. In a final section we will use this reflective notion of responsibility and apply it to business information technology using the important problem of privacy and employee surveillance as an example. It will be shown that responsibility is an inevitable fact of the business use of IT and that the reflective turn of the concept can offer solutions where a traditional approach to responsibility fails.

At this stage it is probably useful to add a few words on the content, scope, and readership of the book. Most people who live in the information society, meaning in western market economies, have encountered moral problems caused by the use of ICT. Many of us will be aware that the changes of the structure in society and business triggered by ICT can have ethical implications. We all know the concept of responsibility, and many of us may be wondering what it means to be responsible with regards to ICT or information systems. In this sense the readership of the book potentially encompasses most of the citizens of the modern world. In a more confined sense, the book will probably be of interest specifically to those people who have an interest in information systems and more specifically in the ethical side of them. This would include academics, be it students or teachers, who are active in the areas of computer ethics, information ethics, etc. It should also be of interest to information systems practitioners who are faced with the ethical impacts of the use of ICT.

To those potential readers who are looking for quick solutions or clear instructions on how to be responsible, a caveat should be added. This book attempts to develop a well-grounded theory of responsibility that is based on the philosophical discourse about ethics. Given that this discourse in its academic form is already 2,500 years old, and that beyond that it is part of every human's experience, it will not be possible to condense this into clear algorithms. The subject of ethics has proven to be highly resistant to unified approaches, and no universally accepted ethical principle exists. This book attempts to use this moral plurality as a starting point and uses the inevitability of responsibility ascriptions as an argument for suggestions on which action can be based despite their fallibility. The idea is thus to produce a theory of responsibility that can live up to philosophical scrutiny, and that can at the same time give indications as to how individuals could or should act. Due to this aim of theoretical and philosophical acceptability, the level of discussion always remains above the level of action. The theory of reflective responsibility developed in this book cannot tell us what to do, but it tries to tell us how we can find out what the responsible thing to do is.

This approach may lead to frustration by those readers who expect quick fixes and easy answers. Unfortunately, however, quick fixes and easy answers are not part of what ethics is about, and they are not to be expected with regards to normative problems. While the book will ideally be eminently practical in that it allows the reader to develop a new perspective on responsibility and consequently new forms of actions and their justifications, it is not practical in the sense of a "how to…" book. On the other hand, information systems is a practical discipline that addresses problems of ICT as they arise in organisational practice. In order to cater to this practicality of the subject area, the book works with a number of examples. These examples are meant to demonstrate what problems can be and how, according to the theory of reflective responsibility, they can be addressed. The reader will hopefully find that walking the tightrope of theoretical stringency on the one hand and practical applicability and understandability on the other has been achieved to his or her advantage.

Acknowledgments

This book started out as an attempt to clarify what it means to be responsible, to act responsibly, to have responsibility. While this is a complex endeavour in itself, it was further complicated by the concentration on the concept of responsibility in business on the one hand, and in information and communication technology on the other. As is probably the case in most academic endeavours, this one became more complicated the more research I did. Most of us seem to assume that certain people should act responsibly, that responsibility is necessary and that the world at large suffers from a lack of responsibility. But the more closely one looks at these statements, the less clear they become. An additional difficulty was that the topic of this book covers several academic disciplines or sub-disciplines and touches on a large number of academic and practical areas and topics. Furthermore, the popularity of the subject, the fact that everybody knows something about responsibility, made it hard to delimit the content of the book.

I would therefore like to thank Birger Priddat, whose research assistant I was at the time when I started work on this project, for helping me focus and for showing me some of the more interesting and worthwhile aspects of economic theory. The interaction with my colleagues at the University Witten/Herdecke, as well as with other researchers engaged in the German discourse on business ethics, helped me appreciate the prevalent topics and also recognise their limitations. Furthermore, I would like to thank Dirk Rustemeyer for keeping me on the track of philosophical thinking and for showing me the dangers of becoming overly prescriptive.

The theory of responsibility developed in this book had taken on a somewhat manifest form when I started to work in the Department of MIS of University College Dublin. It was there that I recognised the value of applying the theory to the area of information systems. On the one hand this allowed a concentration on manifest questions. On the other hand it required incorporating another body of literature on computer ethics, information ethics, Internet ethics, etc. However, it turned out that these writings were in fact quite well compatible with my idea of responsibility and provided a great field of application. During my time in Dublin, I was also put back into closer contact with the academic field of information systems. I would like to thank my colleagues in the MIS Department as well as my colleagues in the German Department for their support and guidance. The German Academic Exchange Service (DAAD) deserves my gratitude for facilitating the three-year stay in Dublin. My particular appreciation has to be extended to Anita Mangan, whose efforts and comments not only enriched the content of this book, but who has played a central part in rendering it understandable.

Furthermore, I want to thank my parents for their continuing moral and financial support, which allowed me to undertake the travels and adventures which led to this book. My wife Barbara, who moved with me from country to country, accepted the fact that academics do not always work the same hours as most other people, and still extended her loving encouragement, which helped me through this work. Finally, there is my son Carl Alexander, who, at this stage in life, does not yet know the difference between good and bad. I hope that when the time comes when he, too, wonders what it means to be responsible, this book will guide him part of the way.

Chapter I

Information Systems and Business Information Technology

This first content chapter of the book is meant to clarify the notions involved in the responsible management of information systems. The focus of this book is the concept of reflective responsibility, which will be developed in the subsequent chapters. However, the application of this theory will be the area of information systems. In order to develop what responsibility means in the context of information systems, we will therefore have to define the notion. This is not an easy task, as "information system" can mean many things. On the one hand there is the academic discipline, sometimes called information systems, computer information systems, management information systems, etc., and on the other hand there is the physical artefact. This artefact, be it a computer, a network, or some other type of ICT, becomes an information system by being used in social settings. Information systems have been defined as "an amalgam of hardware, software, procedures, and activities" (Lyytinen & Hirschheim, 1988, p. 19). This chapter will use another route to introduce the concept of information systems. It will look at three of the constitutive aspects of information systems, namely at business, information, and technology. By analysing these three terms and their composition, it will show what information systems are, and more importantly, why the theory of reflective responsibility is a promising approach to addressing the normative problems raised by them.

Most of us have a pre-theoretical idea what the terms "business," "information," and "technology" mean. It is useful to analyse them with academic stringency, however, because the initial meaning we attach to the terms may be less than clear and it may not be inter-subjectively valid. Some of the ethical problems that seem to resist solution can be explained by a lack of attention to details and definitions. While ethical problems usually cannot be confined to mere semantics, one thing a scholar can do is try to clarify the concepts involved and thereby help structure the discussion and clear up misunderstandings. Apart from trying to do this, the following discussion of the basic concepts also aims to live up to philosophical standards. Philosophy is often defined as the art or the science of language and its use. Philosophers have recognised early that clarity of language and notions is a necessary precondition for the successful solution of theoretical and practical problems. In the context of this text, that means that one should start by defining the terms "business," "information," and "technology."

BUSINESS

The term "business information technology" comprises three words, each of which deserves a short explanation before we look at the combination. "Business" denotes the production and trade of goods and services. It contains several aspects that will gain importance in the course of this argument.

Firstly, there are the two aspects of theory and practice. At first sight business seems to be an eminently practical concept since it deals with real-life facts and figures. It results in real changes in everybody's life. On the other hand there is the theory of business as taught in schools and universities. A book such as this one is obviously mainly focused on theory since it is a part of it. The relationship of theory and practice is a complicated one and in many cases difficult to determine. Especially in business the perception is usually that practice is the prevalent reality whereas theory is there to describe this reality. Theory can be legitimately used to predict some aspects of this reality and to teach newcomers to the field how to behave in it. Many students, but also teachers, would subscribe to this view of theory and practice in business.

However, this distinction of theory and practice is not sufficient. Firstly, theory is a part of the real world. That means that the theoretician is not a mere observer, but has to know practice to describe it. On the other hand, the practitioner always needs some kind of theory to be able to orient herself in her business world and to make adequate decisions.

It is not only simplistic to say that economic theory describes economic reality, but in fact the relationship often works the other way around. Theory can create attention for reality and it can even create reality.

"...economic theory may affect people's conception of the world—their picture of what is acceptable and rational behaviour in their relations to consumer goods as well as to other people, their picture of how various segments of society function as well as of how they should function, their picture of on basis of what kind of information decisions should be made, et cetera" (Helgesson, 1998, p. 54).

We will return to the question of how theory shapes reality because the perception of reality has an obvious impact on the perception of duties, morality, and finally responsibility. For now it should suffice to keep in mind that we should not let ourselves be trapped by the simplistic version of theory and practice.

A further aspect of the term business is the economic level of magnitude. We distinguish between microeconomics and macroeconomics. The first term deals with single economic subjects and the second one with the political economy and society. "Business" usually stands for a meso-level, a level in between the two, namely the level of the company. People doing business studies tend to be interested in practices and procedures that are relevant for the working of a company or, more generally, of an organisation. However, an organisation cannot exist without the individuals as economic subjects who constitute it, and at the same time it is in many ways determined by the societal settings and institutions. Therefore we shall have to consider more than just the level of the company when speaking of business. This is especially true in the case of responsibility, which always involves several dimensions, among them usually individuals, collective entities, and some aspects of society.

INFORMATION TECHNOLOGY

Information technology is a concept that has reached a level of ubiquity which makes it somewhat difficult to define clearly. We all associate many things with IT, from our TV set over the mobile phone that most of us carry by now, to faxes and computers, email, and the Internet. IT has the two roots of information and technology. Information is an entity that we all know something about, but it is hard to define. According to the *Encarta World English Dictionary* (1999, p. 963), information can have several meanings. Firstly, it stands for definite knowledge acquired or supplied about something or somebody. Secondly, it represents the process of gathering and collecting facts and data, and thirdly, it means that the facts and knowledge are made known and published. Finally, in terms of computers, information is contrasted with data, a difference one can often find in literature about IS. Data is usually understood as the brute facts, the way life is, whereas information is data in an organised form that is presented in an orderly and systematic fashion to clarify the underlying meaning. We can see right away that information has points of contact with a good many sensitive philosophic topics such as knowledge, truth, or meaning. Also, it is a rather intangible asset whose properties of being "human, expandable, compressible, substitutable, transportable, diffusive, and shareable" (Cleveland, quoted in Mason, Mason, & Culnan, 1995, p. 41) do not really make description and handling much easier.

Technology, on the other hand, seems easier to manage. Technology is associated with machines, artefacts, with the multitude of things we can use to make our lives easier. However, there is more to technology than just physical objects. Gethmann and Gethmann-Siefert (1996, p. VI) suggest the category of action as a definition, more specifically of action based on objects. While this definition stresses the role of the individual there are others who emphasise the importance of the community, society, and interaction. Rayner (1993, p. 216) suggests a definition of technologies as social systems that are mediated by material and devices. The attempt to combine these approaches can be found in Ropohl's definition where technology comprises utilizable artificial objects, human actions and organizations used to produce these objects, and human actions that make use of them (Ropohl, 1996, p. 84).

There is another view of technology that completely neglects the object side, the artefact. In this view what is relevant about technology is the inherent rationality. For Rapp (1994, p. 19) the most natural definition of technology is that of a certain *modus operandi*, a specific method used to accomplish a given objective. This idea of technology as a relationship of ends and means can frequently be found in the philosophy of technology. Usually the ends are assumed as given and technology is seen as the means of attaining them. A radical example of this is the fact that according to Jonas (1987, p. 164), all technology serves the utility of a user.

Technology's character as a means combined with the supposition of a certain sort of rationality led us to another important property of technology. It can be demonstrated that technology, already in antiquity, was no aimless trial-and-error use of natural objects, but intentional planning according to a design (Breil, 1993, p. 208). The success of this use depended strongly on the quality of knowledge. Thus it is one characteristic of technology to be closely linked to science. This relationship of science and technology can be found in the earliest modern definitions of technology (Beckmann, 1777) up to modern definitions in the context of IT. "Technology is applied science, the use of a discovery in order to find a better tool to make life easier, safer, or better. As science asks 'why?' technology asks 'how?'" (Hauptman, 1999, p. 3). While the direct relationship between science and technology is a simplification of reality (technology is much older than modern experimental science (Lenk, 1994, p. 22)), it is nevertheless useful because it shows the close link between theory and practice that is as constitutive for technology as it was for business.

Apart from these rather abstract attempts to describe the nature and meaning of the term technology, there are some obvious feedbacks to most aspects of life. Technology not only compensates man's shortcomings and produces a certain sort of rationality; it is the driving force behind our modern world (Mittelstraß, 1996, p. 4). The ubiquity and importance of technology have led to the development of several philosophical disciplines that try to deal with the complexity of the topic.

Information technology, to return to our question of interest, is the combination of the concepts of information and technology. In this section it was demonstrated that neither of the two terms is simple and clear-cut. The combination is even less so. The general use of the term "IT" is connected with classical definitions such as, "Information technology is the tangible means by which information is manipulated and carried to its ultimate users" (Mason et al., 1995, p. 80). Often one finds even narrower definitions of information technology, i.e., IT understood as those technologies whose basis are digital switches and microelectronics (Zerdick et al., 2001, p. 111). After all we have seen so far, it is obvious that these definitions are too narrow. Information as well as technology are notions that are fundamentally social and complex. Their combination in "information technology" has to reflect that and cannot be confined to the object side. Even though the object side plays an important part and IT would cease to exist without it, the exclusive concentration on artefacts can lead to many problems, some of which will be discussed later on in this book. Also, information technology is caught up in the complex relationship of theory and practice, of science and application.

BUSINESS INFORMATION TECHNOLOGY

We have now discussed some of the central underlying concepts of information systems. Information systems tend to be based on technology, more specifically on information technology. One could argue that information systems do not necessarily require such a technological basis, but the academic discipline as well as business practice tend to refer to technical systems when they use the term. Information systems find their meaning in organisations, usually businesses; they are based on IT; and they develop their complexity because they are socio-technical systems. Why is it that information systems are of such central importance in business? One possible answer is that businesses are eminently dependent on information. Markets can be interpreted as the (theoretical) places where supply and demand meet. They are therefore subject to functioning exchange of information. Every step of the value chain of a business is dependent on information. On the other hand businesses are also directly linked to technology. Modern ways of production all need technology, and without technology the way we do business would not be possible. Technology also plays an important role in the theory of the economy, where it is used as a factor to explain growth. In fact, the impact of technology on business theory and practice are incalculable.

The concept of information systems is highly complex and warrants attention from different angles. Definitions of business information technology, such as "any activity using information technology which is undertaken by business" (cf. Langford, 2000, p. 227), may give a first orientation, but they are not really helpful because they do not even hint at the levels and aspects of what information systems stand for. Similar to the terms business, information, and technology on which it is based, information systems have a distinct theoretical and practical side to them, and also show relevant differences in their different levels of magnitude.

While it is hard to give a clear and precise definition of IS, it may help to look at their development to gain a better picture of the concept's meaning. Information systems serve a basic purpose, which is the pursuit of wealth, security, recreation, entertainment, and control. Simultaneously, they help avoid destitution, fear, uncertainty, boredom, depression, and chaos. This common root is too wide to be of any practical use in the discussion of the term, but it paves the way for an important argument that will be developed later on. It shows that an information system is not a value-free object, but is intrinsically linked to different conceptions of a good life. It is therefore subject to ethical discussion.

In a narrower interpretation the concept of IS stands for the attempt to use new technologies for the purposes of business. This perspective sees organisations as market driven and having to adapt constantly to the changes and contingencies of the external environment. Here, "IT is seen as a resource to be deployed according to the needs and pressures of that environment" (Scarbrough, 1998, p. 20). The meaning and content of the concept of IS has been subject to change over time and depends on economic theory. Up to the mid-1980s, information systems were used to integrate the organisation's technical and social systems. The idea was to model the organisation and its hierarchy, and be able to control it with the push of a button through the use of IT (Rolf, 1998, p. 46). Changes in economic theory led to another model of organisations and companies, away from hierarchy and bureaucracy towards models of cooperation of more or less independent groups and sub-organisations. This change in economic theory was reflected in IS, which evolved away from centralised computer architectures towards decentralised client-server or peer-to-peer architectures. The general idea, however, has mostly remained the same. ISs are supposed to reflect the organisation and formalise the structure of the company, the relevant information, departments, job descriptions, the structures of governance and control (Rolf, 1998, p. 6). The different sorts of IS "all share this common objective of improving the processes of control" (Mason et al., 1995, p. 243).

Although information systems have been around for over 50 years, they have acquired new importance with the advent of network technology and particularly the Internet. The inclusion of networks, the interconnection of networks, and the use of the Internet in business have led to a virtual explosion of new applications and business models since the beginning of the 1990s. Buzzwords such as e-commerce, e-business, and e-government stand for new concepts that are in the process of revolutionising the way we do business and connect organisations. Despite the end of blind enthusiasm and the resulting burst of the "dot.com bubble" promises held by these, developments are still huge. Reduction of transaction costs, enlargement of markets and reach, as well as rationalisation of business processes are factors that permit the prediction that the combination of information technology and business will remain of importance for the foreseeable future.

We now have a relatively good idea of what information systems are and how the concept is based on these underlying concepts of business, information, and technology. The objective of this text is to find out how information systems as socio-technical entities are related to the notion of responsibility. Before we get to the core of this question, there is another group of concepts that need to be examined more closely. Responsibility is a term with many different meanings that will be discussed later on. However, every sort and instance of responsibility has a moral or ethical aspect. In many cases responsibility is exclusively moral, but even if it is not, it is still of moral relevance. Therefore we will emphasise the moral aspect, and in order to do so, we will have to clarify the terms "ethics" and "morality." We have seen that even a seemingly clear-cut term like information systems has many roots, meanings, and aspects. This is even more so in the case of the fundamental notions of moral philosophy. The next chapter will therefore be dedicated to an introduction to the concepts of ethics and morality.

Chapter II

Ethics and Morality

Academic texts have to conform to certain standards, and one of these is to define the concepts they use. Texts dealing with ethics or morality therefore have to define what these concepts mean. In the case of English text about computer ethics, the definitions are usually done by contrasting the teleological and the deontological tradition. Another possibility is to talk about absolutist versus relativist ethical theories. Frequently, the terms ethics and morality are treated as equal. Arguably, texts on computer ethics are not meant to be expertises in ethics and many readers of these texts tend to be practically oriented. It is often argued that an introduction into the depth of ethical theory will do more to confuse these readers than help them. However, such arguments can be used to blend out problematic aspects of ethics and pretend that there are clear solutions to these problems when these are in fact contentious. This book chooses another route and will spend some time giving an introduction to normative terms that may be unfamiliar to many native English speakers. Furthermore, it will emphasise that the complexity of the problems warrants a more fine-grained use of the terms, and that it is useful to distinguish between ethics and morality.

The terms "ethics" and "morality" have been used to describe philosophical questions of norms and behaviour since the time of Socrates. This section will present two theories concerning the relationship between the two terms. The two approaches will be called "French tradition" and "German tradition," according to the nationalities of the philosophers whose theories are used to demonstrate them. The etymology of the notions does not demand any particular distinction between them. "Ethics" is derived from Greek, "morality" from Latin. Both words refer to the idea of custom and have originally the same content (Ricoeur, 1991a, p. 256). This is why in English texts one can often find the two terms used synonymously.

In contemporary continental European philosophy, one can nevertheless find more than one tradition of distinguishing between the two notions. They will be called the French and the German tradition, despite the fact that neither all German nor all French authors adhere to the German and French traditions respectively. Both of the traditions will be analysed by taking a look at one classical and one contemporary example. For the German tradition we will introduce as representatives Kant and Habermas; the exponents for the French tradition will be Montaigne and Ricoeur.

The purpose of this chapter is to lay the groundwork on which the term responsibility can be developed. Responsibility deals with normative problems, with the responses to ethical, moral, legal, and other challenges. In order to be able to develop a convincing account of responsibility, it is necessary to give a good description of normative theories. For that it is important to avoid simplistic solutions or models. The following account of ethics and morality attempts to show the intricacy of the concepts by contrasting the French and German tradition. This will allow us to observe a great number of aspects and nuances that will later play a role in our theory of responsibility.

THE GERMAN TRADITION

Most of the features that define the German tradition are a heritage of Kant's moral philosophy. The relevant aspects are: (a) the deontological foundation of ethics, (b) the distinction between theory and practice in ethics and morality, and (c) the trust in reason as the basis of ethics. The German tradition is, in other words, the continuation of the project of enlightenment. Both of the philosophers of the German tradition who will be analysed here, Kant and Habermas, believe that the moral quality of an action can be verified. For Kant the instance of this verification is reason itself. Habermas develops the idea further and arrives at a kind of cumulative reason in the form of discourse. Neither of the two sees the task of moral philosophy in the judging of everyday actions but in the provision of a theoretical model, which allows the specification of rules and procedures to judge the moral quality of events or actions.

Morality concerns the everyday actions and decisions. Ethics on the other hand stands for the theoretical and scholarly dealing with morality.[1] In order to arrive at this conclusion, we should now take a more detailed look at the philosophy of the two authors.

Kant's Moral Philosophy: The Foundation of the German Tradition

A lot has been said about Kant's ethics, and this is not the place to repeat it. We will only take a look at Kant's ideas insofar as necessary to prove that the features of German tradition can be found in his writing.

For Kant there is a point of view from which the morality of actions can be judged. This is the viewpoint of pure reason, which shows that Kant meets the last point of my definition of the German tradition, the reliance on reason as the foundation of ethics. Pure reason is in itself practical and gives man the moral law (Kant, 1995a, p. A 57). The moral law in turn is linked to the good. According to Kant there is nothing unrestrictedly good, no other good without qualification but the good will (Kant, 1995a, p. BA 1). The will is good only when it is motivated by duty, which proves that Kant fulfils the first of the three features that we ascribe to the German tradition, namely that his philosophy is deontological. This, of course, comes as no surprise, as Kant is the archetype of a deontological philosopher and usually the first one to be named as a representative of this school of thought.

The idea of duty leads to the core formulation of Kant's moral philosophy, to the categorical imperative. The categorical imperative is distinguished from hypothetical imperatives in that it does not have other ends; it is an end in itself. Imperatives are answers to the question "What should I do?" and differ in the sort of question that they try to answer. An imperative, which presents an action as necessary in itself without reference to anything else is categorical (Kant, 1995a, p. BA 40). Apart from the categorical we can find the technological imperative and the pragmatic imperative. Only the categorical imperative, however, belongs to free action in general, and thus to the realm of morality (Kant, 1995a, p. BA 44). Kant himself offers several different formulations of the categorical imperative which allow for the analysis of important points in his moral philosophy. The formulation of the categorical imperative that is probably best known is:

> *"Act only according to that maxim whereby you can at the same time will that it should become a universal law."* (Translation: Kemerling, 2000)

This formulation shows some of Kant's central thoughts. One of them is the idea that the content of the moral law can be deduced from generalisation. An act is forbidden if it is against moral law, which is the case if it is either logically impossible or self-contradictory to universalise the maxim or to want to universalise it (Maritain, 1960, p. 146).

Another part of this first formulation of the categorical imperative with importance for us is the use of the term maxim. While the moral law is the principle according to which man should act, maxims are the subjective principles according to which man actually acts (Kant, 1995a, p. BA 16; Rohbeck, 1993, p. 86f). This means that the categorical imperative does not look at single acts or rules but judges the underlying maxims. It is thus clear that Kant distinguishes between several theoretical levels in his moral philosophy. This justifies seeing Kant as a representative of the German tradition since he clearly distinguishes between the practice and the theory of morality, between ethics and morality.[2]

Having proven that Kant fulfils the three defining characteristics of the German tradition, we will now proceed to the modern representative of this tradition to Jürgen Habermas.

Habermas' Discourse Ethics: The Modern Version of the German Tradition

There are several problems with Kant's conceptions of moral philosophy which have led to criticism but also to further development of his deontological ideas. One necessary supposition for the adoption of Kant's stance is that situations are unambiguous. Only in an unambiguous situation is it possible to find out what exactly the agent's duty is according to which he has to formulate his maxims. It has been argued by other authors that the ambiguous situations, which Kant chose to ignore, are exactly the situations in which ethics gain importance.

Another frequently named point of criticism of Kant's theories is the alleged negligence of the results of actions. Since the good of an action is only judged by its compliance to duty, and duty can be deduced from pure reason, it seems that in this theory ethics is indifferent to the actual welfare of concrete human beings. This is one of the points where the theory loses its plausibility since the results of an action are of ethical relevance for most of us. Kant's defenders, however, argue that even though considerations of results are systematically banished from the foundation of ethics, they can be found in the maxims that aim at concrete action (Höffe, 1996, p. 189f).

There are a lot of other points that have been criticised in Kant's writing during the last 200 years. There is Marx's criticism that Kant concentrates exclusively on reason and therefore forgets the historical determinants of ethics. Another argument is that Kant's ethics is nothing but a reformulation of Christian theological ethics in the disguise of humanism (Maritain, 1960, p. 149f; Tugendhat, 1984, p. 4).

However, in spite of the criticism, Kant's system has captured some of the important issues of moral philosophy and turned out to be one of the most important moral philosophies. It had and still has a profound influence on the development of moral philosophy, maybe stronger in German-speaking countries than elsewhere, and it is the base of what is called in this text the 'German tradition'. There have been many attempts to improve on the ideas without changing the basic concepts. One of the actual developments that is popular among (not only German) philosophers is the concept of discourse ethics as developed by Apel and Habermas. Habermas' theory will therefore be the second example for a moral philosophy in the German tradition.

Habermas wants to avoid falling back on pre-Kantian notions and losing the level of differentiation between foundation and application of ethics (Habermas, 1991, p. 24). However, he realises that there are several problems with Kantian ethics which have to be overcome. Habermas concedes that the individual is not able to test the universalisability of all of its maxims because it knows neither all of the relevant aspects of reality nor all of the relevant norms in any particular case. Habermas also tries to overcome one problem that Kant himself admitted, the fact that we can never know by experience whether the fulfilment of moral duties is based on moral or other reasons (Kant, 1995a, p. BA 27).

The solution for these problems of Kantian ethics is itself based on a Kantian idea. Kant saw that the notions are one basis of cognition that cannot be obtained intuitively, but only discursively (Kant, 1995b, p. B 92f). Habermas builds on this and uses the recent development of philosophy where language and speech have gained importance in an attempt to remodel the approach to moral philosophy. Discourses in this theory take the place of the categorical imperative. In a description of Mead, which can also be applied to his own writings, Habermas (1981b, p. 145) states that collective objectives and demands can do what the categorical imperative was meant to do. They can serve as a test for the morality of maxims by constituting discourses.

The underlying idea of discourse ethics as Habermas describes it is the notion of communicative action (Habermas, 1981a, 1981b). His theory of communicative action interprets language as a medium of communication and agreement. During the process of communication, the participants refer to a shared world in which they can claim validity for their arguments. These validity claims (*Geltungsansprüche*) can then again be accepted or contested (Habermas, 1981a, p. 148). Within the shared world of all participants, the life world (*Lebenswelt*), the participants communicate in order to reach a consensus (Habermas, 1981a, p. 37). This consensus centres on the inter-subjective acceptance of the validity claims. There are three basic sorts of claims of validity, which correspond to three aspects of the life world. The life world consists of the objective world, which is shared by all of its inhabitants, of the norms and rules that apply to a given situation, and of the speaker's inner world. Accordingly there are three validity claims—the claims of truth (*Wahrheit*), (normative) correctness (*Richtigkeit*), and veracity or authenticity (*Wahrhaftigkeit*).

Since the purpose of this chapter is to demonstrate the importance of the notion of responsibility in the context of ethics and morality, we will now concentrate on the moral implications of the theory of communicative action. One possible starting point for understanding Habermas' ethics is the notion of norms. Norms can be found when an agent does not act solitarily but acts within an environment where he can find other agents. Norms express the factual agreement of a social group. All members of the group know what behaviour is to be expected of the others in given circumstances. For the individual agent this clarifies what he is entitled to do (Habermas, 1981a, p. 127). Norms refer to some kind of underlying value and thus to morality. Morality has the purpose of regulating life in a society. In modern societies where the individualisation increases progressively, the individual subject is entangled in a net of reciprocal dependencies, which leads to a growing vulnerability of its identity. The conservation of this identity is therefore one of the goals of morality (Habermas, 1991, pp. 69 & 223). Morality, on the other hand, is also a mechanism used for the purpose of limiting conflicts in order to preserve the social integration of the life-world (Habermas, 1981b, p. 259).

Habermas understands discourse ethics as the successor to Kant's ethics. The difference to Kant is that the process of moral argumentation takes the place of the categorical imperative. Only those norms can claim validity, which could be agreed upon in a practical discourse by everybody affected (Habermas, 1991, p. 12). The idea is that, given valid norms, everybody can accept the results and consequences following from a universal compliance with these norms. Discourse ethics thus abandons Kant's notion of autonomy, which concentrates on the individual's submission under its own laws. Inter-subjective autonomy takes the place of Kant's individual autonomy (Habermas, 1991, p. 25).

Habermas follows Kant's intuition that the theory of morality is universal and can be deduced from reason. He supposes that there is a "moral point of view" from which questions of morality can be judged impartially (Habermas, 1991, p. 13). However, unlike Kant, Habermas does not think that any one person is able to find and correctly interpret this moral point of view. The place, which the autonomous individual has in Kant's theory, is held by discourse in Habermas ideas. Discourse is the medium for testing whether a norm is impartially justified (Habermas, 1981a, p. 39). Discourses are used to check all kinds of validity claims, and among them the claims of normative correctness. Real discourses, however, do not concentrate solely on any single one of the three validity claims, but can deal with several at the same time. This takes care of the problem that ethical differences in many cases are due to differing perceptions of reality and not only to differing views of moral norms.

A norm can claim to be valid when everybody who could be affected by it agrees that the norm is valid (Habermas, 1983, p. 76). Even though the aim of a discourse is to produce consensus, this does not mean that everybody has to share the same view of the world. The participants of a discourse can also find that they disagree on certain topics. In this case the validity of speech acts would refer to an acceptance of the disagreements (Habermas, 1998a, p. 34).

Even though discourse ethics tries to sort out moral differences and thereby help us coordinate our lives, it cannot tell us what to do. It only offers a procedure to judge morally relevant conflicts from the impartial moral point of view. Discourse ethics can therefore only be formal (Habermas, 1983, p. 113) and is unable to generate practical norms or, in our terminology, to generate morality. Discourse ethics is unable to produce a list of duties or a hierarchy of norms; it burdens the subjects with the task of making their own judgments (Habermas, 1998a, p. 147). It cannot even give criteria for telling whether something was judged from the impartial point of view, as this can only be decided by the affected parties due to the lack of external criteria (Habermas, 1998b, p. 565).

Habermas' discourse ethics can be interpreted as an attempt to reconcile Kant's abstract autonomy and Hegel's substantial morality (cf. Bienfait, 1999). It corresponds with Kant's ethics in that the basis is a formal principle, which is also universal. Moral validity, and this leads us back to the German tradition, is based on a rational procedure (Wellmer, 1986, p. 8).

The rationality of a statement in the case of Habermas stands for its capacity of being criticised and justified, in other words for the validity claims

(Habermas, 1981a, p. 27). Unlike Kant, Habermas does not limit rationality to the individual who then would have to decide which action or maxim can be morally justified. Communicative rationality or reason is no source of norms (Habermas, 1998a, p. 18); it only allows the rational discussion of adequate behaviour and norms.

So far we have seen that Habermas' ethics fulfils two requirements of being put into the category of the German tradition. It differentiates between theory and practice of moral questions, and it is based on reason. The third point, the fact that the German tradition is fundamentally deontological, is certainly not as clear in Habermas' theory. It would be wrong to put him into the same category as Kant, for whom the only thing good without further qualification is the good will. It is justified, however, to say discourse ethics is deontological because it is not exclusively based on consequentialism. That is to say the good will, the intention of the agent, is of importance for the moral evaluation of an act. Veracity, as we saw, is one of the validity claims, which is taken into account in discourses. The deontological aspect of ethics can therefore be said to "hide" in the discourse. Deontological and teleological aspects are not easily divisible since both play their part in determining what is right or wrong. This may be seen as analogous to the impossibility to distinguish between moral and factual claims in a discourse. Both refer mutually to each other.

There is a lot more that could be said about the implications of both moral theories introduced so far. Questions of realization, of sanctions, of ethics and politics or society could be discussed. Since the aim of this book is the analysis of the notion of responsibility, we will leave it here. One thing that may strengthen the claim that there is something deserving to be called a "German tradition" is the fact that the aforementioned features can be seen in the writings of many contemporary authors dealing with problems of applied ethics. Especially the distinction between ethics and morality along the lines of theory and practice is commonplace in contemporary German discussions about applied ethics (for similar definitions, see Bayertz, 1993, p. 18; Ulrich, 1997, p. 43; Steinmann & Löhr, 1994, p. 8; Homann & Blome-Drees, 1992, p. 16). The other two points, the dependence on rationality and the deontological aspect, can also frequently be found in these and other texts.

A different view of the content and relationship of ethics and morality is reflected in another school of thought, which, due to the fact that the following examples come from a French background, will be called the 'French tradition'.

THE FRENCH TRADITION

While the German tradition sees the relationship between ethics and morality as a correlation between theory and practice, the French tradition favours a completely different view of the two concepts. From the German tradition's point of view, ethics is based on reason. Such a final foundation does not seem possible to the French tradition. The deontological aspect, even though it still exists, loses its central position in ethics. Finally, a distinction between ethics and morality is still possible, but it does not run along the lines of the distinction between theory and practice. The entire architecture of moral philosophy is different in this school of thought.

The French tradition has its roots in French moralism. The authors, who can be understood as representatives of this tradition, can therefore be seen as members of the moralistic school. Contrary to what the word might suggest, moralism in this sense does not stand for rigorous enforcement of moral norms, but rather for the attempt of keeping up morality in the face of relativism and ambiguities. We will briefly describe the moral theory of Michel de Montaigne as the classical representative of moralism. While Montaigne is recognised as one of the founders of moralism, the modern author, Paul Ricoeur, is certainly less clear-cut as a moralist. However, we will see that Ricoeur embodies some of the ideas of moralism and that he displays some of the features that make him a representative of the French tradition. The French tradition in this text will stand for the ideas that: (a) ethical theories cannot have a final foundation, but find their justification in the propagation of peace and avoidance of violence; and (b) ethics and morality can be distinguished along the lines of deontology and teleology.

Michel de Montaigne and Moralism

The French tradition in this paper is understood to be strongly influenced by moralism. Moralism in turn stands for the idea that there is no final justification of morality comparable to reason in the German tradition.[3] A wider definition of a moralist that can be found in French literature is that he is someone who contemplates the essence of man, who reflects upon questions of conduct and interaction (Schalk, 1995, p. 20).

> "A 'moralist' in France has typically been a man whose distance from the world of influence or power allows him to reflect disinterestedly upon the human condition, its ironies and truths,

in such a way as to confer upon him (usually posthumously) a very special authority of the sort commonly reserved in religious communities for outstanding men of the cloth." (Judt, 1998, p. 121f)

Moralism in this sense is not confined to a specific period or place in philosophy. However, the notion of moralism is strongly linked to French philosophy of the 16th and 17th centuries. One feature that unites different moralists is their continuous battle against philosophic systems. Life is seen as an infinite whole, which can never be comprehensively described. All-encompassing systems therefore have to be exchanged for other forms of philosophic thoughts. It is obvious that anyone who is considered part of this tradition necessarily has to be on an opposite pole of philosophy from the German tradition, where systematic thought and the attempt to explain everything with one theory are characteristic. Since philosophy is not understood as a system in moralism, ethics has to be justified by other means. The lack of systematic foundation has often led to moralism being equated to relativism.

Michel de Montaigne is one of the most important figures of moralism. His philosophical position is hedonistic. Joy and pleasure are man's final end, no matter what one may think about the means to reach this end. The final end, even of virtue (and thus of ethics), is pleasure (Montaigne, 1976, p. 7). On the other hand there is one fact that threatens our pleasure. This is our inevitable death. Since we know that death is inevitable and that we are necessarily headed in its direction, the worst that can happen to us is being afraid to die. If we fear death, it is impossible for us to do anything. All of our life we do nothing but "build" our death (Montaigne, 1976, p. 26). Death, however, is not to be feared because we don't have to care as long as we live, as we are alive. We don't have to care once we are dead either, because then we will not be able to care any more (Montaigne, 1976, p. 28). Nevertheless death remains the central point of philosophy. Montaigne therefore takes up Cicero's thought and even puts one of his essays under the heading of "philosophise is learning to die." At first sight Montaigne seems to search for a good way to spend his life. Philosophy and science do not appear to have any other purpose than to teach him more about himself, about how to live and how to die well (Montaigne, 1976, p. 115).

However, this apparently harmless and contemplative philosophy has serious repercussions for the perception of morality and ethics. In order to completely understand this, one has to take into account that the reason for Montaigne's philosophy of dying was not only individual death, which looms on the horizon for everybody, but also the downfall of conventional morality at his time.

Philosophy traditionally distinguishes between recognition of truth and the tasks of morality. It speculates on the one hand about being and on the other hand about virtue. Learning to die, however, means that all aims and ends of philosophy are united in a single focus. The difference between word and deed, between theory and practice melts away (Starobinski, 1986, p. 117f). Virtue in this setting not only aims at moral behaviour, but it helps us to hold death in contempt. Thus it allows us to develop the necessary quiet and contemplation to enjoy life (Montaigne, 1976, p. 9). We know that death awaits us anywhere, but we can overcome the fear of it. Contemplating death is therefore contemplating freedom. This is where Montaigne's philosophy becomes subversive for all moral systems. As we realise that dying is no evil, we are free of coercion and constraints (Montaigne, 1976, p. 16).

This philosophy does not lend itself as a basis for ethics. Montaigne does not offer a science that we could learn and no method to find out optimal conduct. His philosophy is rather a well-considered inquietude (Wutenow, 1976, p. 298). Thus Montaigne stands in the tradition of the stoic sceptics. He is no systematic thinker, and the only consistent characteristic of man he admits is his inconsistency (Montaigne, 1976, p. 103). With regard to morality he sees the factual plurality of moral systems and the difficulty of determining which of these systems should be chosen. What he denounces is the "mystical" authority that is attributed to the worldly and religious order of his time. This doubting of the foundations of morality and the lack of an alternative foundation led to Montaigne being called a relativist. This reproach is not quite justified, however, since he does recognise the need for moral norms. He simply chooses what seems to be most useful to public life, and that is the custom, the lived morality (Starobinski, 1986, p. 385). Montaigne's morality is thus fundamentally conservative since he simply accepts the norms that exist on the grounds that the existing norms are always better than no norms at all.

This shows that Montaigne fulfils the first criterion of what we called the French tradition, namely the fact that morality's foundation is to be found in the conservation of peace. Montaigne shares this foundation for the respect of public rules and morality with other French philosophers such as Pascal and Descartes. The formal respect of norms does not rely on their justice, but simply depends on their immediate result, which is public peace (Starobinski, 1986, p. 384).

The second one of the aforementioned criteria of the French tradition, the distinction between ethics and morality along the lines of deontology and teleology, is not quite as apparent in his writings. He does not, in fact, differentiate between two notions the way we have so far. However, it is quite obvious that both of these aspects of ethics, which are often understood to be conflicting, each find a central place in his moral philosophy. On the one hand teleology is obvious in his hedonistic approach to morality in general. Lust is the final aim of virtue and morality. He does not go as far as to propagate the rules of 'do as you will' but, quite on the contrary, his solution is to adhere to existing norms, no matter what their justification. This duty of obeying norms and doing what is expected refers back to the first aspect of the French tradition, the keeping of peace. The idea is that peace can be held when everybody does his duty, which is to obey existing moral and legal norms. Having proven that the moralist Montaigne is part—or maybe better, one of the founders—of the French tradition, let us now proceed to the contemporary philosopher who represents this tradition.

Paul Ricoeur and the Other

Ricoeur can best be understood by looking at the most important philosophical tendencies of the time. He is influenced by phenomenology, by Heidegger, and by the further developments these thoughts have found in France exemplified by names from Sartre and Camus to Levinas. There is a general feeling that philosophy can, at best, have the task of helping analyse situations; it cannot prescribe acts or norms (Ricoeur, 1995a, p. 192).

The *other* holds a central position in contemporary French philosophy.[4] One sign of this is that Ricoeur's most important recent publication on the topic of ethics is titled *"Soi-même comme un autre"* (1990). The title suggests that there is a close relationship between the self and the other. The self implies the other, it cannot even be thought without the other (Ricoeur, 1990a, p. 14). As Ricoeur demonstrates, this relationship between the self and the other has implications for almost every aspect of philosophy. Most important for our purposes is the result of this concerning moral philosophy. The other is understood to be someone who can, like myself, say "I," who sees himself as an agent responsible for his acts (Ricoeur, 1990b, p. 258). Ricoeur emphasises the fact that in many languages the goodness of an action is judged not only by the goodness of its aims, but also by the orientation of the agent towards the other (Ricoeur, 1990a, p. 222).

Ethics consists of three dimensions, all of which have to be taken into account for the entire theory to be workable or relevant. The first dimension is the *soi-même*, the thought of oneself. The underlying question of this reflective thought is that of the good life. It is an example of the Aristotelian tradition where the good life is the final end of ethics. As we have already seen, the reflection on oneself implies the other. In this context the other can mean two things. It is the other whose face I can see, which forces me to take responsibility as described by Levinas. At the same time the other refers to the faceless other or others. This is the anonymous other as the foundation of justice (Ricoeur, 1994, p. 15). The other as the personalisation of justice leads to an emphasis on institutions, which are the third element of ethics.

> *"I define the ethical goal by the three following terms: the aim of the good life, with others in just institutions. The three parts of the definition are equally important."* (Ricoeur, 1990b, p. 257, translation by the author)

Even though Ricoeur's moral philosophy seems to be rather teleological, he does not omit the deontological problem, the question of duty, which has had a big influence on the German, and especially Kantian tradition of moral philosophy. He distinguishes between ethics (*l'éthique*) and morality (*la morale*) along the lines of teleology and deontology. Ethics thus stands for the aim of a life accomplished under the distinguishing mark of actions held for good. Morality, on the other hand, stands for the obligatory side, distinguished by norms, obligations, prohibitions. These are characterised at the same time by the claim for universality and the factual effect of constraints (Ricoeur, 1990b, p. 256). Ethics stands in the Aristotelian tradition of the search for the good life, whereas morality is understood to be the Kantian side of moral philosophy (Ricoeur, 1990a, p. 200). The two aspects, however, do not have the same importance in moral philosophy. Morality only constitutes a limited if indispensable part of ethics. Ethics, the search for the good life, envelops morality.

One central question of this theory is why we need morality at all. If ethics is the search for the good life, why do we need the constraints and duties of morality? Ricoeur's answer to this is clear and straightforward. We simply cannot afford to stay in the realm of the desire for the good life because our actions entail power and power may lead to our inflicting violence on others. The transformation from optative to imperative, from ethics to morality is forced by the existence of violence (Ricoeur, 1995b, p. 18; 1994, p. 16). This characteristic of morality as being the measure against violence is the reason why moral imperatives in many cases have a negative form. Violence in this context is understood to range from the more subtle forms of coercing people to do one's will such as flattery or lies, up to the most drastic forms of violence such as rape, torture, and murder (Ricoeur, 1990b, p. 262).

As a representative of the French tradition, Ricoeur does not try to depict this view of morality as a final foundation of moral philosophy or of moral norms. The search for the good life and the desire to avoid violence are not founded by moral philosophy. In fact it is the other way around. Moral philosophy just takes moral attitudes and convictions as they exist and tries to justify them. A theory, which does not try to argue in one logic chain, but goes back to trying to justify the convictions on which it is built, would seem suspect to many thinkers educated in classical logic as it seems to commit the fatal error of a *petitio principii*. For Ricoeur this is does not pose a problem since this appears to be a feature of all philosophical theories.

> *"I will support at the given moment that every moral theory presents in its argument a circularity of some sort. Maybe this is even the case in every grand philosophy."* (Ricoeur, 1988, p. 216, translation by the author)

Ricoeur obviously fulfils the two criteria of the French tradition introduced earlier—the lack of a final foundation of ethics, and the distinction of ethics and morality along the lines of teleology and deontology. Again, as in the case of the German tradition, this distinction that was only demonstrated with the help of one example can be found in the writings of many contemporary authors (e.g., Wunenburger, 1993, p. XIV; Lenoir, 1991, p. 13), which justifies the use of the term "French tradition."

Now that we have seen several possible relationships between the notions of ethics and morality, we shall return to the question of how the notion of responsibility can be of help to solve problems of moral philosophy and the question why responsibility has become the ubiquitous word that it is. From there we will be able to come back to the moral and ethical problems of information systems and analyse the contribution of responsibility in this area. For this purpose we first have to take a brief look at the problems that arise from the definitions of ethics and morality as they were described so far.

PROBLEMS OF THE DISTINCTION BETWEEN ETHICS AND MORALITY

We now know two ways of distinguishing between ethics and morality. Both find their justification in addressing a specific problem of moral philosophy. It is plain to see that morality and ethics in the German tradition are two fundamentally different concepts. In this tradition it is easy to admit the factual multiplicity and contingency of moralities. In the German tradition the contingency of norms does not pose a threat to ethics understood as the reflection or science of morality. In this way the German approach may help defuse discussions about morality. There are, however, problems linked to this distinction that are not easily solved. One is the question whether the two levels of moral philosophy implied here are in fact sufficient. Since there are many different ethical theories, one can suppose that there should be at least one more level, maybe a sort of meta-moral philosophy or meta-ethics. Another problem is the foundation of ethics on rationality. This heritage of enlightenment has been controversial ever since its introduction. It seems even harder to justify today than ever before. Modern sociological research indicates that there are better models for the explanation of human behaviour and adherence to norms and rules than rationality. One central problem of the German tradition is the question of how exactly the relationship between ethics and morality has to be imagined. If morality really is moral practice, consisting of norms and rules that people follow, what can ethics as a theory of this practice do, what can be its purpose? One possible answer is that ethics can generate the norms and thus produce morality. This, however, would make ethics an eminently practical discipline and therefore nothing but a somewhat more elaborate form of morality. The generation of moral norms always has to be part of morality anyway since the norms have to come from somewhere. If ethics cannot directly produce the norms of morality, then its aim must be more abstract and more general. This is what we have found in the discussion of the German tradition. For Kant, and more so for Habermas, ethics is in fact an abstract exercise. Kant wants to check the possibility of universalising the subject's maxims, whereas Habermas is trying to disburden the subject by invoking a discourse that should test validity claims. In both cases it is often hard to see how the ethical exercises can take effect on moral realities. We need at least one more theory that explains the connection between theoretical contemplation of norms and practical moral action. If this is so then the question remains why we even bother with ethics at all and why we do not simply follow Montaigne's footsteps and accept the given morality.

This leads us to the French tradition where the situation is similar to the German tradition. Here, too, the distinction of ethics and morality serves a purpose, and it is plain to see how it furthers moral philosophy. The two poles of moral philosophy, teleology and deontology, have been present in ethical discussion since the very beginning of systematic thought about the matter. Furthermore they are highly plausible to this day. One underlying thought is that ethics aims at the perfection of one's life and therefore strives for the "good life." Teleology also reflects the intuition that the results of an action are relevant to its moral evaluation. Even the best intention cannot lead to somebody being called morally good if the consequences of his actions are disastrous. The opposite is just as true. If somebody tries to commit a grievous harm and this by accident leads to favourable results, most of us would have difficulties evaluating the action as morally good. Deontology also points towards the universal experience that ethics and morality have something to do with duties. These duties may be positive or negative. They restrict our freedom of choice in that they rule out some possibilities we might want to choose from a purely egotistical point of view.

So, while the French tradition can reflect some of our moral intuitions and explain some aspects of moral philosophy quite well, it also leads to problems. One of them would be the foundation of morality. While the French tradition does not try to offer a final foundation for morality along the lines of the German tradition, it does offer a reason for the introduction of morality, which is the avoidance of violence. While this may seem plausible to many of us, this idea has to contend with the problem that the avoidance of violence may not always be possible, even worse, that it may not always be desirable. Most people would probably be able to picture situations in which violence may be a moral obligation.

The problem of the French tradition that again leads us to the notion of responsibility is its specific relationship between ethics and morality. Similar to the German tradition, it is obvious that the two notions are related, but at the same time it is difficult to see how exactly this relationship has to be imagined. If the teleological aspect of moral philosophy takes precedence over the deontological aspect, as is the case in Ricoeur's theories, then it appears hard to see when and under what circumstances exactly duty and strict rules enter the picture. It would be equally unclear if deontology took precedence when teleology should take over. What, finally, is supposed to happen if the two aspects contradict each other. What are the criteria according to which it is to be decided which one should prevail?

The questions concerning the relationship of ethics and morality touch many issues of moral philosophy, which have been discussed from the earliest occurrences of philosophical discussion. We chose the approach of the two traditions for introducing ethical questions because it shows that there are different ways of defining the concepts and their relationships. Philosophical ethics, this should have become clear, allows different approaches and none of them can claim to be the one truth or to have solved all of the problems. We hope that this way of introducing ethics and morality has proved interesting to especially English-speaking readers because it tends to be disregarded by the classical Anglo-American approach.

The concept of responsibility on which we will concentrate from now on offers one way of addressing some of the problems indicated by the dichotomy of ethics and morality in both traditions. Responsibility is a concept that relies on practical consequences. It offers no final foundation of morality, but is compatible with many theories of final foundation. It is a teleological notion that relies to a high degree on deontology. Responsibility can mediate between ethics and morality; it can serve as an in-between of ethics and morality in the German as well as in the French tradition.

Chapter III

Why Responsibility and Information Systems?

In this chapter we want to show why it makes sense to use the concept of responsibility with respect to the business use of information technology. There are three parts to the argument. At first, we will demonstrate that the development of the moral idea of responsibility is closely linked to modern developments in our societies. Many of these developments have to do with technology and information technology being the latest step in this direction. We will then continue to show that there are several structural similarities between responsibility and business on the one hand and information technology on the other hand. In a last step we will show that this theoretical setting is fruitful because it can rely on a rich background of ethical theories from different fields and perspectives. Before we can do so, however, the next step will have to be a first analysis of the term "responsibility."

A TENTATIVE DEFINITION OF RESPONSIBILITY

The following paragraphs have the purpose of conveying a rough idea of what the term "responsibility" is supposed to denote in this book. They will point out the most important meanings and components without getting too deep into a discussion of contents and problems. These discussions will be the subject of a detailed analysis in the next chapter. The purpose of this tentative definition is simply to give the reader a feeling for the term that will be required to understand why it is a sound idea to use the concept of responsibility in a discussion of business information technology.

The first difficulty when discussing responsibility is that the word is widely used and often denotes different, if not contradictory, facts and relationships. There are scholars who talk of an inflation of the use of the term (i.e., Homann, 1998, p. IX). Others point out that the clarity of the notion decreases with the frequency of its use (i.e., Etchegoyen, 1999, p. 44). If we believe what we hear, then there is little doubt that we live in a time of responsibility. Even terrorists enjoy accepting responsibility for their deeds. At the same time there is an inverse relationship between the readiness of accepting responsibility and the probability of consequences (Ilting, 1994, p. 176). As an illustration of the lack of clarity of the meaning of responsibility, let us look at a short story of a drunken sea captain that originates from H.L.A. Hart (1968, p. 211):

> *As captain of the ship, X was responsible for the safety of his passengers and crew. But on his last voyage he got drunk every night and was responsible for the loss of the ship with all aboard. It was rumoured that he was insane, but the doctors considered that he was responsible for his actions. Throughout the voyage he behaved quite irresponsibly, and various incidents in his career showed that he was not a responsible person. He always maintained that the exceptional winter storms were responsible for the loss of the ship, but in the legal proceedings brought against him, he was found criminally responsible for his negligent conduct, and in separate civil proceedings he was held legally responsible for the loss of life and property. He is still alive and he is morally responsible for the deaths of many women and children (Hart, 211).*

The first thing we can state is that responsibility can have different meanings. It can stand for causality, for ethics, for morality, and for more idiosyncratic facts and relationships. We believe—and will demonstrate this in the following chapter—that responsibility is first and foremost a social construct aiming at ascription or imputation. Important dimensions of this ascription are the subject and the object. The object is ascribed to the subject. Thus, the subject is the answer to the question, "Who is responsible?", and the object answers, "What is the subject responsible for?" This is true for all instances of responsibility. In the short story quoted above, the loss of the ship is ascribed to the storm and the loss of lives to the captain. There are different sorts of responsibility such as legal, moral, or role responsibility, but in any of these cases, ascription plays a central part.

Our next thesis concerning responsibility is that it is always a moral notion. We have already seen the complexity of the concepts of ethics and morality, but we can distil from them that they are used to denote facts and processes that affect the way we live or want to live in a fundamental way. Morality plays a role when peaceful coexistence or personal vulnerability come into play. All different sorts of responsibility affect in some way or another some fact of moral importance and are therefore morally relevant. An obvious example is legal responsibility that generally has moral consequences.

There are quite a few of other dimensions and determinants of responsibility that will be discussed in the next chapter. Nevertheless we will need to present some advanced conclusion of the discussion of responsibility in order to explain why responsibility is a term that can be applied fruitfully to information systems. First of all, the social construct of responsibility depends on communication. It is a means to transport contents of ethics and morality, but unlike most traditional moralities (in the German tradition's sense of the word), it does not give clear directions but is open and leads to unpredictable outcomes. It is by principle a teleological concept in that it aims at the good life and takes consequences of actions into account when giving moral judgment. At the same time it allows the inclusion of deontological ethical thoughts. Furthermore, the consequentialist side of responsibility seems to promise an affinity to action. When we speak of responsibility, this implies that something is going to happen, some concrete measures will appear, that sanctions can be imposed.

With this short introduction to responsibility, which the reader will have to accept for the time being, we can now explain why responsibility has attained the level of importance that it now holds, and we can also clarify why it has a close affiliation to business information technology.

THE RISE OF RESPONSIBILITY

The concept of responsibility is relatively young when compared to other philosophical terms. This recent rise to importance if not ubiquity of the term is more than just a fashion, and it is caused by the combination of social developments and the failure of traditional moralities to address these developments. Ethics and morality have of course never been perfect in dealing with whatever was perceived as moral problems. The rapid and deep changes in Western societies during the last 200 years, however, have been an insurmountable challenge for many traditional ways of coping with modifications of the social fabric. The call for responsibility is linked to the perception that moral norms are deficient in controlling human action (Kaufmann, 1990, p. 72; 1995, p. 88).

It is helpful to see what the changes were that led to the growing importance of responsibility to appreciate why the concept is applicable to IS. One of the roots of social changes, maybe the most important one, was industrialisation with its close connection to science and technology. We have already seen the link between science and technology, but there is another aspect that is important to explain the impact on ethics. From the beginning of enlightenment, science and technology were understood to be positive. While the ancient Greeks saw science as the theoretical contemplation of the world and thus did not attach any moral relevance to it, this viewpoint changed radically with the advent of enlightenment. Francis Bacon was the thinker who most eloquently changed the role of science from value-free contemplation to an active tool for overcoming the shortages of the world (cf. Höffe, 1995). Ever since then, it was clear that science and technology were to serve human needs and therefore every progress in science and technology was a progress for humanity. For centuries this idea was generally accepted even by critical philosophers. Karl Marx for example criticised society and its workings, but he saw technology not as a root of the problem but as a potential solution. This belief in technology, whose shortcomings became visible during industrialisation and its social and ecological results, was irreparably damaged during the 20th century. The first serious hit it took was the first World War, during which destruction was administered on a scale that had been unimaginable before. The wholesale slaughtering of a generation of Europeans in just five years was only possible with the help of technology. The technological enhancement of war was continued in World War II and in most of the following conflicts. Maybe even worse than the intentional use of science and technology for destructive purpose for the belief in the positive properties of technology were the unintentional problems it created. Spectacular technological catastrophes such as the ones in Chernobyl, Bhopal, or a host of others mark one side of this problem. The apparently limitless increase in scope and size of technology entails the corresponding increase in accidents. Worse, however, are those catastrophic results of technology that do not result from a single accident, but from the continuous use of technology conforming to rules and the original intention. This is where we find ecological problems such as global warming and the depletion of the ozone layer, but also problems that threaten the material basis of technology itself, most notably the shortage of natural resources. The conceptual limits of technology are at the same time the limits of progress. We know now that technological advances are not intrinsically good, but that most technological developments are at best ambiguous. While the examples used so far come from the sphere of classical and large technologies, information technology is no exception to this rule. Nowadays, more new developments reach us from the field of IT than from classical technologies, and therefore the ethical problems produced by IT are increasingly coming to public attention. We will discuss some of these problems later in connection to the practical problems of responsibility and IS.

We can state that the originally optimistic view that technological and scientific progress would lead to social progress has been replaced with a more cautious mood, in many cases even with an attitude of rejection of technology. This change in attitude is caused by the results of technology on the one hand and by the realisation of our collective limits on the other hand. Many ethically motivated rejections of technology are based on the fact that modern technology has results of an order of magnitude and with long-range effects that surpass everything mankind traditionally had to deal with. There is a growing sense that our responsibilities must be extended in the same way that our power and our capacity to do damage is extending (Ricoeur, 1995c, p. 64). It is characteristic for our present-day understanding of responsibility that it comprises the multitude and variety of topics and problems that have become subject of human action and decision, and that are therefore believed to be relevant to responsibility (Krawietz, 1995, p. 185).

We have now seen that the development of responsibility as a term to address ethical and moral questions results from the progress in science and technology, and the resulting increase of human power. Jonas (1984) explicitly bases his theory of responsibility on these developments and tries to develop a model of responsibility that is suited to deal with our new power. Technology and power, however, are but two aspects of social change that has led to the apparent insufficiency of traditional morality. In the next section we will discuss some other aspects, all of which create the background of the modern discussion of responsibility and at the same time the setting for capitalism and modern information technology.

SOCIETY, RISK, AND RESPONSIBILITY

In this section we will discuss some of the buzzwords of contemporary social sciences such as risk, uncertainty, complexity, globalisation, and information society. All of them are facets of social change that made our societies what they are today. They are also the reasons for the failure of traditional morality and the ascent of responsibility.

Technology, as we have seen, has several meanings. It is linked to science, it has close relations to economic activity, and it also constitutes a fundamental culture that can be called a technical civilisation (Höffe, 1995, p. 119). This sort of civilisation in which most citizens of Western societies live has several properties that are relevant to our topic.

Technology and Risk

Our lives today seem to be riskier than ever before. We risk them when we use a car, a bicycle, a plane. There are numerous risks to our health, our well-being, and the way we organise our lives. Some of these risks are known, such as pollution, the greenhouse effect, nuclear radiation, and so forth. Others may not even be known, and we are constantly surprised by new risks that we may have been taking for a considerable time without even knowing it, such as the consumption of BSE-infected beef. This view of rising risks stands in marked contrast to the fact that we have a higher life expectation than any other group of humans before and that at least the peoples of the industrialised countries have never known a longer time of peace and prosperity than today. In order to clear up this apparent contradiction, we will have to take a look at the concept of risk and how it affects our lives.

There are several etymological sources of the term risk. On the one hand risk can be deduced from Greek "riza," or root, whose basis is Arabic "risc," meaning divine gift or fate. This stands for an objective mix of chances and dangers in which we always act. On the other hand, there is the Latin/Italian root "risco," meaning the sailing around a cliff. Risk is then produced by humans through the attempt to avoid dangers (Hubig, 1995, p. 102). Another possible root of the term is the Persian "rozik," which means daily salary, daily bread, or fate (Pietschmann, 1992, p. 192). What is important for us here is that risk denotes a non-deterministic causal relationship. The term "risk" is used to "indicate that a consequence follows an event in probabilistic fashion, as opposed to necessity" (Thompson, 1985, p. 302). The philosophical use of the word risk is relatively new, but the underlying problem of lacking certainty is very old and can be seen as a basic constituent of being human. In the history of philosophy, we find the problem discussed under other headings, notably under the word "contingency." Something is contingent, simply said, if it could also be different. It could be different because it is not necessary (Makropoulos, 1997, p. 13).

In a wider sense contingency can be used to describe the world at large. "Contingency is the concept that the world exists but does not have to be there." The notion of contingency denotes the ambivalent areas of indetermination in which actions as well as coincidences are realised (Moran, 2000, p. 356).

Risk is the notion that tries to transform contingency in such a way that it becomes manageable. The most common (technical) definition of risk is the product of the results of an action multiplied by their probability (Pietschmann, 1992, p. 192; Gethmann, 1996, p. 42). This may sound somewhat abstract, but in some technical circumstances both of the factors can be calculated. The fact that this definition of risk is firstly linked to the use of technology and secondly of high ethical relevance can be demonstrated by an example. During the development of the nuclear bomb in 1942, the "father of the hydrogen bomb," Edward Teller, believed that there was a possibility that the first nuclear explosion might ignite the water contained in the earth's atmosphere and thereby lead to the end of the world. According to one of the participating physicists, the probability of this was estimated to be 3:1,000,000 and thus was considered to be sufficiently low to take the risk (cf. Birnbacher, 1988, p. 13). This decision was based on the objective character of risk as mentioned before. Nevertheless it is certainly open to debate whether there can be any justification for risking the existence of the world.

The criticism of the objective definition of risk is linked to both of the factors involved, to probability and damage. We distinguish between subjective and objective probability. Objective probability can be defined as the limit of the relative frequency of an occurrence, whereas subjective probability is a degree of belief (cf. Hausman & McPherson, 1996, p. 225; Gethmann, 1987, p. 1131). While objective probability can be measured, subjective probability is a different form of information. It is not knowledge, but a form of assumption about possible worlds that has been made computable (Priddat, 1996, p. 107). Even objective probability is in many cases hard to come by. An example of the problems in obtaining objective probability is nuclear power plants. The operators of such plants tend to tell the public that they are safe, while their opponents doubt the underlying numbers and probabilities and even doubt the fundamental possibility of calculating such probabilities (Kafka, 1994, p. 151).

The dimension of damage in the objective notion of risk is equally contentious. The problem in this case is that it is impossible to objectify results from decisions because they depend on what is taken into consideration. The range of results from any decision is infinite, and therefore the damage of any decision is also potentially infinite (Kaufmann, 1995, p. 79), which makes every decision infinitely risky.

We can conclude that there is no such thing as an "objective" risk because any description of risk depends on arbitrary decisions about the limits of the results taken into consideration and about the basis of probability estimation. Risk is bound to human beings' mental or physical activities or their results (Banse, 1994, p. 127). What remains is a relative notion of risk. Using the term risk in a relative sense means that the speaker is describing something that has to do with contingency, with the fact that we do not know the future. It also has normative connotations. While risk may formerly have had the sound of courage and adventure today, it is often equated with the potential suicide of the human race (Beck, 1986, p. 28). In the public discourse risk is a negative notion (Holzheu, 1993, p. 265).

A question related to the objectivity of risks is that of their reality. Proponents of an objective concept of risk tend to base their arguments of the objectivity of the measure of risk on the objectivity of the existence of risks. This raises deep metaphysical question about the structure of the world that will be impossible to discuss here. However, one can state without too much fear of controversy that for the purpose of describing the connection between society, risk, and eventually responsibility, 'real' is what affects the outcome of this discussion. In this sense Beck is right when he says that risks are real when they are perceived as real by humans (Beck, 1986, p. 103). This equation of risk with the perception of risk explains why we live in a "risk society" (Beck, 1986), while at the same time the scientific data about life expectancy, health, etc., can be interpreted to mean that we never lived more risk-free than today. It is therefore not the dangers that threaten our existence, but the complexity and incomprehensibility that grow. Therefore, decreasing dangers do not result in an increase in security (Kaufmann, 1995, p. 87).

If risk is no objective entity but related to perception, and at the same time is not something idiosyncratic but socially relevant, then the best way to describe it may be to see it as a social construct of ascription. Technology increases the reach of human actions and their results. This not only leads to a better knowledge of causal chains but also to more complexity. The capacity of shaping social relationships increases, but at the same time complexity increases. One possible way of dealing with this in a quasi-moral fashion is the ascription of risks. A result of this development is that many things that used to be accepted as fate now move in the perimeters of human control. Dangers are thus transformed to risks (Birnbacher, 1995, p. 143). Risks, unlike dangers, are constituted by human actions and they are therefore inherently moral.

This brings us back to the problem of responsibility and information systems. We have now seen that the development of the notion of risk as a description of social settings and relationships is in large part due to science and technology. On the one hand they produce risks in the objective sense by producing new dangers such as nuclear explosions or the greenhouse effect. On the other hand they produce risks by illuminating causal chains and thereby increasing the possibility of ascriptions. What is true for technology in general is also true for information technology. It produces some qualitatively new dangers that we will talk about in later chapters. Maybe more important in the context of risks, however, is that IT allows us to handle complexity in new ways. IT stabilises social constructs such as organisations and bureaucracies and thereby opens new ways of ascription. At the same time it allows us to model on a greater scale and thus find new causalities. The entire area of climate protection and global pollution is only manageable with highly complex mathematical models that require advanced information technology. If we can say today that driving a car produces CO_2 and that this is a cause of global warming, which in turn will lead to the melting of polar ice with a consequent flooding of low-lying countries such as Bangladesh, then we have an example of a risk that could only become visible through the use of IT. This kind of reasoning is morally relevant. On the grounds of the causal chain just described, I can say to any person driving a car: "You are (partially) responsible for the flooding of Bangladesh." Of course this is a problematic imputation, but the fact that it is possible and has a certain kind of plausibility is due to the scientific quality of the underlying model.

A problem with the business part of IS and risk is that risk plays an important role in economics and the economy, but the perception of risk in this context is completely different from that in technology. Economic activity is based on uncertainty, and risks are the lifeblood of business. In economic contents the positive side of risks are generally accentuated. Risk is no longer the product of probability and damage, but of probability and profit. It is highest praise for a manager to say that she is willing to take risks. This, of course, conflicts with the negative perception of risk in technology. The different views of risks by business people and technicians is expressed by the famous "put on your management hat," a sentence used to convince a senior technician to put aside his technical objections and think about the management side of a decision, which eventually led to the explosion of the Challenger space craft.

The same ambiguity is part of information systems, where uncertainty and contingency are interpreted differently depending on the point of view. While the technician may not believe that a certain hardware or software is developed and tested sufficiently, market constraints may force a company to sell it anyway. The fast pace of development in the IT sector thus results in a conflict of interest that apparently tends to be won by business. Proof of this can be seen in the multitude of programming errors or "bugs" that we find in even the most sophisticated and expensive software.

Strategies of Handling Risk

There are different ways in which one can react to risks. In this section we will look mainly at the individual strategies that will then lead us to the aggregate strategies as they can be observed in societies. The first and most obvious behaviour when faced with risk is to simply ignore it. Escape from hazard and coincidence, from contingency in our terms, is an old remedy of philosophy. According to Rorty (1994, p. 55), such different philosophies as stoic refrain from passion, Zen-Buddhist lack of will, Heidegger's dispassionateness, and physics as absolute perception of reality serve this purpose.

However, man escaped animal's determinism and he has won the freedom to make decisions. This, on the other side, makes him uncertain. He is confronted with such a mass of information that he must try to do something to overcome insecurity (von Cube, 1995, p. 103). The next strategy of dealing with risk and uncertainty is thus their elimination. Enlightenment, science, and technology can be interpreted as attempts in this direction. Unfortunately these attempts were all doomed to failure. Even in the case of objective risk, the measures taken to eliminate it have proved to be unsuccessful. Scientific risk analysis cannot eradicate ambivalence and uncertainty (Renn, 1996, p. 252). The production of more and better knowledge cannot be counted as a contribution to the elimination of uncertainty (Wiesenthal, 1990, p. 47).

The impossibility of eliminating uncertainty extends beyond the area of genuine uncertainty, that is to say that we do not know the future, and covers the more manageable area of risk in the narrower sense. Risk, defined as 'damage x probability' and caused by human action, is not eliminable either. There is no option of total security in modern societies (if there ever was) (Krawietz, 1995, p. 209f). As Lübbe (1998, p. 109) points out, the prohibition of producing risks for others would result in a general standstill of life. The catch is that every decision is bound to produce risk. It is impossible to decide risk-free because in any decision the alternative can be judged as a risk as well. The risk of option A is always opposed by the risk of option B, even if option B means doing nothing (Wiedemann, 1993, p. 57). Many authors therefore agree that due to the impossibility of eliminating all risks, we have to accept them. This does not mean that we may not try to minimise them or to increase our knowledge about them. However, there is no point in trying to completely eradicate risks. This is true for all decisions in general (Kleinwellfonder, 1996, p. 26) and for decisions involving technology in particular.

If the inevitability of risks leads to their acceptance, then the next step is to ask which risks are acceptable, for it can certainly not be our conclusion that every risk should be taken. This is the step where ethics and morality enter the picture, and where responsibility will later find its justification. Why are risks ethically relevant and why did we spend this much space discussing them? An example might serve as an answer to this. When someone who is completely isolated from the rest of the world, for example Robinson Crusoe, were to take a risk knowingly and willingly, there is not much we can say about the moral consequences. If Robinson decides to hunt a tiger on his island or to take a swim in bad weather, then he may endanger himself, but such an action is not immoral.[5] The situation changes, however, as soon as Robinson is no longer alone. With the arrival of Friday, not only his daily routine changes, but also his moral duties. Since Friday may need Robinson for survival or comfort, the risks that Robinson takes now acquire a moral quality. If Robinson willingly puts his life on the line, then Friday is affected and the moral quality of the action changes. We can continue the variation of the theme and find that things may again look different in case Robinson has a family or is a village chief or the President of the USA. What is the difference between the cases and why does the moral content change? The ethical evaluation of risks has in a large part to do with the question whether the taker of the risk is at the same time the person affected by it. If this is so, as in the original Robinson example, then risk is ethically neutral. If we risk something and exclusively get the good as well as the bad rewards, then there is no need for an ethical discussion about the risk. This situation changes when the person profiting from the risk is not identical to the one having to pay the price. Again, technology is a good example for this. People who decide about development and deployment of technology in our society are rarely identical with those who operate it who are again different from those who suffer the potential consequences. Before we proceed to the question of how responsibility can address these ethical problems of risk, we should enlarge our perspective from the individual to society.

Risk is, as we have seen, no longer an individual notion, even though individual interpretations and perceptions influence it. In fact, risk is a shared experience of many, if not all humans in industrialised countries. Life under uncertainty and the resulting need for security are uniting features of modern societies (Banse, 1996, p. 19). Risk is on the one hand the form in which the future in decisions is made visible and rational (Luhmann, 1990, p. 29). On the other hand this rationalisation of risk has led to a new concept of society, the risk society. The term risk society was introduced by Beck (1986), and one of the reasons for its immediate success was the simultaneous nuclear catastrophe in Chernobyl. In effect the risk society is that social order in which nothing can be risked any more because so much is being risked already. The other side of the risk society is the insurance society. All systems have to function reliably because the dangers grow with the size of the system (Guggenberger, 1992, p. 44). The risk society is somewhat similar to the class society in that the riches accumulate in the upper classes whereas the risks have to be faced in the lower classes (Beck, 1986, p. 46). In this sense the risk society embodies the moral problems of risks because those who profit are not the same as those who pay. This brief introduction into the risk society has served as an introduction to the next point, to the connection of individuals and society in the light of the development of IT.

Society, Modernity, and IT

The risk society with its particular reaction to risk is only one aspect of the changes we find in modern societies. It is a manifestation of the changes of society in modernity. Risk and uncertainty can be seen as the most important aspects of modern societies. There has never been a cultural present that knew less about its future than ours (Lübbe, 1993, p. 33). This pervading theme of uncertainty is part of the definition of modernity. The term modernity is difficult to define. The word "modernus" was used during the late 5th century to distinguish Christian present from heathen past (Habermas, 1998c, p. 197). Ever since, it has been used to signify the intentional discontinuity between new and old. For Max Weber modernity stood for the principle of defining ends, and to produce and use adequate means to meet them (Rohbeck, 1993, p. 49). Daele sees the increase of contingency as a main feature of modern culture. By increase of contingency he means the translation of realities in possibilities, of limits to options of substance to function, of absolute values to mere preferences (Daele, 1993, p. 172). We will not try to include all possible meanings of modernity, post-modernity (cf. Lyotard, 1993), second modernity, and whatever other terms have been invented for it because the definitions are too disparate. Important for our purposes is to note that modernity is defined by a huge increase of knowledge that paradoxically leads to decreasing knowledge of the future. The central form of dealing with this uncertainty is the category of risk (cf. Bonß, 1995).

Since the topic of this book is the relationship of responsibility and information systems, we have to take a brief look at the impact of modernity on the normative structures of society. One feature of the normative side of modernity is the loss of certainty. From the beginning of enlightenment and then increasingly during industrialisation, traditional moral certainties were lost. The total reliance on God (or the church) for moral guidance became less tenable. For Max Weber this was the background of his explanation of the rise of capitalism that served as a worldly replacement of religion (cf. Beck, 1986, p. 135). It is clear that modern societies destroy old forms of social commitments. That does not mean that modern societies have to disintegrate into individualism (Priddat, 1998, p. 88), but it does mean that they become less personal and more institutional (Wieland, 1999, p. 117). The institutionalisation of ethical values and their transformation into legal values are reasons why the subjects do not experience them any more (Mai, 1996, p. 247). This is probably the reason why many, especially conservative authors speak of a loss of values. In fact values are not simply lost, but they change. The apparent change towards individualism and egotism is not a sign of decadence, but an objective necessity in the face of expanding spaces of free disposition that modern societies entail (Lübbe, 1993, p. 33).

One last societal development that is important for our topic is that of the information society. The term "information society" denotes all of the different aspects that result from technological development and the resulting problems as described above. At first sight the most important characteristics of the information society are the structural and organisational changes induced by IT. It can be defined as a form of society and economy in which the production, storage, processing, transmission, spread, and use of information and knowledge—including growing technological possibilities and interactive communication—play an increasing part (Mittelstraß, 1997). If we look at the amount of information produced in our society, and the fact that more and more people in western societies are employed dealing with information, then we can conclude that "Our society is truly an information society, our time an information age" (Mason, 1986, p. 5).

It would however be simplistic to interpret the information society as nothing but a sort of organisation using certain technology. To overcome this myopic interpretation, it is helpful to ask why we collectively decided to develop our society or societies into information societies. According to Mason et al. (1995, p. 32), there are four motivations for humanity to "embark on the ascent of information"; these are: "(a) the pursuit of wealth and the avoidance of destitution, (b) the pursuit of security and the avoidance of fear and uncertainty, (c) the pursuit of recreation and entertainment and the avoidance of boredom and depression, and (d) the pursuit of control and order and the avoidance of chaos." We see the recurring theme of uncertainty but also some other factors of moral relevance such as wealth and power. The reason we mention all of this here is that we want to make it clear that all of the developments connected to business and information technology are not just facts that can be described and accepted. All of the individual and societal developments discussed so far, from modernity, information society, risk, and uncertainty to the driving role that economy and technology play in them, have a moral angle. All of the moral angles allow different ethical interpretations and have been analysed with different ethical theories and tools. There is one concept, however, that can be found in the works of different authors from different backgrounds that seems to be especially suitable to address the issues at hand. That concept is the notion of responsibility.

RESPONSIBILITY AS THE ANSWER TO OUR PROBLEMS

Responsibility has become a key word of modernity. Whatever the deeper reason, the success of the term responsibility results from the fact that the normative challenges to human action under the conditions of modernity are growing. New developments need to be reflected constantly, with regard to their normative implications and responsibility is seen as a moral construct that can meet the challenge. This is why Hastedt (1994, p. 176) can state that modern societies need to rely on a general assumption of responsibility. The ascription of responsibility is the functional equivalent of legal or moral norms in such situations in which general norms are no longer applicable because of the complexity of the situation (Kaufmann, 1990, p. 71). The reason for the success of responsibility is thus the increasing awareness of the complexity of reality. This complexity leads to difficulties in applying traditional norms and thereby to a decrease of the collective validity of traditional morality. This development can of course backfire on responsibility, as a certain rest of accountability is necessary if responsibility is to be ascribed. So, while responsibility is a result of increasing complexity, it is at the same time dependent on the reduction of complexity to be viable (Spaemann, 1975, p. 331f). This is a general problem to which we will return in later chapters.

The facts that we talk about here are not new. It is one of the oldest ethical propositions that one should think about what one does and consider the results. What is new about it is that the reflection in our complex civilisation is hard scientific work (Sachsse, 1972, p. 124). As we have seen, the scientific attempts to tackle uncertainty and complexity can be found under the label of risk. If the rise of importance of the term responsibility is linked to uncertainty and complexity, and responsibility is seen as a moral answer to them, then the concept of responsibility should be viewed as the solution to moral problems posed by risk. Indeed, one can often find this view. From a general norm that each person is "responsible to those whom his actions affect, and he is morally bound not to harm others unless there is some overriding reason for doing so" (De George, 1999, p. 308), we progress to the postulation of responsibility for risk. Responsibility gains its specific relevance where classical tools of implementing norms fail (cf. Bayertz, 1995b; Kaufmann, 1995). It is important to note that since risks have to do with uncertainty, they are necessarily future occurrences, and therefore responsibility for risks is a specific form of responsibility, prospective responsibility, or responsibility *ex ante*. This sort of responsibility that will be discussed in more detail during the next chapter is the reason why responsibility is perceived as a potential solution for the normative problems produced by risks of technology (cf. Bayertz, 1995a, p. 45; Ricoeur, 1995c, p. 69).

Interestingly enough, the relationship between responsibility and risk is mutual. Not only is responsibility often perceived as a solution for moral questions of risk, but at the same time every ascription of responsibility is a risky endeavour. Risk is inseparable from responsibility, and it can even be said to constitute one of its most important ingredients (Etchegoyen, 1999, p. 149). Responsibility usually has some aspect pointing to the future and tends to be connected to some sort of sanction, which always comprises the possibility of going wrong, of ascribing actions or results on wrong grounds, according to non-viable norms, etc., so that the process of ascription can be said to be risky in itself. This also means that responsibility by its very foundations is a fallible construct.

We can now see why responsibility is related to business information technology and why it makes sense to address the moral problems of IS using the term responsibility. Both business and technology produce risks and are at the same time ways of dealing with them. Information technology has the express purpose of helping us deal with the increase of information that constitutes the reason for the increase in risks. IT is a tool for dealing with complexity and reducing it. It should help us understand larger amounts of data and transform them into information that is useful to us. In this sense IT is one of the factors that turn uncertainty into risk. This is true for general risks as well as for specifically economic risks. Information systems, we can summarise, create risks at the same time that they reduce them. If this is true and we accept the property of responsibility as being a remedy for the moral problems of risks, then the ascription of responsibility emerges as the preferred method for dealing with ethical and moral problems created by IS.

Apart from this argument there are several other reasons why responsibility may appear as a good solution for moral problems of IS.

THE SIMILARITY OF INFORMATION SYSTEMS AND RESPONSIBILITY

Another reason for the popularity of responsibility, especially in business contexts, is that the root of the term can be found in its legal use. Legal responsibility is a clear concept in business that is commonly recognised to firstly set and enforce the rules and secondly solve conflicts. Most business students must attend some lectures about commercial law. Knowing and being able to apply the concept of legal responsibility makes it easy for economic subjects to transfer their knowledge to the idea of moral responsibility.

Another point is that responsibility as a moral notion has a more positive ring to it than most other words from the realm of ethics and morality. While businesspeople may object to the idea that they should act morally or consider ethical questions, they will generally agree to the suggestion that they are responsible. This is due on the one hand to the acceptance of legal responsibility and on the other hand may be caused by other types of responsibility such as role responsibility. Being a CEO or manager is often defined by the responsibilities involved. Engineers and technicians have technical responsibilities, and workers at the lower end of a hierarchy tend to know what they are responsible for.

Also, there are several material and structural similarities between IS and responsibility. The first one is that all of these terms are morally charged and that they point toward a consequentialist idea of morality and some underlying theory of the good life. Responsibility is a consequentialist notion because it uses the results of actions as the basis of ascription. Business as well as IT are consequentialist in that the end result is generally considered to be more important than the process of getting there. Business is justified by its promise of producing an efficient allocation of resources, which in turn is supposed to produce maximal welfare. Maximal welfare is usually considered morally good because it enables people to choose what they consider the good life. Similarly, technology is meant to facilitate everyday chores as well as more complicated work with the purpose of giving man freedom from labour, misery, etc., to allow him to live his life according to his wishes (Kissling, 1995, p. 424).

While all of our terms are compatible with a morality of the good life, they remain formalistic in that they do not tell people what exactly it is that constitutes a good life or how to achieve it. The ethics of responsibility thus corresponds to IS in that it is open. Responsibility ascriptions as social constructs are not unequivocally predictable. The same is true again for business where we know some organising principles, such as the principle that organisations in markets have to make profits[6] without knowing how to do so.

Another important point linking business, IT, and responsibility is their reliance on communication. All three of them are social constructs and social products and therefore are clearly dependent on communication. Furthermore, responsibility consists of communication and would cease to exist without it. IT on the other hand is generally understood to be an attempt to improve channels of communication, an effort to provide new means and to help reach this goal. Business, finally, is also a social construct that uses communication to reach its goals and depends on IT to do so.

Furthermore, all of the terms involved promise to lead to action. While ethics is often perceived as a hobby for philosophers, theologians, and other groups of people who have a lot of time on their hands, responsibility seems to imply immediate action and results. Again legal responsibility is probably the reason for this perception because it delivers results quickly and visibly. This appeals to businesspeople as well as technicians and facilitates the application of responsibility in the sphere of IS.

The summary of this chapter is that responsibility is a notion that holds the promise to facilitate the analysis and solution of ethical and moral problems in the area of information systems. This is due firstly to the fact that technical and social developments have culminated in a situation where traditional morality no longer seems to be able to fulfil its role. The decline in the relevance of traditional morality was accompanied by a rise of the importance and popularity of the term responsibility. Responsibility is perceived as a solution to modern moral problems because it allows us to deal with uncertainty and risk. On the other hand it is closely related to information technology, which is also a tool to reduce complexity. All of this takes place in a society where human interaction is increasingly mediated by social systems, the most important of which is probably the economic system. Responsibility holds the promise to allow us to discuss morality and facilitate ethical reflection, and it does so on a social basis. This helps it overcome the solipsistic attitude that was one of the reasons for the failure of morality. We see that this is a rather ambitious picture. Responsibility is supposed to help us in several highly contentious tasks that take place in an uncertain environment. The decisive question that this book wants to answer is: Is it possible that the notion of responsibility can live up to these expectations, and if so, what are the practical consequences? In order to answer this, we will use the next chapter to give a detailed analysis of the notion of responsibility and the theoretical problems it entails.

Chapter IV

The Theory of Responsibility and Information Systems

In the broadest possible sense, responsibility is "but a set of practices that we use to describe and understand individual and social behaviour" (French, 1992, p. IX). In order to understand how we can use the term as a description and what results from the description, one must be aware of possible definitions, implications, dimensions, conditions, etc. In this chapter we will therefore attempt to describe all these different features of the word. In a first step we will look at the overall definitions that can be found in the literature and the implied objectives of its use. This part will also contain a first reflection on how responsibility relates to ethics and morality. The next part of this chapter will analyse the conditions that are commonly named for the ascription of responsibility. This will then allow us to discuss the classical dimensions, namely subject, object, and instance. From there we will proceed to take a look at the other relevant determinants of responsibility such as type, temporal dimension, sort of imputation, and the limits of ascription. As a summary we will extract the implications that most sorts and definitions of responsibility share. In total this chapter will lay the theoretical groundwork needed for addressing the problems that responsibility in information systems pose, which will then be discussed in the following chapters.

DEFINITION OF RESPONSIBILITY

Even though a definition is usually thought to be a rather brief process with a clear and concise phrase as result, the definition of responsibility is more complex. The term responsibility has many different meanings, which makes it very hard to grasp. There are different ways to react to such confusion. On the one hand one can give up in the face of such an obstacle and decide to give one's own definition. The advantage would be the clarity that is derived from proceeding in this way. The downside is that much of the ordinary language meaning is lost. On the other hand one can therefore try to pay attention to the general use of the word and try to distil the relevant core. In this chapter we will attempt this latter method. It is useful to distinguish between the meanings and objectives of responsibility. Meanings and objectives often refer to one another. However, in some cases they can even become contradictory. The somewhat extensive discussion of these two aspects will find its justification later on in the book when it will become useful in explicating and solving some of the detailed problems such as the question: "Who can be subject of responsibility?"

Meanings of Responsibility

We have already seen that there is a multitude of possible meanings of the term responsibility. Another factor that complicates the definition of the word is its inflationary use. This follows from what was said so far. If responsibility is perceived as a moral notion that helps us cope with the problems of the modern world, then it is only natural that it is in high demand. The lack of clarity is thus a result of its positive potential and general recognition. Another problem is the overextension of the term. Some theoreticians of responsibility make claims that are so wide that they become meaningless. In order to overcome these problems, it is imperative that we define the term and narrow it down. The different ways in which it is used in everyday life should be helpful in this endeavour.

A first and clear hint to the content of responsibility comes from its etymology. Responsibility comes from the "response," from answering. We can find this as the heart of responsibility in the work of many authors. "'Having a responsibility' is interwoven with the notion 'Having a liability to answer', and having such a liability or obligation seems to imply" (French, 1979, p. 210). The idea of a liability to answer is also reflected by Lewis (1972, p. 124f) or Collste (2000a, p. 125). This etymological root of the notion is reflected in other European languages as well. The French *"responsabilité"* also stands in a literal sense for "being able to respond" (Etchegoyen, 1993, p. 45; cf. Trigeaud, 1999, p. 94; Ricoeur, 1990a, p. 195). And the same is true for the German *"Verantwortung,"* which is based on *"Antwort,"* the answer (cf. Lenk & Maring, 1995, p. 247; Lenk, 1991a, p. 64; Schwartländer, 1991, p.

19). Answering is in itself already an ethically charged idea because it presupposes language, someone to whom one must answer, some kind of relationship, respect, etc.

The second common meaning of responsibility is not as clearly ethical. It is the use of the term for describing a causal relationship. In this sense responsibility can again have a wide range of meanings. Depending on whether we say that a natural disaster, a rogue state, or a mass murder was responsible for human deaths, the term means something different. One thing all of these meanings have in common, however, is that somebody or something caused something. While causality does play a role in responsibility, the limitation to causality is definitely too narrow. Most authors who refer to it do so as just one aspect of responsibility (cf. Goodpaster & Matthews, 1982, p. 133; Weckert & Adeney, 1997, p. 89; Johnson, 2001, p. 174).

The use of responsibility as a means to establish a causal relationship is in fact part of a wider meaning of the term. It is part of the central idea of imputation or ascription (Ricoeur, 1994, p. 24f). This meaning can again be demonstrated to be one of the etymological roots of the notion. While the word "responsibility" is relatively new in ethical contexts, its central theoretical problem of ascription (Latin: *imputatio*) has a long history (cf. Schmidt, 1992; Schwartländer, 1991). The purpose of a responsibility ascription can be understood to be the production or a relationship between several entities. In this book these entities are called "dimensions." The two most important dimensions are the subject and the object. The object is the entity that is being ascribed to the subject. To remain within our examples, if we say "the mass murderer is responsible for the deaths," then the mass murderer is the subject whereas the deaths are the object. The process of ascription generates the relationship between the two. If we agree on the ascription, then we can say that it was not the disaster and not the state that caused the deaths, but the mass murder. One purpose of a theory of responsibility as it is being developed here is to develop and justify criteria for such an imputation (Bayertz, 1995b, p. 64f).

The fact that responsibility is first of all an ascription allows several immediate conclusions. Firstly, an ascription is clearly a social construct. While the same may be true for every other moral, ethical, or legal term, in the case of responsibility there can be no doubt that it depends directly on those who are involved in the social process of ascribing. The social construct of a responsibility ascription is used to establish a relationship that has no independent metaphysical reality as such, but is always and without doubt dependent on everybody involved. Secondly, the character of an ascription is that it depends on and is constituted by communication. In order to realise an imputation or ascription, there needs to be some sort of communication between the affected parties. This is another hint of the ethical relevance of responsibility. Where there is communication, several ethical conditions must be fulfilled which will be discussed later.

Another important aspect of the idea of ascription is that it is concerned with consequences. When responsibility is ascribed to someone or something, then this generally means that some sort of consequence is taken into consideration and is made public (cf. Gehlen, 1973, p. 151; Ricoeur, 1990a, p. 341; Zimmerli, 1991, p. 83). This is one of the more important properties to which we will return on several occasions. Whenever one speaks of responsibility, there must be some sort of consequence to speak about.

The meanings of responsibility discussed so far were rather formal and limited in their approach. Responsibility was understood as a propensity to answer, as causality, or as the social construct of ascription referred to specific individuals or situations. There is also a wider view of responsibility as a human constant, as a part of what it means to be human. Birnbacher (1995, p. 165) shows that responsibility as part of morality can be of existential importance in providing meaning and orientation. Being responsible for someone or something can ease uncertainty concerning one's behaviour and one's self. In this sense responsibility is a key term of modernity because it explains man's behaviour towards himself and others. It is a sign of the creative relationship among humans who understand themselves as competent to form themselves and their environment (Bender, 1994, p. 132). Some authors go so far as to describe responsibility as one of the differences between man and animal (Taylor, 1995, p. 27). As Neuberg (1997, p. 2) points out, the difference between a human society and a pack of wolves is that we can treat each other differently, we can recognise one another as moral persons. Responsibility is thus constitutive for humans because it is based on specific properties, abilities, and conditions. Among these conditions are some that we generally see as genuinely human such as free will, the ability to recognise others as fellow humans, etc. (Böhret, 1987, p. 6). The human properties that allow responsibility are so close to the core of humanity that they are sometimes seen as part of human dignity. According to Lenk (Lenk & Maring, 1995, p. 249; Lenk, 1994b, p. 118), a human being can only be a moral person if he or she is able to accept responsibility. On the other hand human dignity demands that man as a free and acting being assume responsibility.

There is one last meaning of responsibility worth mentioning, because it often interferes with other interpretations and at the same time causes or expresses them. This is responsibility as a moral sentiment. The most extensive analysis of this view of responsibility has been done by Wallace who defines it as follows:

> *"To hold someone morally responsible is to view the person as the potential target of a special kind of moral appraisal. People who are morally responsible are not seen merely as acting in ways that happen to be good or bad; they are not just causally responsible for certain welcome or unwelcome happenings, the way a clogged drain might be said to be responsible for the unfortunate overflowing of a basin. Rather, the actions of morally responsible people are thought to reflect specially on them as agents, opening them to a kind of moral appraisal that does more than record a causal connection between them and the consequences of their actions."* (Wallace, 1996, p. 52)

This view of responsibility goes back to Strawson (1997), for whom moral responsibility can be understood in terms of certain social practices. Responsibility stands for a certain emotional reaction to what an actor does (cf. Fischer, 1999, p. 93).

This understanding of responsibility has the advantage of describing one important aspect that is often overlooked by other approaches. When we say: "A is responsible for X," then this usually contains an emotional aspect. We feel that A's behaviour was adequate or not, that she should be punished or commended. Whatever the specific case, a certain measure of emotional attitude towards A is involved. Another advantage of this definition of responsibility is that it solves several fundamental problems, especially the question of freedom as a condition of responsibility. The weakness of the approach is that it is self-contained, that it has no external consequences. While this facilitates its strengths, it leads to a loss of the original intention of using the term. In order to clarify this, we will use the next section to discuss what the purpose of responsibility might be.

Objectives of Responsibility

The social construct of responsibility only comes into existence because the people involved in it think it is worthwhile. Responsibility ascriptions thus always have an objective. In order to be able to decide most of the detailed questions about responsibility in IS, it is important to know this objective.

Usually responsibility ascriptions lead to sanctions, whether in the form of punishments, rewards, blame, or praise (cf. French, 1992, p. 18; Lenk, 1998,

p. 263). In most cases that are discussed in the literature, the negative aspects are emphasised and thus the attribution of punishment is often seen as the "main reason we are interested in attributing moral responsibility" (Velasquez, 1991, p. 122). The same is true for most other kinds of responsibility, most notably for legal responsibility (cf. Bayertz, 1995b, p. 22). The difference between the two are "the criteria for evaluating the outcome and the sanctions following a blameworthy action. In law, the criteria for evaluation are formally decided and legally institutionalised, while in morality the criteria for evaluation are according to some established informal ethos and the sanctions are, not institutionalised, blame" (Collste, 2000a, p. 126). While most scholars agree that the purpose of responsibility ascriptions is the attribution of sanctions, mostly punishment, it is far less clear what the purpose of that punishment is.

Maybe the oldest and most widely spread reason for punishment is retribution. It can be found in its purest form in the Old Testament, and "an eye for an eye" still counts as a valid argument in many parts of the world. Finding a justification for retribution is somewhat difficult. Fauconnet (1928, p. 142) offers an explanation for retribution that is based on the idea that punishment rectifies the wrong in the eyes of society. Punishment is thus not aimed at the offender, but at those who witness the offence. The idea of retribution can be interpreted as a metaphysical notion, that is to say that a bad has to be counterbalanced by a good, in this case represented by the punishment. Another explanation of retribution is the motive of revenge. The great critic of responsibility, Nietzsche, believes that wherever we are looking for responsibility, we are in fact looking for revenge (Nietzsche, 1987, p. 229).

However, retribution does not have to be based on revenge. As Höffe (1996, p. 235f) demonstrates, Kant's legal theory is also based on retribution, but it is aimed at the weaknesses of utilitarian thinking. Kant's justification of sanctions is based on his concept of justice. Justice for him is universal and results from pure practical reason. It is not to be tainted by considerations of utility. Punishment is justified by justice and that means that every punishable act must be punished according to its severity. Hart observes a change in emphasis in modern retributive theory from "the alleged justice or intrinsic goodness of the return of suffering for moral evil done, to the value of the authoritative expression, in the form of punishment, of moral condemnation for the moral wickedness involved in the offence" (Hart, 1968, p. 235). The latter argument can also be found in theological contexts and has been stated by Pope Pius XII (1987, p. 221).

While the idea of retribution is old and has many notable supporters, it seems to be losing some of its appeal, at least in some parts of the world, among them Western Europe. The main criticism of retaliation for the sake of retaliation is that it does nothing to change events. If we punish someone for something she did, then this will not change anything about what she did. Most authors therefore emphasise the role of deterrence as the prime motivation for punishment. Deterrence and retribution are of course connected because "retribution, the public sense that justice has been done, itself constitutes a deterrent to potential malefactors" (Staddon, 1999, p. 160). Retaliation serving as deterrence can thus help stabilise social morality and under this condition was even accepted if not practised by Gandhi (French, 1992, p. 27f).

Some authors prefer to leave aside the idea of retribution all together and concentrate instead on the question of how the ascription of responsibility and sanction can improve social life. This idea is not new either. "Even Plato thought that looking back to the past deed (except as a symptom indicating what was likely to cure or prevent) was irrational. To measure punishment by reference to it was, he said, like 'lashing a rock'" (Hart, 1968, p. 163). Punishment according to the prospective theories is supposed to facilitate human coexistence by enforcing law or morality (cf. Bayertz, 1995a, p. 22; Schlick, 1930, p. 33; Fauconnet, 1928, p. 152). In its clearest form this intention is often called the "economy of threats" (cf. Wallace, 1996, p. 54; Hart, 1968, p. 40). The idea is that the subject of responsibility knows the possible outcomes of the planned action and attaches a probability to them. He is then able to calculate an expected value for the utility of the outcome. If the expected value is negative, then the subject will refrain from acting and deterrence is successful. This idea is very strong in the utilitarian tradition starting from Bentham's writing about justice and punishment.[7]

The idea of the economy of threats has the advantage of being highly rational and thus acceptable for many philosophers. However, it also contains several weaknesses. One of the central difficulties is that it overestimates the abilities of real agents. In order to work as intended, the economy of threats has to take for granted that the agent knows which alternatives are open, knows their consequences and the resulting utility, can ascribe or estimate a probability for each of the alternatives, and knows how to do the maths behind it. We have already discussed the problems of probability and will later on come to the problem of knowledge of results. It should be plain to see that no single human being is able to fulfil the prerequisites for the economy of threats. If people cannot fulfil them, then it is questionable whether the idea makes sense at all. What remains is an external view that does not take the internal states of the agent into account and just looks at the results. From the point of view of methodology, this is admissible since the economy of threats explicitly aims at real social consequences and only stipulates the agent's internal states in order to gain credibility. The ethical validity of the economy of threats approach thus boils down to the empirical question whether it is successful.[8] This opens the door to critics of punishment for reasons of deterrence such as Menninger (1987, p. 233), who states that the strategy of fighting crime by threatening terms of imprisonment has failed completely. Proponents of punishment therefore need to use some other sort of argument. Consequently, Lord Denning, a proponent of capital punishment, told the Royal Commission on Capital Punishment:

> *"It is a mistake to consider the object of punishment as being deterrent or reformative or preventive and nothing else...The ultimate justification of any punishment is not that it is a deterrent, but that it is the emphatic denunciation by the community of a crime: and from this point of view there are some murders which, in the present state of public opinion, demand the most emphatic denunciation of all, namely the death penalty'."*
> (cited after Hart, 1968, p. 170)

A last objective of responsibility ascriptions, that in some cases is similar to sanctions but driven by different motivations, is restitution. For the responsible agent it is in some cases of no difference whether she pays a fine or settles the damages, but the intention is different. Restitution has more clearly the goal of facilitating social life by giving some kind of compensation to the victim. While restitution will in many cases not make the victim whole again, it can do so better than punishment. Some authors believe that restitution is the first objective of responsibility, and punishment only holds the second place (Höffe, 1995, p. 21).

We now know several objectives of the sanctions resulting from responsibility, several reasons why a person or group of persons would go to the trouble and attempt an ascription. These motivations are important if we want to understand the details and problems of responsibility ascriptions, and in many cases they can help solve those problems. On the other hand they pose a problem of their own because in some cases they are not compatible. Retribution, revenge, restitution, and social change can be conflicting goals. If for the sake of retribution it may appear necessary to impose the most serious punishment, at the same time the goal of improving collective quality of life may lead to much more lenient measures. The objectives of responsibility also determine the approach to specific cases. Let us take a brief look at the question whether we should punish the insane, that is to say people who to our knowledge have no control over their actions. From the viewpoint of retribution, this may make sense. On the other hand it is impossible to deter someone who cannot control his or her action. Thus it would seem that from the point of view of the economy of threats, we should not punish them (which is Bentham's argument). Hart (1968, p. 19) demonstrates that the social good may still be served by punishing them, because they may not be deterred but their example may deter others. We see that the objectives determine the ascription of responsibility. According to Becker (1976, p. 68):

> *"Actual criminal proceedings in the United States appear to seek a mixture of deterrence, compensation, and vengeance. I have already indicated that these goals are somewhat contradictory and cannot generally be simultaneously achieved...."*

One way to shed some light on this confusion may be to return to the normative foundations of responsibility which we will do in the next section.

Responsibility, Ethics, and Morality

Earlier on, during the discussion of the French and German tradition of moral philosophy, we said that responsibility is a moral notion. Now, after having introduced the notion of responsibility in some more detail, we can take the next step and see how responsibility fits in with the different theories of moral philosophy.

There is some ambiguity as to whether responsibility is always and exclusively a moral notion or maybe even no moral notion at all. This ambiguity is caused by the different meanings and definitions of ethics, morality, and responsibility. Many authors would follow Lewis, however, when he answers the question of what responsibility means:

> *"It means simply to be a moral agent, and this means to be an agent capable of acting rightly or wrongly in the sense in which such conduct is immediately morally good or morally bad, as the case may be."* (Lewis, 1991, p. 23)

While Lewis continues by saying that we cannot say what rightness, moral worth, and their correlatives mean, Etchegoyen (1999, p. 43) goes the opposite way and states that responsibility is the contemporary expression of the true morality.

Both of these statements tell us that responsibility and morality are closely related, but they do not really help us with the ethical classification of responsibility. Obviously ethics, morality, and responsibility are not equal, or else it would not make any sense to discuss them separately. A first difference is that moral rules tend to be expressed negatively, whereas responsibility is characterised by positive instructions. Moral rules frequently tell us what to refrain from doing ("Thou shalt not…"), while responsibilities are often things we have to do (cf. Birnbacher, 1995, p. 151).

Other than that, responsibility can be used to express all sorts of moral theories and ideas. In the most general sense, responsibility stands for a relationship between two parties in which one party does something that affects the well-being of the other party (Ladd, 1992, p. 291). There is one meaning of the term ethics, however, that is ruled out by the use of the term responsibility, namely purely descriptive ethics. Responsibility as an ascription has the explicit purpose of accusing someone, of looking for retribution, deterrence, or maybe for rewards. Either way it is not neutral and by its definition never can be neutral (cf. Höffe, 1995, p. 21).

The rest of this chapter will be used to show how responsibility is related to different ethical theories. Responsibility is not equal to any of the concepts discussed so far, but it has areas of interaction with all of them. As a first example we can take a look at virtue ethics. This is the ethical tradition with the longest history, with Plato and Aristotle being the first great representatives. Virtue ethics is one of the traditions still frequently discussed today because it contains some aspects that are generally plausible. The underlying idea is that humans should live virtuously. There are many reasons why one should live this way. Traditionally virtue is seen as the path to the good life. Responsibility fits in here because it can be interpreted as a virtue. If acting responsibly is defined as taking a course of action such that its aim is the prevention of harm to others, then responsibility becomes a disposition to a certain sort of action and thus a virtue (Ladd, 1992, p. 297). This definition of responsibility is not exactly the same as the one we have used so far, but it is certainly translatable into our terms.

But responsibility is not only a virtue; it can also be described in the terms of teleology and deontology. While at first sight there seems to be a contradiction between teleology and deontology, this does not apply to responsibility. The term responsibility seems to have replaced the formerly dominant term of duty as the central concept of moral philosophy or become a sort of duty itself (cf. Ropohl, 1987, p. 154; Schwartländer, 1991, p. 17f; Bochenski, 1991, p. 24; Bayertz, 1995b, p. 33; van Luijk, 1990, p. 40; Kettner, 1995, p. 311).

Responsibility, understood in a broad way as a representation of morality, always has to do with duty and intention. If responsibility is viewed from its objective of improving human coexistence, then it can be interpreted as the duty to avoid harm (cf. Hager, 1990, p. 60). "Responsibility and obligation are closely related. In general, we have an obligation or a duty to fulfil our responsibilities, and we are responsible for fulfilling our obligations" (De George, 1999, p. 110). As De George is quick to point out, responsibility and obligation are not the same. According to Jonas (1991, p. 194), responsibility is a specific case of obligation that is characterised by an external relationship. Another link that responsibility holds to the deontological ethical tradition is its reliance on conditions that are classically associated with deontological ideas such as freedom and autonomy, which will be discussed later on.

On the other hand responsibility is also clearly related to teleology. There are several arguments that support this claim. The first one is that the object of responsibility must be human life and human dignity (Kissling, 1995, p. 424). If one supports this statement, then responsibility aims at the good life and is thus teleological. Another hint towards the teleological quality of responsibility comes from the importance of consequences. Consequentialism is one type of teleological ethics that is characterised by its reliance on consequences for the ethical evaluation of facts or actions. The ascription of responsibility is always grounded on consequences, be they in the past or future. Assuming responsibility means that the subject agrees to accept the consequences of his or her actions (Sinn & Zimmerli, 1986, p. 35). On the other hand, successfully solving problems, thus dealing with consequences, can be seen as the quality mark of responsibility (Kaufmann, 1992, p. 76). It is doubtful that Etchegoyen (1999, p. 52) is right when he says that consequences are the only and exclusive foundation of responsibility, but it is generally accepted that consequences play an important role.

Responsibility is also close to the French tradition of moral philosophy as it was introduced earlier. The duty to answer for the consequences that one has caused is always a duty towards someone else, thus to the other who plays such an eminent role in the French tradition. It is therefore no surprise that especially French authors emphasise this aspect. The answer, the heart of responsibility, first of all presupposes the existence of the other (Etchegoyen, 1999, p. 83; 1993, p. 210; Philippe, 1991, p. 235). This relationship between myself and the other is based on equality. The fact that I answer means that there is someone who is similar to me in that she has the same basic aptitudes and rights, that she is a moral person like myself. There are also other concepts of responsibility that put the stress not on equality but on the opposite, on the fact that there is responsibility even if the other does not recognise me. In the extreme it is the other's death and death in general that is the cause of all responsibility (cf. Levinas, 1983, 1984; Malka, 1984). While this is a very specific theory of responsibility that we will not be able to discuss here in more detail, the fundamental idea that responsibility is based on the other and that its moral quality arises in large part from this relationship can be found in other philosophic traditions as well. A bridge between the German and the French tradition in this respect is built by Ricoeur (1994, p. 24f), who sees the similarity of Jonas' approach to the French thinkers. For Jonas, responsibility is the solicitude for another being that is recognised as obligation in the face of its vulnerability (Jonas, 1984, p. 391).

Most theories of responsibility converge on the fact that when we are responsible, have responsibility, act responsibly, the other plays an important role. What makes the ascription of consequences morally relevant is that they have an impact on others. The moral relevance of the other can again be justified by deontological ideas (Summer, 1998, p. 109) as well as by teleological or other moral theories. Responsibility can thus be defined as an ascription based on the fact that a moral being is affected (Neumaier, 1994, p. 170). This importance of the other means that the agent can never determine the scope and scale of his or her responsibilities since it is always determined by others. Others are affected and thus are the reason for responsibility ascriptions. At the same time they are involved in the process of ascription, in the imputation of sanctions and the realisation of the results.

This description of the moral roots of responsibility was supposed to show that the term does not belong unequivocally to any specific moral theory, but is compatible with most of them. It was thus also meant to demonstrate that the apparent contradiction between ethics of responsibility and ethics of disposition (*Verantwortungsethik, Gesinnungsethik*) that was famously put forward by Weber (1992) is not as divisive as it seems at first sight. Weber distinguished between the two approaches to ethics saying that one, the ethics of responsibility, considered the consequences, whereas the other aimed mainly at intention or mental states when making ethical judgments. Even though Weber himself pointed out that the two aspects are not mutually exclusive but in fact depend on one another, one can find this putative confrontation in many texts about responsibility. We hope to have made clear that it is neither relevant nor true and that responsibility combines the different aspects of duty, obligation, and consequentialism while also offering possibilities to accommodate other ethical theories and schools.

The multiple possibilities of explaining and justifying responsibility are one of the central strengths of the term, but at the same time are also one of its weaknesses. Responsibility always suffers from a certain ambiguity and is always open to different interpretations. It is also impossible to give a final foundation for it. Unlike some of the ethical traditions that try to anchor their theories in reason, love, peace, or whatever else, a theory of responsibility always has to accept that there is no final foundation. Responsibility is the expression of morality, and without morality there is no responsibility. Therefore responsibility always contains an element of decision that cannot itself be explained in other terms (Berger, 1994, p. 137). The alternatives to that are describing responsibility as simply part of human nature (Neuberg, 1997b, p. 16) or to seek a foundation in metaphysics (Jonas, 1984; Levinas, 1984).

PROBLEMS OF RESPONSIBILITY AND INFORMATION SYSTEMS

We now have all of the theoretical background to understand what responsibility can mean in the field of information systems and at the same time recognise the problems that this poses. In order to understand what the different problems of responsibility and IS are, we should look at some brief scenarios that revolve about different applications of responsibility and IS:

- The CIO (Chief Information Officer) is responsible for the development and functioning of the company's information systems.
- Programmer Smith assumes (is ascribed) responsibility for not eliminating the bug that resulted in the loss of vital data.
- Electronic commerce is responsible for a huge potential in savings due to the decrease in transaction costs.
- Computers and computerised trading are responsible for the globalisation of financial transactions.
- The central computer of the air defence system was responsible for the decision to fire the rocket and shoot down the airliner.

We see that responsibility and IS can be combined in a number of different ways that are not necessarily related to one another. Computers can play the role of the subject as well as the object of responsibility. They can have different temporal directions, they can be descriptive, normative, reflexive, transitive, and so on. In the following subsections we will discuss most of these aspects insofar as they are relevant to the use of computers and IT in business. In the first step we will concentrate on the conditions of responsibility.

The purpose of the next few sections is to recapitulate the literature on responsibility and demonstrate the difficulties it entails. It will become clear that it is almost impossible to construct a case or an example of responsibility that fulfils all of the conditions, has an acceptable subject and object, that follows the reasoning of moral philosophers, and at the same time has tangible results. Not only are some of the commonly named ingredients of responsibility contradictory, it is even doubtful whether the notion holds any promises for those cases that it was designed for. The great moral questions stemming from social change set off by technological developments mostly seem resistant to the notion of responsibility. This is why Apel (1980, p. 229) can say: "A universal, i.e., intersubjectively valid ethics of collective responsibility thus seems both necessary and impossible."

Briefly, what we intend to do in the following pages is demonstrate the limits of responsibility in order to lay the foundations for the subsequent development of a theory of reflective responsibility.

Conditions of Responsibility

Conditions of responsibility are those circumstances, traits, or properties that have to be fulfilled in order to render the ascription of responsibility viable and acceptable. The bulk of these conditions refer to the subject. The subject is the person, group, or other entity that is responsible. Generally it is understood to be the grown-up human in her capacity as a person. We will look into the questions concerning the subject in the next section after discussing what conditions it is supposed to fulfil.

It is without a doubt one of the central tasks of any theory of responsibility to determine what the conditions of responsibility are. They are necessary to determine who or what can act as subject, object, or instance. They are also the foundation of the discovery of excusing circumstances and a successful ascription. Depending on the theory of responsibility one talks about and the corresponding objectives of the ascription, the conditions that have to be fulfilled vary. There is, however, a group of circumstances often cited as conditions that seem to be necessary for most theories of responsibility. In a first step one can distinguish between "objective" conditions that are independent of specific subjects and the "personal" conditions that have to be fulfilled by a subject in order for it to play its role. One of the most commonly named objective conditions is that of causality.

Causality

We have already mentioned that one of the meanings of responsibility can be causality. The limitation of responsibility to purely causal relationships is too narrow to be of any real interest. Nevertheless, there is a close connection of responsibility between responsibility and causality that can be expressed by naming causality as a central condition of the ascription of responsibility. Causality is never the only condition, but it is generally recognised as a *conditio sine qua non* of responsibility. "A necessary condition an agent must satisfy to be held morally responsible for a decision is that the agent must figure in the causal chain resulting in the decision or be capable of such figuring in the causal chain" (Bechtel, 1985, p. 298). This necessity of the subject to figure in the causal chain is true for moral (cf. Jonas, 1984, p. 172; Ulrich, 1997, p. 74) as well as legal responsibility (cf. Moore, 1999).

Causality, however, is a problematic concept. In our everyday life we may not be bothered by its intricacies, but if we want to realise valid ascriptions of responsibility, we find that it is difficult. The first problem is that the nature of causality is unclear. Is it something that can be found in the objects or is it just in our perception? Is it maybe just one of our own habits, forced onto us by evolution as a programme with life-enhancing properties (Riedl, 2001, p. 76)? Another problem is that it cannot be limited. If we look at the physical image of cause and effect, we find that every effect turns out to be a cause for the next generation of effects. Whenever we talk about causality and look at a certain effect and look for its causes, we have to be aware that this distinction is always temporal and may change quickly. On the other hand it is also impossible to find the first cause for any given effect because that in turn was caused by something else. When De George (De George, 1999, p. 111) says that "the causal chain sometimes is a long one," he palliates the situation. It is not only long, it is infinite. We therefore have to be aware that every causal relationship that we use as the basis of a responsibility ascription is itself just that, an ascription. Being the start of a causal chain as a prerequisite of responsibility, as Rötzer (1998, p. 18) puts it, is only a way of describing that we have to posit a point at which we start the ascription.

But even if we accept that causality is nothing but a construct with the purpose of explaining things and ultimately imposing judgments and sanctions, we still have the problem that there are no clear rules to follow in this construction. There are different sorts of causality. For example, it can be direct or indirect (Ladd, 1992, p. 293). Direct causality is what is intended, obvious to the agent and the observer (even though what is obvious to me does not have to be obvious to you), and follows in a straight line. Cases where this sort of causality exists are generally cases where responsibility ascriptions do not pose too difficult a problem. However, normally this is not the case. Most ethically relevant developments today are not intended, not caused by a single person or group, and do not follow a straight line. The obvious example in this work is computer networks, especially the Internet. The Internet has a pervasive influence on our daily lives, on the way we do business, on the way we interact. Causalities in the Internet are hard to come by, however. There is no clear answer to questions like, "Who built the Internet?" or "Who is in charge of the development so far and who determines how it continues?" The Internet is a good example of an artefact that was built by a collective that was never constituted formally. Many people have participated for many different reasons, and the result that we see today is cumulative and did not causally result from anything or anybody that could be easily described in hindsight. Collective and cumulative action is thus one example for a loss of causality that leads to difficulties with the ascription of responsibility.

Apart from the fact that there is no single person or group to whom one could ascribe causality, another problem with the Internet is that it was not explicitly intended the way it is used now by anyone. When we look at the Internet today from an economic point of view, we see a universal platform used for e-commerce and e-business that promises huge improvements in the way we do business and equally huge cost savings by facilitating information and interaction, and lowering transaction costs. This was not intended by the founders of the mainly military ARPA net, nor by Berners-Lee when he thought up the World Wide Web. One can see that even if we suppose that the philosophically fundamental problems of causality are overcome by using a constructivist approach, causality is still a problem because it may be next to impossible to construct causality for cumulative action or unintended results. These problems will return later on in the discussion of the subject and object of responsibility. For now we will leave these questions and proceed to the next condition of responsibility that is often seen as contradictory to causality, to freedom.

Freedom

It is generally agreed that responsibility presupposes freedom. For a subject to be responsible, it must have (had) alternatives to the actions it did or will do. Without such a margin we cannot speak of responsibility (cf. Picht, 1991; Frankfurt, 1997).

"Traditionally the most influential view about the sort of free-dom necessary and sufficient for moral responsibility posits that this sort of freedom involves the availability of genuinely open alternative possibilities at certain key points in one's life. With-out this sort of alternative possibility, it is alleged, one is com-pelled to do as one actually does." (Fischer, 1999, p. 99)

Responsibility and freedom are in a relationship of mutual reference. Responsibility is based on the supposition of freedom, and freedom leads to responsibilities (Bayertz, 1995a, p. 12). Freedom can even become an object of responsibility because the subject has to ensure its freedom. If I give up my freedom to choose between alternatives without a good reason, then I may be held responsible for the loss of liberty (Wunenburger, 1993, p. 174). The relationship between freedom and responsibility may be even clearer when we look at the negative side. It is not plausible to ascribe responsibility for something that the subject had no freedom to decide, that happened as an act of fate (Birnbacher, 1995, p. 169; Sänger, 1991, p. 76).

This apparent unanimity of authors on a basic point is probably based on common sense. In cases where there is no choice, it does not make sense to hold someone responsible. If, for whatever reason, we could agree that it would be a moral duty to float one foot above the ground, then we still could not hold people responsible for not doing so because it is simply impossible for humans. Similarly we only hold people in IS responsible for things that they are free to change. The programmer is not responsible if the hardware does not work correctly, and the CIO is not responsible if an earthquake destroys the company's information system. On the other hand these examples lead us to the question of the limits to which freedom goes and how people are supposed to evaluate their choices. The programmer might have had the freedom to check the hardware first and the CIO might have known that in California earthquakes are a frequent occurrence.

There are other more philosophical problems of freedom. One is the distinction between freedom of action and freedom of will. Even if we follow Höffe (1995, p. 23) in saying that freedom of action is not problematic because it results from mankind's anthropological constants such as lack of instincts and intelligence, which necessitate free action, it is much less clear whether humans also have a freedom of will. In our context this means that even if an external observer might discern several alternatives that the subject could choose and thus conclude that it is possible to ascribe responsibility to him or her, it is not clear whether the subject knows about these alternatives and perceives the possibility of such a choice. If the subject does not see the alternative, then it is doubtful whether he or she can really be described as free and therefore whether responsibility is appropriate. Usually, when freedom is mentioned as a prerequisite of responsibility, both sorts of freedom—freedom of will and of action—are implied (cf. Koller, 1996; Bayertz, 1993, p. 31; Voland, 1998, p. 47). On the other hand the subject may feel perfectly free to decide what she does, but an outside observer may be capable to completely predict what she will to. This might suggest a lack of freedom.

> *"In other words, subjective and objective meanings of free will need not, and in general do not, coincide. The feeling of freedom can perfectly well coexist with perfect predictability and perfect determinism."* (Staddon, 1999, p. 148)

This leads us to the most frequently discussed part of the question of freedom, to the relationship of freedom and determinism. In the world of physics, there is neither freedom nor coincidence. Everything can be reduced to cause and effect. This has led the French philosopher and mathematician Laplace to stipulate that if there was a demon that knew the location and momentum of every particle, then this demon could perfectly predict the future. While modern physics and Heisenberg's uncertainty principle indicate that it is impossible to gather the required information, even in theory, this does not change the principle. Human beings live in this world of physics, and a strong theory of determinism assumes that we as physical beings are thus completely determined by the laws of cause and effect. Even our thoughts and in this case my writing about them are nothing but predetermined. This may contradict my feeling that I am writing because I decided to do it and could just as well do something else, but that feeling is of course itself an effect caused by the movement of electrons, atoms, or molecules in my brain, and those movements are subject to predetermined paths. Fisher calls this "causal determinism," which is defined as:

> *"...the claim that a complete statement of the laws of nature and a complete description of the (temporally non-relational or 'genuine') facts about the world at some time T entail every truth about the world after T."* (Fischer, 1999, p. 99f)

There are also weaker forms of determinism such as social determinism. In these theories we find statements to the effect that we are much less free than we think and that even those things that we may perceive as intimate personal decisions are in fact determined by our social background. Bourdieu (1998) spends a considerable effort showing that matters of taste—of our likes and dislikes in music, art, etc.—are to a great extend predetermined by the social status of our parents, our formal education, etc.

The clash between determinism and responsibility is not a new one. "A perennial subject of dispute in the Western philosophical tradition is whether human agents can be responsible for their actions even if determinism is true " (Meyer, 1999, p. 250). Many authors hold that if a strong determinism is true, we lack the freedom of will and action necessary for an ascription of responsibility. But the alternative is no better. If we move away from determinism, the solution seems to be to give humans the opportunity to do things that are not caused by anything outside of them. Apart from the fact that this would ascribe attributes of the divine first mover to humans (Chisholm, 1997, p. 49f), it also leads us to problems of causality. The freedom to do things that are not caused by anything or anybody would tear apart causal chains. This would then in turn lead to problems with the first condition of responsibility, with causality. This ends in a dilemma. If determinism is true, we cannot make a difference in the world and can therefore not be responsible. If it is not true, then causality does not work any more and we may make a difference, but nobody will know about the reasons, and therefore responsibility does not make sense either.

The position that sees responsibility and determinism as mutually exclusive is often called 'incompatibilism'. There are many good philosophical texts on this topic that we will not be able to discuss here.[9] One solution to the dilemma is to move away from the strong determinism towards a weaker one. "Responsibility depends on a degree of determinism, namely, predictable response to contingencies of reward and punishment (reinforcement contingencies)" (Staddon, 1999, p. 173). Wallace (1996) also argues for the compatibility of determinism and responsibility on the basis of his concept of responsibility as a moral sentiment. To ascribe responsibility, which means to have distinctive moral feelings towards someone, does not require that person to be free.

The problem of freedom and determinism is a very old one, and we will not be able to solve it here. If we want to keep on talking about responsibility, that of course means that the philosophical position of this paper must be compatibilist. For us, a constructivist position seems most appropriate. Starting from Kant's observation that man's freedom can be proven as well as his lack of freedom (cf. Kant, 1995b, p. B566ff), one can ask how that is possible. A constructivist solution would be to say that we can never observe the world itself and determine the possibility of freedom within it. The only thing we can do is analyse our models of the world. Differing models can lead to different solutions. In this case, the physical model of the world does not leave any room for freedom. Our own experience, however, is another model that is no worse than physics, and some of us do occasionally feel free in certain respects. If we follow the constructivist credo and give up hope that we can ever see the world as it is and that we will always have to work with self-constructed models of differing adequacy for different problems, then we may be able to combine two apparently contradictory world views. The conclusion for this text is that one can recognise the problem of determinism and still believe that the ascription of responsibility makes sense. This may be done by Wallace's strategy of interpreting responsibility as a moral sentiment or by another strategy, for example by concentrating on the presumed social utility of responsibility ascriptions.

One particular aspect of determinism with important implications for our topic is technological determinism. This is the doctrine that technological development follows laws that are akin to natural laws in that they are unchangeable and can at best be described but never changed. This is a necessary consequence of a strong determinist theory. One can also hear this kind of thought from others who would not subscribe to a strong determinism. Indeed, the development of computers and information technology appear more similar to natural growth than to controlled and intentional developments. There are even so-called laws that describe this development. The most important one of these laws is probably Moore's law, which says that the number of transistors on a computer chip doubles every 18 to 24 months. The better known result of this law is that the speed of micro-processors doubles every 18 to 24 month at a constant cost (Pitt, 1999, p. 119). Another law is Grosch's law, which says that the computational power of computers rise with the square of the cost (Zerdick et al., 2001, p. 116).

While especially Moore's law has worked for more than 30 years despite regularly recurring objections that we would soon come to a natural end of the development, one should nevertheless be careful to compare these computer "laws" to natural laws. The danger in calling them laws is that they may be accepted as unchangeable and thus cease to be subject to ethical discussions. Another case in point is the development of the Internet. There are many ethical pros and cons to this artefact, some of which will be discussed later on in the book. These ethical issues should give rise to a discussion about the way we want the Internet to be developed. Do we want it mainly as an economic means, do we want to use it for educational or political purposes, do we want central control or complete freedom? All of these are valid questions, and their answers determine how societies go about developing technical infrastructure, rights of access, etc. However, if we accept that the development of the Internet follows some kind of economic, technical, or other law, that it is thus predetermined, then these ethical discussions will not take place and this is in itself a moral fact that would need to be discussed.

We, as a society and as humankind, have to realise that we can control technical developments and that we have to take responsibility for them. Apart from the argument of technological determinism, we can also find the thesis of technological constraints. This is a weaker thesis in that it says that, originally, technological development followed human intentions, but the original development now requires certain technological advances. This argument has more validity than the pure determinism because it can point to some facts that are hard to ignore. Following a majority of philosophers of technology, we should keep in mind that technology is made and shaped by humans, and that humans therefore keep responsibility for it (cf. Rohbeck, 1993, p. 204; Guggenberger, 1992, p. 37; Murswik, 1991, p. 160). Even admitting that not all choices are open to us, that we are for example unable to return to an agrarian society without great losses, one still has to admit that the use of technology for good or bad is up to human beings (Walther, 1992, p. 85).

Freedom, as we have seen, implies that there is the freedom of choice and the possibility to act. Consequently, one can find this ability to act as another possible precondition for responsibility. The ability to act, in order to be wholly convincing, should be based on an theory of action. A theory of action in turn will generally have to make the same assumptions as a theory of responsibility. The agent is usually imagined as possessing a certain degree of freedom of will and action, intentions, imagination, means to achieve objectives, control over her actions, and the ability to correct mistakes (Zimmerli, 1991, p. 84). The ability to act can thus be seen as a criterion of responsibility that is similar to but weaker than the criterion of being a person that will be discussed later on (Maring, 1989, p. 38).

While the questions of causality and freedom are probably the most complex ones with the longest philosophical history, they are not the only conditions of responsibility. The next one to be discussed here is the question of power.

Power

Power as a precondition of responsibility is a mix of the first two conditions, of causality and freedom. When we say that power is a condition of responsibility, that usually means that the subject had the power to do whatever responsibility is ascribed for at any particular moment. This includes some sort of causality, and it also implies that the subject did it voluntarily, that she did it according to her free will. Another way of saying this is that having control over something is the condition for being held responsible for it (Nida-Rümelin, 1998, p. 31).

Power as a precondition of responsibility is a wide notion including capabilities, personal qualities, and so forth. It is not restricted to political power in the sense of being able to make others do one's bidding. However, this sense is also included. One can find that power in the narrower sense also has an influence and that most authors agree that more power leads to more responsibility (cf. Lenk & Maring, 1990, p. 50; Birnbacher, 1995, p. 152). The correlation of power and responsibility corresponds to what was said earlier on about the correlation of responsibility and technology. The fact that technology increases our ability to do things, to cause changes, and also to know about these changes, makes it a prime reason for an increase in responsibility (cf. Lenk, 1997, p. 77; Küng, 1997, p. 99; Ricoeur, 1995c, p. 64).

It is of course hard to practically determine who had the power to do what and whose doing the result was. Therefore one can often find the condition of power expressed negatively, that is to say that a lack of power is accepted as an excuse from responsibility (cf. De George, 1999, p. 121). "…you cannot be held responsible for something over which you have no control" (Staddon, 1999, p. 146). Fain suggests that for someone to be held solely responsible, that person not only brought about the result, but "it was in his power to prevent the situation from occurring" (Fain, 1972, p. 29).

Apart from causality and freedom, power is usually presumed to be linked to personal attributes of the subject that would enable him or her to make use of this power. There is a host of these attributes that will be discussed in the next section.

Personal Qualities

We all know that responsibility ascriptions differ with personal qualities of the subject. If I shoot my neighbour, I will most probably be held accountable for that, whereas this would probably be different if my one-year-old son did the same thing. The reason for this is that an adult and a child have different personality traits that are relevant for being a subject of responsibility. There are different abilities that a person needs in order to become responsible, and according to Kaufman (1995, p. 88), these can be grouped in moral, cognitive, and communicative abilities. Without wanting to rank these attributes, we will just briefly describe them, starting with emotions.

Emotions play a complex role in responsibility depending on the prevailing theory. For theorists like Strawson or Wallace (cf. Wallace, 1996, p. 8) who see responsibility as a moral sentiment, and according to Stocker, also for Aristotle it is "constituted by, and in this sense secondary to, certain emotions and emotional reactions" (Stocker, 1999, p. 196). Other theories of responsibility also have a link to emotions. Humans often need to cross some personal threshold before they start acting responsibly. That threshold can be a personal concern that changes the perception of a social dilemma to a personal one (Bierhoff, 1995, p. 225) and it is linked to emotion. As long as we do not feel that we are concerned, we will not be willing to assume responsibility.

Another point where emotions are of relevance is the social utility of responsibility. Going back to the purpose of responsibility, one finds that a frequently named reason for invoking it is social change. This social change is to be engendered by affecting the motivation of agents, which in turn is done by giving incentives to do or refrain from doing certain things. This intellectual exercise can only be fruitful if there is some sort of transmission that brings it to action. The transmission mechanism in question can be emotion. There is no use in the agent knowing that a certain punishment awaits her for some behaviour if this knowledge cannot impress her and make her act accordingly. The following quote that concerns emotion's role in ethics in general can be transferred to responsibility as well:

> "Indeed, emotions serve specific roles in the moral life. As expressive capacities, they function as a medium by which we signal our moral interest to others, such as when we express compassion when a friend suffers, or grief at her loss; as sensitivities, they are the receptors or antennae by which we, in turn, pick up signals of moral salience or interest. They are the modes by which we track moral relevance." (Sherman, 1999, p. 297)

Furthermore, one can be held responsible for one's emotions. There are emotions that are viewed as positive, such as love, mercy, or compassion, and emotions that are regarded as negative, such as hate, anger, or ingratitude.[10]

The subject must dispose of more than just emotions. Another important property is intention. Nature and degree of intention influence the outcome of responsibility ascriptions. Sanctions will differ depending on whether I shot my neighbour on purpose or whether I did it accidentally while cleaning my gun. Intention relates back to the other conditions already discussed. It implies causality, knowledge of this causality, and the freedom to change things. The discourse concerning intentions is well developed in the legal tradition where determining and judging intentions are an important part of the process of imposing sanctions. It is therefore little wonder that a philosopher of law like Hart uses an elaborate theory of intentions:

> *"Intention is to be divided into three related parts, to which I shall give what I hope are three self-explanatory names. The first I shall call 'intentionally doing something', the second 'doing something with a further intention', and the third 'bare intention' because it is the case of intending to do something in the future without doing anything to execute this intention now."*
> (Hart, 1968, p. 117)

The legal aspect of intentions is often discussed under the heading of "*mens rea*" (a guilty mind), which in Anglo-American law seems to be a condition of criminal proceedings. According to Hart (1968, p. 114), the *mens rea* requirement includes all of the mental or intellectual elements that the perpetrator must fulfil, but intention is the central one among them. Long (1999, p. 129) sees the difference between responsible and non-responsible wrongdoers in the presence of malicious thoughts in the former. Intention, however, is not limited to the legal concept of responsibility but applies to all other sorts as well. More generally, " We say that some person P is responsible for the outcome O of an action A, when P has intentionally caused A in order to achieve O" (Collste, 2000a, p. 125). According to Rötzer (1998, p. 18), responsibility, in a strong sense of the word, means that in addition to being causally responsible, one must have intended something knowing the potential consequences.

Intention as a condition of responsibility may be a plausible thought, and the examples given above explain why this is so. On the other hand intention is also a serious problem for the ascription of responsibility because it is by definition unknown. All those cases in which responsibility is ascribed to the subject by someone other than the subject itself have to deal with the problem that they have to rely on the subject's description of her intentions or on her behaviour. Both may be misleading. The subject can lie in order to escape prosecution, she may be unaware of the real reasons for her actions or her motivations, and intentions may be too complex to be adequately understood. Behaviour can be a good guide for the judgment of intention, but it can also be misleading. When I threaten you by pointing my gun at you and saying that I will now shoot you, this may express my intention to murder you, but it can also mean that I am kidding with you and that I think the gun is not loaded and you probably know that. Any responsibility ascription that takes the intention of the subject into account is therefore also an act of judgment and it is not least of all for that reason fallible.

Another problem of intention as a necessary condition of responsibility is that in many cases where responsibility might be called for, there is no discernible intention to be found. As we have seen, the rise of the concept of responsibility is closely linked to the technological development and the moral problems resulting from that. Neither these developments in general, nor the spectacular occurrences that stirred up discussion about technology, are clearly intended by anybody. If intention is perceived as necessary for responsibility, then we can disregard the concept for technological catastrophes such as Chernobyl, Bhopal, Three Mile Island, or the Challenger explosion. It would make even less sense to search for responsibility for the underlying development of technology and resulting problems such as the depletion of the ozone layer or the greenhouse effect. Intention is thus another condition that has to deal with theoretical and practical problems and whose stipulation can endanger the ascription of responsibility.

The condition of intention implies the next condition, which is knowledge. It makes no sense to speak of the intention of a subject if he of she has no knowledge of the expected outcome of an action (cf. Hubig, 1995b, p. 62; Wehowsky, 1999, p. 94; McGary, 1991, p. 83; Hassemer, 1990, p. 64). "To hold an individual responsible for an action requires that he be aware of the nature of the action, in the sense that he is not doing A in the belief that he is doing B" (Held, 1991, p. 90). The knowledge required for responsibility, however, goes beyond knowing what one is doing at a given moment. Knowing about the results of an action requires foresight, judgment, and again contains an irreducible aspect of contingency. Another sort of knowledge required is the knowledge of the relevant rules. If the subject is not aware of moral, legal, or other standards, then she may not realise that something she is doing can result in responsibility ascriptions which may endanger the validity of these ascriptions. On the other hand a lack of awareness does not always preclude responsibility from being ascribed. Someone coming from a cannibalistic society might not realise that in Western democracies, it is generally regarded as bad practice to eat the dead. He would still have to suffer consequences from such an action even if these consequences might be of a different quality from the ones a native citizen of such a society would have to put up with.

While knowledge is a condition of responsibility, it is also an object of responsibility. We not only need knowledge to be able to act responsibly, it is also a duty arising from responsibility to acquire the necessary knowledge to be able to act responsibly. We can thus also be held responsible for a lack of knowledge. This goes for individuals who can be required to acquire certain kinds of knowledge for certain roles, and it can also be true for societies that may feel an obligation to fund research to gain knowledge.

The inverse relationship between knowledge and responsibility is valid as well. Ignorance may be an excusing condition for responsibility, but it can also be the object of responsibility. Some sorts of responsibility that are linked to certain roles require the holder of the position to keep up with current knowledge, and a lack to do so can lead to the ascription of responsibility. This is true for all of the positions that carry an "expert" status. One area where this status is of great importance is the area of technology in general and thus also the area of computing and IT.

> *"Special knowledge coupled with the power of position gives computer professionals efficacy; they can do things in the world which others cannot. Thus, they have greater responsibility than others."* (Johnson, 2001, p. 73)

Ignorance, finally, can be divided into several groups. First of all there is the fundamental ignorance defined by proofs of impossibility to know something. Secondly, there is ignorance concerning the results that can be overcome by learning of the pertaining facts and relationships. The third form of ignorance is that where the results are known in principle, but unknown to the subject in question. The fourth form is that there is knowledge of results, but not all of the causes may be known (cf. Zimmerli, 1994a, p. 184). These different forms of ignorance might be judged differently and lead to different results in responsibility ascriptions.

Another condition the subject has to fulfil is that it needs to have the faculty of reason. Reason can be understood in the Kantian sense as enabling us to see the world as a world of freedom and an infinite task (Schwartländer, 1991, p. 19). Reason in this sense is what enables us to conceive of the categorical imperative and to follow it. Other concepts of ethics and morality also build upon reason. It can be understood as the faculty that allows us to develop our idea of the good life, which we then follow. Reason is one of a multitude of character traits and capacities that a subject of responsibility is often understood to need. In Wallace's view of responsibility, it is the "powers of reflective self-control" (Wallace, 1996, p. 190) that the agent needs in order to be a subject. For Höffe (1995, p. 293), it is a combination of reason, sensitivity, and conscientiousness, without which responsibility remains a wish.

Many of the traits that the subject should have are usually ascribed to persons. For this reason some authors say that only persons can be subjects of responsibility. "We can assign responsibility only to persons" (Baier, 1972, p. 50). All of the other conditions of responsibility discussed so far can be subsumed under the idea that they are necessary to make us persons. Freedom, for example, is not an end in itself, but it is freedom that makes us persons or morally accountable agents, which is the reason why we long for it and why it is necessary for responsibility (cf. Wallace, 1996, p. 3). Apart from the conditions already mentioned, there are others that need to be fulfilled to allow us to speak of persons and to consider moral responsibility.

One ability a subject must have is that it can render the ascription of responsibility useful in the sense that the purpose of the ascription can be fulfilled. What this is depends on the definition of the purpose but, as we have seen, responsibility often stands for the attempt to bring about social change by administering sanctions. If those sanctions or punishment are to fulfil their role, then the subject must dispose of the mental capacity to understand them and react accordingly. Wallace describes these rational powers that he calls "powers of reflective self-control" as follows: "the power to grasp and apply the principles that support the moral obligations we accept, and to control one's behaviour by the light of such principles" (Wallace, 1996, p. 188). This requirement relates back to the faculty of reason, but also to questions of freedom and causality. The subject must be able to learn from the consequences of her behaviour, which in turn means that she must be aware of the causal relationships (Staddon, 1999, p. 150). To stay within the terms introduced earlier on, the subject must be able to understand the economy of threats and to act accordingly.

This comprises two aspects that lead to consequences, the mental aspect and the physical aspect. In order to be able to act accordingly, the subject not only needs to meet the conditions mentioned so far, most of which are part of her "nature," but she also needs a personality, developed through the process of socialisation, education, and formation. The development of the personality includes pedagogical aims, among them the training or instilling of a sense of responsibility (Hager, 1990, p. 60f; Dehner, 1998, p. 95; Böhret, 1987, p. 6). Education holds a central point in the enabling of individuals to be moral or ethical agents (Severson, 1997, p. 26). It is thus also necessary to engender humans with the ability to act responsibly. Since this development is part of the long process of socialisation of an individual, it is part of the responsibility of the group or society in question, but we will return to this later.

Most of what was said so far refers to the mental capacities of the subject, to the *mens rea* requirement of responsibility. There is, however, also another side to it. *Mens rea* in itself is not punishable by law, and in moral philosophy it is contentious whether a guilty mind in itself should and could be the basis of a responsibility ascription. Usually there also needs to be a guilty deed that needs to have been done; it is this what is also called the *actus reus* requirement. In relation to the condition that the subject must fulfil, this can be interpreted to mean that only the mental and physical unity that characterises human beings can be the basis of responsibility (Velasquez, 1991, p. 114). Only a being with both of these aspects can act freely knowing about the limits to its freedom and can therefore be responsible.

This should suffice as a discussion of the conditions of responsibility. One thing should have become clear by now, that is that these conditions are hard if not impossible to meet. They require a huge amount of abilities on the part of the subject. It is questionable whether anyone can fulfil all of them, but it seems clear that they are too high an aim to be attained even by the majority of persons who so far have been regarded as the typical subjects. The next step will therefore be an analysis of who or what is generally understood to be possible subjects. This discussion will underline the problems of responsibility. It will become clear that the traditional subjects of responsibility are often unable to fulfil the conditions, while other entities that might be able to fulfil the conditions are not recognised as subjects.

The Subject of Responsibility

Who is the subject of responsibility? There are many potential answers to this question, but one of them is clearly the traditional and the most widely accepted one: it is the human individual. One also often hears that it is the person. Let us start with the human individual. Many authors define responsibility and human individuals as mutually dependent. "Responsibility belongs essentially to the individual" (Lewis, 1991, p. 17; similar: Rapp, 1991, p. 23). On the other hand the human individual is characterised by his or her capacity to be responsible (Lenk, 1994, p. 43; Neuberg, 1997b, p. 2). From here it only seems to be a short step to say: "The subject of responsibility is the person." However, the concept of the person is a complex one and has led to a number of problems for theories of responsibility. It is therefore worthwhile to spend a little time on the analysis of the concept of the person and personhood.

The Person as Subject of Responsibility

One can find an interdependency between person and responsibility similar to the one between individual and responsibility. "We can assign responsibility only to persons...only persons who have failed in this responsibility can be responsible for something that has happened" (Baier, 1972, p. 50). While this sounds convincing it remains to be seen what exactly a person is. The term is derived from the Latin "persona" and originally stood for the *dramatis personae*. It then became a term used in Roman law where it referred to anything that could act on either side of a dispute (cf. French, 1979). The concept developed other meanings and today can be interpreted to stand for unity and duration, rational agency, and self-awareness (French, 1979). The person is one of the possible functions of the ego (next to ontological unifier and ultimate agent) and according to Flynn (1984, p. 10) is the centre of moral ascriptions. This, it seems, is the most important function of the notion of a person. It is a construct that fulfils the conditions of responsibility discussed earlier. Responsibility is only possible if past actions and their results can be ascribed to the subject. This requires that successive acts are linked and that they can be understood as acts of the same actor. The term "person" is supposed to achieve this goal. It is a legal and moral construct that is necessary in order to identify the substance that remains throughout the sequence of acts which is necessary to hold a subject responsible (Bayertz, 1995a, p. 13). The construct of the person also stands for the property of freedom. It is defined as free in the sense that it can decide against the given alternatives, that it can transcend the given reality (Priddat, 1994, p. 272).

Persons are created or constructed for certain ends, and according to these ends there are different sorts of persons, the most important ones being the legal person and the moral person. The most important one in terms of factual relevance is the legal person. While there may be discussion about the metaphysical status of legal persons, they are clearly defined by law. The legal person is an entity that is subject to legal rights or obligation. "Legal personhood is always something conferred, never merely the result of the act or acts of parties" (French, 1992, p. 134). Legal persons are not necessarily natural persons. Companies, organisations, or states can be subjects of legal ascriptions, which is generally recognised and does not produce philosophical problems. A more controversial point is the moral person, which can be defined analogous to the legal person but which runs into philosophical objections as we will show later on. Before discussing the philosophical problems of moral and legal persons, we will take a brief look at two examples of individual moral responsibility that are relevant to this discussion. The examples are the scientist and the engineer/technician and their personal responsibility. For questions relating to responsibility in IS these, two can be considered important because they embody the groups of people who are usually considered responsible for IT, the computer professionals. Computer professionals tend to have a scientific background and work in a technical environment. Furthermore, many of the traditional approaches to ethical problems of computers and information technology specifically address this group and hope to be able to solve the problems by guiding the individuals who work with computers according to ethical principles.

Since technology is often understood to be the application of science, it makes sense in the case of responsibility to look at the responsibility of the scientist first and then at the responsibility of the engineer. An ethics of science cannot be reduced to questions of the responsibility of the individual scientist. However, for now we will limit ourselves to this aspect because the aim of this analysis is to show the shortcomings of individual responsibility. Concerning the responsibility of the scientist, there are two possible extreme positions. Either the scientist is completely responsible for the results of his or her research, or he or she is not responsible at all. The latter position is based on the idea of the amorality of science. Science is understood to be a good thing, to further progress and welfare, and thus not to be in need of further justification. A scientist working in this generally positive environment does not have to worry about ethical implication of research. Prof. L. F. Fieser, one of the co-developers of Napalm, is a good example of this position. He stated in the *New York Times* (27 December, 1967, quoted in Lenk, 1991b, p. 7) that he regarded his job as completely technical and that he did not consider ethical implications. In his opinion it is the distinction between development and use of scientific results that counts. The scientists therefore bear no responsibility for what happens with their research, only those who use these results. The example of a military researcher dealing with weapons of mass destruction was of course chosen because it is not convincing. It is easy to construct even more drastic examples of scientists doing nothing but research and still being morally responsible. A physicist helping a dictator to build nuclear bombs or a chemist helping a terrorist organisation to develop chemical weapons would probably be considered cases in point even by the staunchest defenders of a moral freedom of science. Once we recognise, however, that scientists can be responsible for the results of their work, we run into the problem of determining who is responsible for what. If the physicist working for the dictator is morally responsible for a potential use of these weapons, how about the physicist doing the same sort of work in a democracy? And what about Otto Hahn, who discovered nuclear fission? One possible way out that some scientists use is the distinction between basic research and applied research. One can never know what the results of basic research will be and therefore there can be no responsibility for the results of basic research. Applied research on the other hand has a clear goal, and at least the intended effects of this research can be attributed to the involved scientists. However, the boundary between basic and applied research is blurring. In fields like genetics or computer science, the two are hard to distinguish. Meyer-Abich (in Lenk, 1991b, p. 26), for example, argues that the nuclear bomb was a direct result of basic research and that therefore those scientists who collaborated on the Manhattan Project are responsible for the dead of Hiroshima and Nagasaki.

Therefore, the other possible extreme solution would be to hold scientists responsible for everything that results from their work. Carl Friedrich von Weizsäcker, one of the German scientists working in nuclear physics under Hitler and arguably one of those who were responsible for Germany's failure to develop a nuclear bomb, believes that scientists are responsible for the results of their research, if not in legal terms, then at least in moral terms (von Weizsäcker, 1991, p. 95). The reason for this responsibility is that the scientist is never just a scientist. He or she is always a human being and part of society, and as such he or she has the normal moral duty to consider the result of actions with regard to their impacts on other people's lives (von Weizsäcker, 1964, p. 8).

While this argument appears convincing to many contemporaries, who, in the light of the problems and destruction caused by science, believe that there should be someone responsible, it is at the same time limited. The fundamental fact that the future is unknown, in combination with the limits of individual knowledge, preclude the individual scientist from being responsible for all of the results of his or her work. It is not plausible that Otto Hahn is quintessentially responsible for not only Hiroshima and Nagasaki, but also for the subsequent cold war and any future use of nuclear weapons. Neither would anyone hold Berthold Schwarz, according to legend the inventor of gunpowder in Europe, responsible for the millions of victims of guns over the last few centuries.

The answer to the question of the responsibility of the scientist is somewhere in between the two extremes of complete responsibility and no responsibility at all. Most authors agree on this fact. However, they do not at all agree where in the spectrum between the two extremes the true solution is supposed to be (cf. Lenk, 1984, p. 102; Hegselmann, 1991, p. 218; Mohr, 1995, p. 105; Rapp, 1994, p. 157). An interesting fact concerning scientific responsibility is that the code of scientific conduct in fact seems to be the only sort of morality that has worldwide validity. Scientists can therefore be said at least to be responsible for the adherence to this code (Eibl-Eibesfeld, 1997, p. 149). Also, this existence of a moral code should make scientists prime contenders for an overarching responsibility. If scientists are recognised to be unable to fulfil responsibilities, then what other groups should be able to do so?

Another group that might be considered a prime example of responsibility are those people whose work builds on science, the technicians or engineers. Among them one can find some of the potential subjects of responsibility in or for IS. For this group the same sort of arguments counts as for scientists, with the exception that they do not have the potential excuse of doing basic research. It is generally recognised that engineers have some sort of responsibility for the results of their work. At least in their role as citizens and participants of public life, they share the same responsibilities as everybody else. This general sense of responsibility also extends to their professional role. On the other hand they have to deal with more severe limitations of their freedom of action. Engineers tend to be employed by large organisations, and their degrees of freedom within these organisations are usually fewer than those of scientists. Therefore they may lack the ability to assume responsibility even in those cases in which they have the necessary knowledge (Ropohl, 1987, p. 162; 1996, p. 114). Again, as in the case of the scientist, one can conclude that the engineer is neither completely responsible for the results of his work nor is he absolved of every responsibility. In order to better realise responsibility, many authors have therefore suggested to stop concentrating exclusively on the individual and to look instead at the organisation that the individual is working in.

> *"We not only need moral people. Even more importantly we need moral structures and organizations. Only by paying more attention to these can we adequately resolve the questions of the ethical responsibility of engineers in large organizations."* (De George, 1991, p. 164)

Others, however, fear that this may lead to the decline of the idea of individual responsibility towards an ethics of institutions, and that this development would miss the nature of ethics and morality (Zimmerli, 1991, p. 79). In order to understand the two positions, we will use the next section describing the strengths and weaknesses of individual responsibility and the exclusive definition of the person as subject.

Strengths and Weaknesses of Individual Responsibility

The reason why individuals are generally seen as subjects of responsibility is that only they seem to fulfil most of the conditions discussed above. Individuals have the personal qualities required such as emotions, intentions, the faculty of reason, self-control, a propensity to react to punishment, and so forth. Many of these attributes can be summarised as having a conscience, which is one of the most frequently named reasons for individual responsibility (cf. Wehowsky, 1999, p. 21; Etchegoyen, 1999, p. 55). Closely related to the conscience is the ability that is the root of responsibility, the ability to answer. Only humans act morally because they recognise the other as a moral subject, and only they feel the need to answer and thus to assume responsibility. Furthermore, individual human beings are generally seen to be free in their will and action. This is not to deny the factual constraints under which everybody lives, but it implies that everybody can at least imagine alternatives to his or her actions that might enable them to act differently.

The strongest argument, however, for a limitation of responsibility to natural persons or individuals is of a metaphysical nature and pertains to the definition of the term. The argument is that only human beings have the metaphysical status to be able to assume or be ascribed responsibility. Therefore the only definition of the subject of responsibility that makes sense is the one defining the individual as subject (cf. Zimmerli, 1987, p. 107; 1991, p. 86; 1994a, p. 183; 1994b, 12; Breil, 1993, p. 230; Downy, 1972, p. 69f).[11] If this argument is true, then it does not make any sense to even discuss the possibility of other potential subjects. The problem with this point of view is that the individual does not fulfil all of the conditions. In fact, life in modern societies seems to contradict the idea that individuals are responsible for what happens. Individuals also do not have the capacity to satisfactorily deal with the consequences of responsibility ascriptions.

The classical model of responsibility that admits only individuals runs into severe problems in a world where organisations, institutions, or other collectives become the relevant actors (cf. Bayertz, 1995a, p. 53). Individuals are not able to deal with the most important problems of responsibility that we face today because they lack the knowledge of causal chains and the power to do anything about them. Speaking of global problems such as hunger relief or environmental protection, French (1992, p. 79) says: "Individuals are virtually impotent with respect to any of these problems, despite the best of intentions." Irrespective of questions of responsibility, many authors agree that the important agents are no longer individual human beings. Human beings still act within organisations, their responsibilities, however are usually limited to their tasks within these organisations. Especially with regard to the design and development of complex technologies, individuals can no longer know the results of their action and thus lack the prerequisite of being held responsible. This is certainly true for the area of the design of computer software and hardware. The single programmer who works in a large company is not able to assess the functionality of her source code in the context of the entire program. It is this development that Hubig (1993, p. 282; 1995, p. 98; 1995b, p. 61) calls the "loss of the subject."

In some ways this development may even appear to increase the possibility of responsibility. Human beings in modern industrial societies are freer than they have ever been. Economically and sociologically they dispose of degrees of freedom unknown before. Since freedom is a condition of responsibility, one might think that this development should be positive for the practice of responsibility ascriptions. On the other hand this new freedom also signals a loss of individual importance. Human beings can be replaced in their functional roles in organisations. Individuals are but cogwheels in the greater gearboxes of social life (Wehowsky, 1999, p. 20). "Anyone can be replaced at any time. The positions endure" (French, 1992, p. 143).

The loss of the subject, the decrease of apparent importance of individual human beings in societal decision making, is frequently described with the model of systems. Systems are understood to be complex entities that consist of human beings, but develop their own logic and are relatively independent of single individuals. If individual responsibility is possible at all with respect to systems, then this refers to responsibility within the system (Hubig, 1995, p. 98). The software engineer can thus be responsible for the reliability of the software she is programming, but she cannot assume responsibility for the social system constructed around computer use.

The systems in society are not only an expression of complexity; they also contribute to it. Different systems are interrelated and influence one another in ways that are hard to understand for the individual. This is another reason why institutions and organisations become the prevalent decision makers (Lenk & Maring, 1995, p. 243). Unlike individuals, they can increase their capacity of acquiring and dealing with knowledge.

This description of modern society is not as new as it may seem. The question whether the individual can be responsible is probably as old as moral philosophy. Furthermore, the idea of social systems taking over and leaving humankind powerless is also not confined to our days. For Marx (1998) the economy was the sole reason for social developments, and the individual, whatever he or she did, could not change the flow of events caused by economic laws.

There are several possible ways to react to the dilemma of individuals losing their role as agents. The first solution is to recognise that collectives are the relevant agents, while still insisting on individuals as subjects of responsibility. Not surprisingly, this solution is chosen by those authors who see responsibility confined by definition to the individual (Sinn & Zimmerli, 1986, p. 35). This approach, however, not only seems to be too narrow to be useful, it can even be seen as explicitly dangerous (Hengsbach, 1993, p. 19). Responsibility ascriptions looking exclusively at the individual necessarily overlook most of the important moral and social problems we face today. If we want to hold on to the idea of responsibility as a moral notion, then we should enable it to deal with structural questions and problems of collective actors (Ströker, 1996, p. 19).

Apart from these practical problems of individual responsibility, there are theoretical reasons why the use of the term "person" as the sole possible subject of responsibility is not satisfactory. The first group of objections against the concept of the person is that it is opaque. The person, as we have seen, is the main competitor of the individual in terms of being a subject of responsibility. However, one should only use the term "person" with highest caution. The problem is that the term is ambiguous, multifunctional, and leads to a tendency to mix questions of facts and values. Locke's legal understanding of the person is that the human being can embody different persons within a lifetime that are responsible for different actions. Human beings thus only exist in certain phases as persons: neither the newborn nor the old person in a state of dementia is a person. Collste (1998, p. 86) criticises Fletcher's criteria of personhood that would have the same effect of excluding some human beings that do not meet criteria of rationality or self-awareness. On the other hand, some Catholic moral theologians tend to see the fertilised egg as a person. It is thus enough to have the characteristic human genes. Another example of problematic definitions of the persons that no longer seem viable is given by Feinberg (1991, p. 63), who reminds us that the "fiction of conjugal unity" was only given up by American law in the 1840s. Before that, women did not have a separate legal identity from their husbands.

The flip side of this uncertainty regarding the definition of the person is that it is often defined as the being that is capable of being ascribed moral actions (cf. Kant, 1990). The person and responsibility are conditions of one another; they depend on their mutual existence (Ilting, 1994b, p. 96). According to Habermas (1998a, p. 107), culture, society, and person each presuppose the others. In effect, we have to admit that the person is nothing but a social construct with the explicit (if maybe not sole) aim of ascribing responsibility. Therefore, saying that persons are potential subjects of responsibility is true, but it is also tautological. It does not help us determine who persons are and which sort of entity can be considered a person. In the next section we shall see how this uncertainty concerning the concept of the person has led to the development of a highly controversial theory of moral personhood that might also include collective subjects.

Collective Responsibility

The problem with collective responsibility is that the two sides—those who favour it and those who are against it—are opposed in a way akin to what one can usually find between the factions of a religious war (cf. Ropohl, 1994a, p. 187). The idea of collective responsibility is not new at all. The biblical idea of the original sin is certainly an example of early concepts developed in this direction. Collective responsibility in this sense can be seen as the norm rather than the exception in less developed cultures. One could therefore argue that the discussion about collective responsibility is a step backward in our cultural development. However, the classical ideas and paradigms of collective responsibility, as embodied in the doctrine of the original sin, are not helpful for our modern problems (cf. Neuberg, 1997c, p. 254). We therefore see new developments in this field that are based on the hope of establishing a new sort of ascription that would include collectives as subjects.

The reasons for this development are the same as those discussed in the last section as the problems of individual responsibility. The central problem is the loss of the subject. The individual can neither change the course of the world, nor can he or she generally even change the course of a company. Engineers do not decide the development of IT and users do not decide the development of the Internet or infrastructure. Even those developments that can be traced back to a single decision have to deal with the problem of who made the decision. Teams, groups, commissions, and so forth make most important decisions. Reducing these decisions to individual acts is in most cases neither possible nor plausible. The problem becomes worse when one looks at developments that cannot be traced back to clear decisions. Neither environmental problems nor political developments nor technological progress are subject to any one decision that might have been altered. Nobody who bought a refrigerator in the 1970s did this deciding that the ozone layer should be destroyed by the chlorofluorocarbon. Nobody working on nuclear physics intended the cold war and the overkill capacities eventually produced by the two sides. And nobody using a computer intends the sweeping social changes that are a result of the general use. This is the reason why French (1992, p. 97) can claim that no "sensible responsibility relationship" can exist for this sort of problem.

Corporate Responsibility

The way out of this dilemma seems to be the expansion of the notion of responsibility to collective subjects. "Collective responsibility is the kind of answerability incumbent either on social wholes or on individuals by virtue of membership in such ensembles" (Flynn, 1984, p. 124f). This expansion alone, however, does not solve the problem either. As the quote indicates, there are different sorts of collective subjects and thus of collective responsibility, each with their own theories and difficulties. The sort of collective responsibility that is most widely discussed in the literature and that has the greatest impact on most of the questions relating to businesses or information technology is usually called corporate responsibility. The idea behind it, which may seem natural to many of us, is that there is a type of collective entity, embodied by the form of organisation that is usually called a corporation, that can be held responsible by itself. While this idea is anything but new in the legal sphere, it is still a controversial issue when it comes to moral responsibility.

In order to be able to talk about corporate responsibility, it is imperative to define what a corporation is. A first approach might be to see it as systems that first of all try to insure its own survival (cf. Apel, 1988, p. 208). According to Velasquez (1991, p. 123), there are three things we have in mind when we speak of corporations: "(a) the fictitious legal entity, (b) the organization as a structured set of relationships, and (c) the organization as a set of human beings." For Werhane (1985, p. 31) a "corporation is an association given legal status by a state charter to operate as a single unit with limited liability over an indefinite period of time. A corporation is originally created by a group of individuals for a specific purpose or purposes."

Corporations can also be defined as purposeful systems with a governance structure (Maring, 2001, p. 112). It is clear that corporations consist of human beings and without these human beings they would cease to exist. On the other hand corporations seem to exhibit signs of their own will and in many cases they keep on being even after all of their members have changed. The same collection of individuals that collaborate within the corporation would not produce the same outcome if they worked together randomly, without the "umbrella" of the corporation (Maring, 1989, p. 37). Many authors agree that corporations, even though they consist of human beings, can still be said to have the ability to act (Werhane, 1985, p. 50; Maring, 2001, p. 133f).

We have tried to show elsewhere (Stahl, 2000) that the fundamental question that decides whether we admit corporations as responsibility subjects is in fact a metaphysical one. Authors who admit any sort of metaphysical existence of corporations independent of their members tend to hold them responsible. Those theorists that propose a reductionist view, that is to say, believe every aspect of a corporation can be reduced without remainder to their individual members, generally do not believe that they can be held responsible. In view of the factual power of corporations and their apparent agency, many philosophers go a middle way and concede that corporations have some sort of moral responsibility, but that this is not the same as individual human responsibility (cf. Lenk, 1998, p. 281; De George, 1999, p. 196).

There are in fact some good reasons why corporations may count as subjects of responsibility in cases where individuals are no longer able to act in that role. Corporations are frequently better prepared to fulfil the conditions of responsibility discussed earlier. In many cases they have the necessary power and they make the relevant decisions. Depending on one's point of view, one can discern in corporations the preconditions such as intention, projection, the ability to decide and to act (Bayertz, 1995b, p. 55). They not only have more power and clearer decision algorithms than individual humans, they also have a longer life span (Böhret, 1987, p. 9). Political institutions, just like economic organisations, may survive their members by centuries. They may therefore be able to assume responsibility that would not have a human counterpart left. One example of this are the payments made by German companies and the German government to former slave labourers from the Second World War, 60 years after the war. It would be hard if not impossible to find out which human might be responsible, but it is comparatively easy to see which company benefited from the slave labour, and most of the companies accepted the responsibility and made the payments, even though none of the former decision makers are still left in power.

A counterargument against corporate or organisational responsibility is that corporations cannot be moral because they do not have a conscience and therefore do not have the ability to deal with moral facts and arguments. The opposite is true, however. First of all, corporations can react to moral facts and interpretations, as many of the scandals in recent years show. Shell's initiative of publishing a triple-bottom-line report, dealing with the financial, social, and ecological balance sheet, shows that the moral pressure that was brought to bear upon Shell did influence the decision process deeply. Institutions and organisations can at least fear moral discourses (Hubig, 1995, p. 108). Corporations can even be better in fulfilling moral obligations because they have more options in dealing with realities and their abstractions (cf. Wiesenthal, 1990, p. 72). Therefore Goodpaster and Matthews (1982, p. 133) can say: "A corporation can and should have a conscience. The language of ethics does have a place in the vocabulary of an organization."

Another condition of responsibility that corporations fulfil is the ability to answer. Corporations can communicate, and for many of them communication is even the main line of business. If they can communicate, they can answer to specific questions of specific stakeholders and these questions include moral ones. This answerability is the basis for some concepts of corporate responsibility (cf. Homann & Blome-Drees, 1992, p. 171).

Answering is a particular sort of action and if the answerability of the corporation is admitted, then it is only a short step to the admittance of general agency of corporations. As already mentioned, the assumptions of agency by corporations is closely linked to a tacit underlying metaphysical theory of corporations. Many authors, however, prefer not to discuss the metaphysical side and concentrate on the more easily observed aspect of acting on the part of corporations. Werhane (1985) or Lenk and Maring (1995) base their theories of corporate responsibility on the corporation's ability to act. This solution allows the introduction of corporate responsibility without having to discuss the problems of metaphysics and personhood. Since agency also implies intention, it fulfils another one of the central preconditions. Agency as the foundation of corporate responsibility also solves another problem, namely the question of the underlying morality. Since corporations may exhibit intentions but their motives are complex and hard to discern, it is easiest to subject them to some sort of consequentialist moral norm as background of the responsibility ascription.

> "...their actions, not their motives, are the proper object of moral evaluation." (De George, 1999, p. 196)

The criterion of being an agent is weaker than the one of being a person, and it allows the use of responsibility ascriptions (Maring, 1989, p. 38).

Some authors, notably Peter French, do not confine their concept of the corporation to the aspect of agency, but go further and describe it as a moral person. The starting point of French's and similar ideas is the legal person. The law treats corporations as persons because they have the relevant features of "personhood, including a method for forming intentions and a capacity to act" (May & Hoffman, 1991, p. 3). Legal persons are entities that have rights or are recognised in law. In the case of legal persons, it is clear that they are not something natural but social constructs.

> *"Legal personhood is always something conferred, never merely the result of the act or acts of parties."* (French, 1992, p. 134)

Legal persons are the subject of legal responsibility. Accordingly moral persons should be the subject of moral responsibility.

French compares legal and moral personhood, and concludes that both can be applied to corporations. Corporations can be said to have a personality that is not identical with their employees' personalities (French, 1992, p. 140). Corporations can show intentions, make decisions, act responsibly, enter into relationships, and they can be punished. The emphasis in French's theory lies on the fact that corporations have something akin to intention. The mechanism by which they form intentions and realise them is called the Corporate Internal Decision (CID) structure. It is this CID that determines the personality of the corporation (French, 1992, p. 139). French speaks of persons as non-eliminable subjects of responsibility ascriptions, and the corporation fits the description. "In short, corporations can be full-fledged moral persons and have whatever privileges, rights, and duties as are, in the normal course of affairs, accorded to moral persons" (French, 1979, p. 207).

Many philosophers have attacked this extreme view of the corporation as a moral person as being comparable to the human being. French himself no longer advocates it. The idea of corporations being morally responsible, however, has gained credibility and is now quite widespread. De George uses a Kantian argument, saying that corporations are not ends in themselves and therefore not moral persons. Nevertheless he concedes that they can act intentionally and thus be held morally responsible for their actions (De George, 1999, p. 195f).

Summarising the problem of corporate responsibility, one can say that the only really contentious issue is whether they can be held responsible in a moral sense. This question is basically a metaphysical one and is hard to solve by arguments because it deeply impacts on what we perceive as real and as fiction. However, corporate responsibility is the sort of collective responsibility that is easiest to handle. Firstly, we can find definitions of corporations; secondly, at least corporate legal responsibility is clearly established; and thirdly, corporate responsibility is part of our everyday way of dealing with responsibility issues. The statement that Microsoft is responsible for the functioning or non-functioning of their new system software does not need to be explained. In the area of software we may bemoan the fact that corporations do not live up to their perceived responsibilities, but that does not mean that we doubt their responsibilities. In fact, the opposite is true. We can only talk about the shortcoming of corporate responsibility because we collectively accept that the idea makes sense. Unfortunately, there are sorts of collective responsibility that are much harder to handle and that have a huge impact on questions of responsibility in business in general and with regard to the use of IT in particular.

Other Forms of Collective Responsibility

Corporate responsibility—contentious as it may be—has the advantage of being part of our everyday communication and can thus be seen as generally recognised. Furthermore, corporations not only have a social reality, but are also defined by law and therefore subject to clearly defined rules of legal responsibility. The same cannot be said for other forms of responsibility that result from collective action or are caused by collectives. The problem we are driving at here is the constitution of a collective subject that is usually called a group. Among groups one can distinguish between groups that have something like a collective consciousness or collective purpose and those that do not, that are thus purely random. This is a similar distinction to the one Held (1972) suggests between organised and unorganised groups. An organised group:

> "...has a method for deciding to act: it has officials who can act in its name, or a voting procedure to arrive at its decisions, or customary procedures to guide its actions. The possession of such a decision method by a collection of individuals, is, we might say, that which transforms a collection of persons into an organised group or collectivity." (Held, 1972, p. 105)

An organised group that is subject according to this definition can be said to have an internal decision structure and could therefore be described using French's CID. "A group collectively internalises responsibility when, but only when, members willingly take responsibility for themselves as a group" (Schmidtz, 1998, p. 8). It can then be subjected to the same arguments as a corporation. Examples in our field of interest might be the members of a computer club, a citizens' action committee on data privacy, or any special interest group with an appropriate internal structure.

The most important questions in the case of such group responsibility are:

1.   How is the group constituted?
2.   How far does the behaviour of group members differ from the individual behaviour of these persons?
3.   What is the relationship between the responsibility of the group and the individual responsibility?

Question 1 is important because, unlike in the case of corporations, this is generally unclear for groups. A group can have an enduring existence, but it can also be constituted for certain tasks. Most groups are less formal, so it may be difficult to determine whether they really have a decision structure. If groups have an internal decision structure, then they are able to act and thereby fulfil at least the requirement for being held responsible.

When a decision structure is not clearly visible, there may be other facts that hint at the possibility of a group's responsibility such as a common "way of life" (Cooper, 1972, p. 90). Another clue could be a shared culture that is produced by the group and accepted by its members (May, 1991, p. 246). This sort of group consists of individuals who voluntarily come together for some purpose, and who willingly and knowingly constitute the group. The problem with regard to responsibility that this type of group faces is similar to the problem of corporate responsibility. It is a question of metaphysics, whether one wants to recognise the independent existence of this sort of group or not. Many philosophers struggle with this question and try to find a way out that allows them to preserve their metaphysical views while at the same time allowing for the plausible claim that this sort of group can be responsible. Lübbe (1998, p. 127), for example, emphasises that collectives are nothing but the sum of their members, but at the same time she has to admit that there are cases where the result of group action is not the same as the action of the group's constituents. This is the reason why collective responsibility seems not only possible but even necessary. Individuals in groups act differently from those acting alone. There is, for example, a tendency to collectively accept risks that an individual would be loath to accept (cf. Lenk, 1994, p. 130). The reason for this increased acceptance of risks may in fact be the question of the distribution of responsibility. As members of a group, people feel that their actions have to be accounted for by all of the members, not only by them alone. The distribution of responsibility is therefore one of the criteria that Held offers for distinguishing organised from unorganised groups (Held, 1991, p. 97).

"A collective responsibility in this sense is one that is distributed to each and every member of the group of individuals sharing it:

the same responsibility falls to each and every one of them."
(Goodin, 1998, p. 146f)

This sort of organised group can be considered a candidate of collective responsibility. Examples for such groups are all sorts of assemblies of people with similar interests who voluntarily come together and view themselves as a group.

More difficult to handle are groups that lack an internal structure. Examples in this area might be the group of the users of the Internet, users of home computers, etc. The members of these groups usually neither know the other members, nor do they care a great deal about them. The decisive difference between the two sorts of groups is that in organised groups, members are aware of their membership and consider themselves members, whereas in unorganised groups, membership is usually not voluntary and members do not consider themselves to be members. In organised groups the description of the member from the point of view of the environment corresponds to the members' description of themselves, while this is not so for unorganised groups. Unorganised groups are usually defined from the outside, and that definition is controversial because it constitutes the group without taking into account the potential members' views. Since this process is more or less random—everybody is always part of an infinity of virtual groups that only come to existence by being named—the entire process of assigning responsibility becomes apparently random and thus loses its moral validity (cf. Bates, 1991, p. 107).

Group responsibility poses several serious problems that do not exist in the case of corporate responsibility. A central problem is that a causal ascription is hard, if not impossible, to realise if the results at which the ascription aims are cumulative (Bayertz, 1995b, p. 54). Examples could be the environmental degradation caused by millions of automobiles or the changes in society caused by the Internet users. Every single one of them can rightly say that his or her contribution to the problem is minimal and that without him or her the problem would remain the same. Briefly, in the case of group responsibility, it is hard to establish a convincing relationship between individual agents and the object of responsibility. We now have a sufficiently detailed insight into the different sorts of collective responsibility to summarise the problems it produces.

Problems of Collective Responsibility
The central problem for those who accept the possibility of collective responsibility is how to determine the relationship between individual and

collective responsibility. Most of the authors who admit collective responsibility do so with the more or less explicit supposition that it is not the same thing as individual responsibility and that it should not replace individual responsibility either. Both aspects are generally seen to have their strengths and weaknesses, and they should complement one another (Mai, 1994, p. 166; Hubig, 1994, p. 157; Spinello, 1997, p. 26). If one agrees to this view and allows for collective responsibility while at the same time insisting on the irreducible individual responsibility that every citizen in a democratic state has to assume (Kettner, 1995, p. 321f), then the central question becomes: How is responsibility distributed between the individual and the collective?

Several models are offered in this regard. According to Cooper (1972, p. 86), there are three ways in which group responsibility can be related to individual responsibility. First, there is the case where the group is responsible but none of the individual members are. Second, some of the individuals can be responsible but this does not exhaust the responsibilities of the group. Finally, "there is the tricky case where one does hold each member of a group individually responsible, yet still feels that the responsibility of the group is something more than the sum of all these individual responsibilities" (Cooper, 1972, p. 86). Similar ideas can be found in other texts (cf. May & Hoffman, 1991, p. 4; Lenk, 1987, p. 127; Seebass, 2001, p. 86). This sort of idea makes sense because it reflects our everyday experience. When a company does something bad, it can be held responsible. At the same time there usually is someone within the company who is also personally responsible for the misdeed. On the other hand it is usually not plausible to condemn the entire company and every single one of its members personally. A distribution of responsibility between collectives and individuals is therefore a convincing idea.

The downside is that this theory does not provide us with clear instructions on how to deal with the distribution of responsibility. First, there is the possibility that the individual, even though she might have knowingly and willingly caused something, can hide behind the responsibility of the collective. Viable collective responsibility would have to guard against this possibility (Böhret, 1987, p. 9; Maring, 1989, p. 32; Lenk & Maring, 1996, p. 240). Second, there is the pragmatic objection that it will be impossible to determine what part of the responsibility should be ascribed to the individual and what part to the collective. To this there does not seem to be an easy answer because any answer would have to rely on a complete theory of responsibility which, if it is possible at all, could only be applicable to a specific case because the relevant dimensions change from case to case.

Summarising the problem of collective responsibility, one can say that it is confronted with several difficulties. Originally, the concept of responsibility was developed with the individual person in mind (Homann, 1998, p. IX; Breil, 1993, p. 230). Overcoming collective responsibility was in fact a progress in moral theory and social practice. The notion of responsibility indicates the individual should be the subject. At the same time, the social developments which led to the importance of responsibility seem to marginalise the individual. Relevant actors today are increasingly collective actors. But even if one admits the concept of collective responsibility, there are no easy answers. Collectives as subjects of responsibility can again be divided into different groups. Among the collectives that are candidates for the role of a subject of responsibility, the most prominent one is the corporation. Firstly, corporations and organisations are the most visible actors in today's societies, and secondly corporations have a precedent in responsibility; they are established as subjects in legal responsibility. This is the reason why most literature on the subject refers to this case. However, there are other collectives that also act, whose acts have results but that are not usually recognised as subjects. In the case of these more or less organised groups, the theory of responsibility runs into even worse problems than in the case of corporations. The most important questions here are: Is collective responsibility just an excuse for the individual who does not want to assume her responsibility? and Even if collective responsibility is admitted in these cases, how should we model the relationship of individual and collective responsibility?

Where does this leave the question of responsibility and business information technology? It seems that the entire question of trying to find a subject that is responsible for IS is highly contentious. On the one hand we have individuals who might be responsible for IS. These might include programmers, hardware specialists, systems analysts and management from IT management, and the CIO (chief information officer) to general management and the CEO. However, none of these individual candidates fulfils the conditions. They usually do not have the necessary knowledge about what consequences their actions will have. They lack the power to stop what is happening and they are frequently changed so that there is no personal continuity to the roles. The only ones for whom there might be exceptions to this problem are the highest level of management, who may have power and the opportunity to know about and change things. These few individuals at the top, however, have the problem that they have to deal with a multitude of facts and aspects, not only from the IT area, so that they quickly come to the limits of their capacities.

On the other hand there are collective actors that can overcome these problems. First of all there are companies—producers of software, hardware, and services—that make their living in the area of IS. These without a doubt have a great influence on what is happening in the market, and they also have good intelligence concerning the results of their actions and other future developments. While these corporations seem the ideal candidates for being subjects, they lack some of the qualities that are often considered necessary. It is unclear whether they can really act or whether collective actions are in fact nothing but the aggregate of individual actions. Also, they lack the personal qualities usually associated with responsibility. Corporations have no personality, no conscience, and no feelings, which is why many scholars do not want to accept them as subjects.

Finally we have potential collective subjects that are even harder to grasp than corporations. There are groups such as the group of computer users, hackers, data workers, or information professionals that might be described as being responsible for IS. Among these groups there are some with a higher degree of organisation such as the computer professionals and some that have no discernible organisation at all such as the group of computer users. These groups too can be said to be responsible for some aspects of IS, but in their case it is even harder to see what they are responsible for and which consequences such an ascription might have.

There seems to be a great number of candidates for responsibility in IS, but not a single one of them is able to fulfil all of the conditions. Using the classic theory of responsibility developed so far, responsibility seems to be a rather useless concept in IS because there does not appear to be anyone or anything that could rightly and bindingly be held responsible in the sense that this ascription would be valid and viable.

For the sake of completeness, we will dedicate the next section to a last candidate of being as subject, a candidate that obviously lacks some of the conditions but that nevertheless has been discussed in the literature and that may develop with technological progress.

Computers and Information Systems as Subjects of Responsibility

The case for computers as subjects of responsibility could be made similar to the case for collective subjects. The most important aspect is that computers appear to make decisions that might be considered objects of responsibility. Some of the most convincing arguments along this line come from the military. The modern military is highly dependent on information systems for reconnaissance, assessment of the situation, and correct reaction. Nuclear forces everywhere have an extremely short warning time, and reaction to threats must be immediate. Human beings are not able to react as speedily and are not able to process the necessary information in the same amount of time. So, in fact computers make decisions or they at least prepare the information that serves as the basis of decisions. While the military is the most obvious example of this, many other information systems serve similar tasks in more mundane environments. Expert systems, decision support systems, or executive support systems are all examples of information systems that either make decisions or at least strongly influence decisions.

Apart from this fact, the next argument that may be used to ascribe responsibility to computers is that it is often impossible for humans to understand how and why the decisions made by computers came about. This is due to the size and complexity of modern computer systems. The attempt to reduce computer decisions to the acts of individual human beings is doomed to failure. Even if it were possible to identify the line of source code that caused a certain decision, it is impossible to forecast how exactly any piece of software would interact with other programmes. Thus, Weizenbaum (1976, p. 239) can say:

> *"...no human is responsible at all for the computer's output. The enormous computer systems in the Pentagon and their counterparts elsewhere in our culture have, in a very real sense, no authors."*

Johnson (2001, p. 188) identifies the same factors, scale, and complexity of computers, the "many hands" involved in their development, and the mediation of human decision making as factors contributing to a "diffusion of responsibility."

From the weaknesses of traditional models of responsibility and the facts just described, Bechtel has drawn the conclusion that one might consider computers and information systems as potential subjects of responsibility with whom humans might share responsibility (Bechtel, 1985, p. 297). The main thrust of Bechtel's argument is that computers are flexible and might be constructed to be adaptable. If they were they might be able to learn and to act appropriately to their environment. If computers ever reach this stage of development, it would appear appropriate to Bechtel to assign responsibility to them. Other authors go even further in their assumptions of what computers can or cannot do. For Stewart (1997) it is conceivable that computers take over the function of judges in criminal courts. Computers and expert systems might be used to evaluate evidence and to come to conclusions as to who the perpetrator was and what the fitting punishment is. These arguments for information systems as responsible agents hinge on whether they can fulfil roles that were designed to be filled by humans. This in turn leads us back to metaphysical and anthropological questions, and the question of what it is that makes humans subjects of responsibility. For diehard behaviourists this question is easily answered. For them it is a function of input and output. If something reacts in a certain way to given stimuli, then this is the base of judging the qualities of that entity. That means that if a computer passes the Turing test, which means that it is impossible to determine whether answers given originate from a human being or from a computer, then the two are functionally equal, and consequentially, if humans can be responsible, the computer should be so as well (cf. Lenk, 1994, p. 51).

There are also good reasons against the admittance of computers as subjects of responsibility. The first one is the definition of responsibility as pertaining only to humans. The second one is based on that and could be described as a general unease resulting from the elevation of computers to subject status. While the sentence "the computer is responsible for..." is one that can frequently be heard, few people would go so far as to describe information systems as morally responsible. In most cases this sort of exclamation stands for the exasperation resulting from a malfunction of computers and at most means causal responsibility. Finally, computers are even less able to fulfil the manifold conditions of responsibility than human beings. Their knowledge base is limited (even if it may be vast) and in most cases they are not able to learn (yet). They may have some power in the sense that they influence events and they are part of causal chains, but they cannot intentionally change the course of events. Clearly computers lack freedom and personal characteristics. While freedom is a contentious issue for humans, it is clear that it is lacking in computers. A computer's reactions are determined. Furthermore computers do not have the necessary feelings, fear of punishment, empathy, or reason, all of which have been cited as conditions of responsibility. For all of these reasons, it seems ludicrous to speak of (moral) responsibility of computers. However, there are aspects to the topic that might warrant attention. Firstly, the development of computers is progressing at such a speed that it seems hard to predict where exactly it is heading. Who is to say that computers never will be able to develop self-awareness, consciousness, and maybe even a conscience?[12] It is a recurring theme of science fiction literature that technical creations develop a life of their own and that humans have to deal with it despite their initial lack of willingness to do so. From the world-dominating computer systems in the *Terminator* movies, to the friendly if somewhat unworldly android Data in the "Star Trek" series, we find examples of the topic. We so far lack any sort of categorical tools for dealing with this which in itself may turn out to be a problem of responsibility one day.

There is one conclusion one can draw from the question of responsibility and computers at this point. The development and design of computers and information systems should reflect the need for responsibility. This refers to responsibility within the design process, but even more to questions of clarity, accountability, and the distribution of responsibilities between users and computers (cf. Bechtel, 1985, p. 297; Lenk, 1998, p. 469).

Having talked at length about the subject of responsibility, the intermediate conclusion we can draw at this point is that responsibility and IS do not seem to give clear instructions or hints concerning concrete behaviour. The combination of conditions and problems, and the different candidates for the status of being subjects all seem to be more or less contradictory. However, the subject is only one of the central dimensions of responsibility. In the next section we will take a closer look at the second most important dimension—the object of responsibility.

The Object of Responsibility

The object is that which the subject is responsible for. As diverse as the different candidates for the status of being a subject were, they are outdone by the complexity that one finds when looking at the object. Object and subject are closely related. Depending on who or what one admits is the subject, the potential objects vary. The candidates for being an object of responsibility in IS are legion. The functioning of a computer program, the accuracy of data, the organisational change within a company, and questions of the quality of life are potential candidates, as well as the global information infrastructure or the use of potentially faulty information systems in nuclear defence systems.

In this section we will start by recalling some of the conditions that a potential object has to fulfil in order to be admissible as an object. After that we will discuss a few typical objects as they can be found in the literature, and finally we will take a look at some of the fundamental difficulties that are generated by responsibility ascriptions on the side of the object.

Conditions for Being an Object of Responsibility

These conditions mirror the general conditions of responsibility as discussed in Section 5.2.1. Some of the properties that the subject should have must be reflected in the object in order for an ascription of responsibility to become viable.

Sinn and Zimmerli (1986, p. 35) develop a list of criteria that an object of responsibility would have to fulfil in order for an ascription to make sense. These criteria limit what is admissible as an object to things that are within the power of a subject. Among this list, one finds a temporal limitation to objects that do not exceed the human life span. Also the order of magnitude of an object and its intensity must be manageable. Furthermore the foreseeable results of the object in temporal, technical, social, and all other respects must be assessable and limited. In other words, the subject must have the object more or less well under control.

But what is it that responsibility is eventually ascribed for? Usually it is the result of an action. To begin with, the action itself can be seen as the object of responsibility. Following Apel (1988, p. 132), an action can only be described as such by looking at the results, be they intended or unintended. In this sense the term "action" implies responsibility. On the other hand not all of the results of human actions are always thought to be objects of responsibility. In fact many authors try to limit responsibility to those actions and their consequences that were intended.

> *"Certain conditions have to be fulfilled for being responsible for an action. An agent has an intention and through acting[,] he/she wants to realise the intention. The consequences of the act are supposed to realise the intention."* (Collste. 2000b, p. 190; cf. Spaemann, 1975, p. 324)

De George speaks of doing an action knowingly and willingly, which means that the subject had a choice, knew what it was doing, and did it deliberately (De George, 1999, p. 111). Similarly, Wallace emphasises the aspect of choice as crucial for being an object. This choice does not have to be a rational or conscious one, it is only necessary that the agent has the power of self-control that would have facilitated this choice as a conscious one (Wallace, 1996, p. 190).

What one can see reflected in these conditions is the realisation of the general conditions discussed earlier. The aspects of action, choice, and intention point towards the questions of causality, freedom, and power, as well as the human agent's ability to deal with them. As will be shown later, these conditions are as controversial on the level of the object of responsibility as they were on the general level. In order to show how these problems manifest themselves, the next section will be dedicated to a discussion of some of the most important and frequently discussed objects.

Some Objects of Responsibility

What is the object of responsibility? In the most general sense, it is the other. Responsibility, whatever the subject, whatever the circumstances or the specific objective, always aims at improving social life, and by doing so aims to improve life for all of the members of society or at least the majority of those individuals that are directly involved in the ascription. In this sense responsibility relates directly to the French tradition of moral philosophy and its emphasis on the other as the underlying reason of morality. Responsibility for the other can mean that no harm be done to her, that her dignity be respected, that her utility be maximised, etc. Starting from these general observations, one can also try to distil more specific objectives that relate to morality, such as advancement of peace, environment, or the chances of future generations (Zimmerli, 1994a, p. 7).

One particular example of the other that one can also be responsible for is the self. The first object that the subject can be held responsible for is its own capacity of being a subject. This is a thought that is prevalent in the French moral philosophy and that has consequences for any theory of responsibility. According to Weil (1998; 1960, p. 152), I am responsible for who or what I am at present. If I am not who I think I ought to be, then I should have decided to change; if I am lacking knowledge necessary for being a responsible agent, then I would have had to acquire it. I am responsible for my own conduct. In a more fundamental way, Sartre (1997, p. 105) sees us as responsible because we are sentenced to freedom, and we are responsible not only for us but because we create the world and we are thus responsible for everything. While Sartre's view is somewhat extreme because it endangers the concept of responsibility by overburdening it, the idea of responsibility for oneself is certainly part of our everyday understanding of responsibility. We hold people responsible for what they are and that includes not only their action but even more so their character and their personality. "We praise individuals for their compassion, think less of them for their ingratitude or hatred, reproach self-righteousness and unjust anger" (Sherman, 1999, p. 294).

While the first object of responsibility is the individual human being, the person, and particularly the person who is the subject, another frequently named object is the aggregation of all of these human objects, the human race of the existence of humans. This object is especially relevant because it is closely linked to technology and the development of the concept of responsibility. Human survival is one of the newer objects of responsibility. In most of the classical philosophical approaches to morality, one finds considerations of the individual, the person, or the self. None of them deals with the question of humanity in general because it was unalterably given. The conceivable end of the human race used to be in the hands of God and therefore out of the reach of philosophers. Since that situation has changed with the advent of modern technology, especially with the nuclear threat and in the light of World War II (Tugendhat, 1990b, p. 6), moral philosophy has had to add it to the list of responsibility objects.

Modern theories of responsibility tend to give a considerable amount of attention to human existence as an object of responsibility. Hans Jonas (1984), for example, who started the responsibility debate in the German speaking area, saw it as the fundamental problem that a morality of responsibility would have to address. Many scholars and maybe even more laypeople agree that the preservation of humanity is a high, if not the highest, ethical goal. It is thus our responsibility to ensure that human existence is not endangered. Plausible as this may seem, however, it is hard to justify from a philosophical point of view. Human existence is a fact, and it is always a problem to draw conclusions about norms from facts. One of the solutions to this dilemma offered by Jonas is that the highest norm is that there should be the possibility of norms. Thus the first responsibility is that there be responsibility.

Ignoring the subtleties of this debate, one can certainly count on broad support when stating that human existence must be protected. In the 1970s and 80s, questions relating to this were usually asked in the frame of the cold war and the possible nuclear annihilation of humanity. While this is technically still as much of a possibility today as it was fifteen years ago, the threat seems less probable from a political point of view and the situation is not perceived as threatening any more by the large majority of the population.

Today, when we speak of threats to humanity, we think more of potential changes of the nature of mankind, of environmental problems, and subsequently of threats to future generations. The first threat is that to the nature of mankind, and it is posed by progress in science, especially in genetics. Having deciphered or at least spelled out the genetic code of humans, it is only a question of time until we will be able to modify our genes according to our wishes. Where this will lead eventually is completely open, but there is no doubt that this development has the potential to change humanity at its roots. Genetic control of humanity is therefore one of the main reasons for Jonas' demand for a new responsibility (Jonas, 1987, p. 162). While the consequences of this are not yet clear, it seems obvious that humanity has recognised its own nature as an object of responsibility. This corresponds to the responsibility for the self on the individual level.

Another point where humankind slowly sees that it must take responsibility is the area of the environment. Environmental degradation, global warming, the depletion of the ozone layer, problems of the provision of drinking water, etc., make themselves felt all over the world. Even though ecocide is an old phenomenon that even Plato complained about (cf. Mohr, 1995, p. 32) and even though it seems to be part of human nature (Eibl-Eibesfeld, 1997, p. 38), overpopulation and shrinking resources make the problem more urgent. Again, the protection of the environment, just like human existence itself, is not a very contentious object of responsibility. The exact content and justification of environmental protection, however, are very much subject of debate. The arguments can be divided into anthropocentric and physiocentric ones. Anthropocentric arguments say that we must protect the environment because failing to do so will hurt or even wipe out ourselves. It is thus a matter of pure self-interest to make sure the environment is in order (Breil, 1993, p. 202; Lenk, 1994, p. 38; Lenk & Maring, 1995, p. 245). Another anthropocentric defence of environmental protection is a perceived Kantian duty that we have towards ourselves in view of nature (Birnbacher, 1980, p. 111f; Tribe, 1980, p. 36; Hubig, 1995, p. 154).

This sort of argument is based on a dichotomy between man and nature, between culture and nature, that does not convince everybody. Firstly, our nature and environment are by now so much shaped by mankind that the discrepancy between culture and nature does not seem relevant (Hastedt, 1994, p. 202). Secondly, humans are themselves part of nature and therefore everything we do can be considered natural. Furthermore, many people are unhappy with the anthropocentric defence of environmental protection because it treats the environment as a means to our ends, while they have a perception of nature as having intrinsic value. This remoralised view of nature (van den Daele, 1993, p. 173) contradicts the classical description of nature as merciless and indifferent. It is usually expressed as part of a theological or transcendent worldview where creation is holy and mankind has no right to interfere with the process of creation (cf. Schweitzer, 1991, p. 120; Devall, 1997, p. 23; Ehrenfeld, 1997, p. 173). Such a transcendent foundation of environmental protection may sound convincing to many of us, but it has the disadvantage of being binding only to those who share the transcendent presuppositions.

Depending on the justification, the idea environmental protection leads to vastly different implementations. If the environment only needs to be protected for the sake of mankind, then trade-offs are possible between the environment and other human needs or wants. A holy nature as an expression of God's creation would have to be treated differently.

Another object of responsibility that is accepted as unanimously as nature and that leads to difficulties at least as serious is the future, more exactly future human generations.[13] Future generations are linked to the environment because they are often invoked as a justification of environmental protection. Traditional ethics never had to worry much about future humans because it was certain that they would come and there was nothing one could do for them. Future generations are thus a relatively new object of responsibility comparable to the environment. And as in the case of the environment, the argument for the protection of future humans is deeply plausible. Human beings will procreate as all species do. Since there is no reason to think that today's humans are better or more privileged than yesterday's or tomorrow's, we must assume that they will have the same rights and obligations. Among them is the right to a happy and healthy existence, which presupposes that we leave them a world in which a dignified existence is possible.

When one looks at the argument, however, one finds that that it is hard to specify what exactly is meant by future generations and how they can be an object of responsibility. It starts with the fact that it is impossible to give reasons for a right to live for someone who has not even been conceived yet. If such an individual right cannot be found, then how do we justify the right of a collective? But even if one concedes that right, the next problem is that one of the central features of morality, reciprocity, cannot exist with future generations. In the case of the immediately succeeding generations, there is the reciprocity that is evident in the classical roles. The parents raise their children until they are independent, and later on the children care for the parents when they are in need. An analogous relationship to humans more than two or three generations away is not possible. So if there should be responsibility for future generations, it would have to be iterative, from generation to generation.

Another problem is that we do not know what the needs and wants of future generations will be and how we can cater to them. The assumption is usually that their nature will be like ours and that they will thus want to live in a world similar to ours. However, it is obvious that this argument is not valid. If it were true, then we should never have evolved from cavemen, and yet most of us prefer living in a world with hospitals and telephones. So, purely conservative arguments using future generations as reasons to slow or stop development are misleading because they make assumptions that cannot be verified. These problems explain why French (1992, p. 98) can say: "It is very difficult to see how any relationship deep enough to support responsibility assignments can exist between any persons existing today and distant generations."

The environment as well as future generations combine epistemic and normative uncertainty when used as responsibility objects. They are thus two examples for a typical property of responsibility ascriptions in modern society, the property of risk. During the introduction of the concept of responsibility, it was pointed out that the term responsibility can be understood as a reaction to the impotence of traditional moralities when faced with risk. Since risk played a part in the ascension of the concept of responsibility in public discourse, it is not surprising that one sometimes hears the suggestion that risk is an object of responsibility or even the prototypical object where the concept of responsibility can show its powers (Bayertz, 1995a, p. 46). The idea of responsibility for risks, however, refers to a lot of the principal problems of responsibility: Who is responsible for risks, which actions or results must be considered risky, to what point do we consider risks, is it possible to take responsibility for risks that others must take, how can the ascription of responsibility for social risks be realised…? These questions relate back to the objects just discussed. Can we ascribe responsibility for risking the well-being of future generations or even for risking human existence? To better understand these questions, one should reflect on the problems that a potential object of responsibility can face.

Problems of the Object of Responsibility

The object of responsibility is relatively uncontroversial in all those cases where the subject intended something and this intended result is what responsibility is ascribed for. It becomes problematic if there is either no discernible subject for a clearly defined object, or if the object itself is either unclear or not intended. These cases are related to the conditions of responsibility, especially intention and knowledge. As we have seen, the growing complexity of social life is one of the main reasons for the success of the idea of responsibility. At the same time complexity threatens the very idea because it undermines the applicability of the conditions. If we say that a situation is complex, then this implies that causalities are unclear, that knowledge about it is uncertain, that outcomes cannot be assessed, and that consequentially a potential subject cannot know what will result from its actions. While the growing complexity leads to an increase of topics and areas that humans can be held responsible for (Krawietz, 1995, p. 185), it diminishes at the same time the ability to assume responsibility. In the risk society it becomes impossible to ascribe damages to any particular person because they lose their spatial-temporal limits. Potential damages reach proportions where it is impossible to compensate for them, and therefore there are no longer even plans to do so (Beck, 1998a, p. 79). This leads to the "organised irresponsibility" where individuals are no longer expected to assume responsibility because they would not be able to live up to it anyway (Wehowsky, 1999, p. 20). Three factors can be identified as the prime causes for this development: cumulative effects, side effects, and the problem of acting and omitting.

The cumulative effects have already been mentioned. Most of the facts that are seen as necessitating responsibility are of a collective nature and come about through collective action. The discussion of collective subjects of responsibility reflects this fact. A particularly difficult case is the problem of environmental protection. For our topic of business information technology, there are economic as well as technological problems that also originate from the collective nature of these processes. Our collective way of doing business, for example, leaves a considerable part of humanity in poverty. Some 30,000 children a day starve or die of curable diseases. On the other hand it is hard to point to any one individual whose action could be considered responsible for that. The use of information technology seems to promise a remedy for some of the questions of international distribution, but at the same time it produces a digital divide that deepens the distance between rich and poor. Again, it is not possible to say that any one user of IT should be held responsible for that. So, collective responsibility, especially responsibility without even a discernible collective subject, that is to say group responsibility, aggravates all of the problems of the object mentioned so far. It impedes the discovery of causalities, it hides the individual, it can mask problems of risk and uncertainty. However, it is not the only problem of the object.

Another problem that is at least as serious are side effects. It is clear that the subject is responsible for intended actions and their results (Ropohl, 1994b, p. 113). But how does an ethics of responsibility deal with unintended results? To answer this question it is imperative to first define these unintended results or side effects. They are presumably called side effects because they do not appear in the straight line from intention to final end, but materialise in some other area that can be defined as being beside the main point. Such a definition would recur exclusively on the subject's intention for determining which causes are effects and thus objects of responsibility, and which are side effects with an unclear status of responsibility. However, the exclusive limitation to the subject's intention is not sufficient. First, one may not know the true intentions of the subject and the subject may lie about them or be unaware of them. Second, the quality of the side effects can make them the primary result, whether intended or not. A nuclear power plant produces electricity that is used in a moment for purposes that tend to be forgotten in a minute, and at the same time it produces nuclear waste that will be radioactive and fatal for tens of thousands of years. Saying that the electricity is the main result and the nuclear waste a mere side effect seems euphemistic. Spaemann (1975, p. 323) points out that the dichotomy of intended and unintended results is not sufficient either. Every action can have at least three kinds of results: the intended ones, the unintended but known and accepted ones, and the unforeseen ones. In this sense the nuclear waste would be unintended but known, whereas the effect of the CFCs on the ozone layer was not only unintended, it was also completely unforeseen.

The question of which effects to ascribe to an action and thus to a subject goes back to other problems discussed earlier. Which are the causal chains that have to be taken into account, how can we determine them, and how can we have knowledge of them? Causal chains do not end, and even the most irrelevant action taken today may have serious repercussions later on. Therefore, if responsibility meant being answerable for every consequence of an action, then this would sentence us to complete inactivity because the mere attempt to find out about all of the results is by definition an infinite endeavour. On the other hand it is easy to see that complete inaction would also produce results (at least we would all starve to death), which would also required the ascription of responsibility. This then leads us to the next big problem of the object of responsibility—the question of doing and omitting.

It is clear that omitting to do something can have consequences that may in turn lead to responsibility ascriptions and to sanctions. If I have the opportunity to save someone from certain death without too much risk to myself, then I am expected to do so. If I omit doing so, then I am liable for punishment. However, there are problems with this model. The first one is that it is hard to determine who omitted to do what. Actions ascribed to an actor can usually be determined quite clearly through a description of physical acts that then lead to consequences. Omissions are more virtual. Depending on the point of view, an actor's activity might easily be described as typing on his computer. At the same time he can be said to omit making love, saving the environment, repairing his motorcycle, or reading a book. Omitting is virtual and thus potentially infinite. Another problem is that of causality. While, despite the theoretical problems with causality, it is clear that certain actions lead to given results, the same can often not be said about omissions. Omissions as negative entities seem to lack a relationship to causality (Picht, 1991, p. 31). Another problem is the question of intention in omissions. While intentional omissions are similar to actions in many ways, the inclusion of everything one does not do and does not even think about in the potential objects of responsibility again leads to an overstretching of the notion. However, many of the contemporary problems of responsibility result from such unconscious omissions and lack of attention. Cumulative effects threatening the environment, for example, are often omissions. We omit to think about the potential effects of using a car or we omit giving to charity, thereby producing results that we are unaware of.

This example shows that doing and omitting are a problem of definition. When is something an action, when is it an omission? Whenever I do something, I omit to do the opposite. So, what is the definition of omissions? Birnbacher (1995b, p. 24) suggests that action and omission should be defined as contrasting concepts; that means that an action cannot be an omission at the same time and vice versa. However, actions can contain omissions, and one can omit by acting. When I see someone drown, I can walk the other way, which is an action, and thereby omit to save the person. Since the consequences of omissions are often the same as those of actions, at least from a purely consequentialist viewpoint, it seems to make no difference whether the subject's actions or omissions led to the result (Bayertz, 1995b, p. 46). Some authors have drawn the conclusion that for responsibility purposes, actions and omissions are therefore equal (cf. Rohbeck, 1993, p. 278; Rachels, 1997, p. 195). On the other hand, the history of western ethics shows that there has always been a clear distinction between the two. The prohibition to do damage has always been stronger than the commandment to do good. This is, for example, one of the pillars of medical ethics since the times of Hippocrates (Höffe, 1995, p. 80).

While it may be more difficult to prove responsibility for an inaction or omission than for an action (Etchegoyen, 1999, p. 94), the most clearly defined example of responsibility, legal responsibility, shows that there is a difference in social evaluation between the two. Omissions are punishable by law, for example in the case of negligence, but they are punished differently from actions. But does this help us with questions of responsibility and business information technology?

Information Technology as an Object of Responsibility

Technology in general and information technology in particular is an object that reflects all of the problems discussed. Technology has always been developed as a means, but it often develops results that were not intended and not foreseen (Rohbeck, 1993, p. 16). It is typical for modern technologies that their development is neither planned nor linear. Instead, typical characteristics are anonymity, inherent dynamism, and complexity (Mohr, 1995, p. 105). Technology produces results, but few of them are intended. In fact, the side effects are often the key reason for thinking about technology at all. The most important single problem that technology produces is probably the degradation of the environment. A considerable part of the literature dealing with philosophy of technology and technology assessment addresses this point. Technology was intended to improve our circumstances, make life easier and more comfortable, a task that it achieved in many respects (cf. Wild, 1991, p. 45). At the same time technology threatens the very basis of our existence. To make matters worse, our growing knowledge and power have led to situations where it is highly plausible that omissions can be more dangerous than actions and the threats we have to assess can come in equal parts from doing and omitting (Lübbe, 1998, p. 183). All of this has led to the call for responsibility in the area of technology and subsequent attempts to come to grips with the problems, to institutionalise some form or other of responsibility for technology. The entire area of technology assessment can be understood as such an attempt to realise responsibility for technology.

Information technology forms a part of this problem, but a part with growing importance. On the one hand IT is a necessity for most modern forms of production, and therefore the problems may not be caused by IT but they are aggravated by it. At the same time IT contributes to the epistemological side of the problem by allowing new forms of information gathering, modelling, and predictions. It thus helps transform side effects to known effects that responsibility has to be assumed for. The increasing use of IT also poses environmental problems of its own due to sometimes poisonous materials needed to produce it and the increasing energy consumption necessary to keep the computers running. Finally, the effects of IT on the social environment are probably the most serious ones and the least researched ones. What does it mean that people are available 24 hours a day, that the limits of work and leisure are blurring, that we communicate increasingly using electronic means, that networks promise us infinite information which at the same time exceeds our capacity to understand?

We will return to the question of information technology as an object of responsibility later on. Right now we are still in the process of demonstrating the difficulties of the classical concept of responsibility. It should have become clear in this section that determining an object is not only difficult in the sense that the participants of the process of ascription have to agree, but that there are also inherent problems that complicate the whole process. Before introducing a possible solution to this problem, the theory of reflective responsibility, we need to continue the discussion of the relevant aspects of responsibility, the next of which is the instance.

The Instance of Responsibility

The instance is the third classical dimension of responsibility, next to the subject and the object. It is more frequently mentioned in German literature about responsibility than in English texts. The idea of an instance, however, plays a role in most theories of responsibility. The instance is that entity which is external to the relationship between subject and object, and which at the same time has a fundamental influence on it in that it decides about the ascription. It might therefore also be called the authority responsibility. The subject is ascribed responsibility for the object before the instance. Since responsibility is a social process involving many potential parties, it makes sense that there be someone or something with the authority to finalise the ascription and the resulting sanctions. Some authors go so far as to suggest that responsibility can only make sense if it produces tangible results, which in turn seems to presuppose the existence of a powerful instance (Lübbe, 1985, p. 59).

The paradigm of responsibility that makes the instance most clearly visible is a legal court. The accused is the subject, the object is that which the subject is accused of and the instance is the judge. In most other types of responsibility, it is less clear who or what the instance might be. One can distinguish between internal and external instances (cf. Birnbacher, 1980, p. 111f; van Luijk, 1990, p. 41). The most frequently named external instance next to the judge is God. For a secular theory of responsibility, however, God as an instance produces the problem that He can only be effective for those who believe in him, a group which in modern societies does not constitute a sufficiently large majority to justify this sort of ascription. Furthermore, as soon as one speaks of God, a whole host of theological problems arise. A secular theory of responsibility should recognise God as a motivation for many agents to act in specific ways, but it cannot rely on him as a binding instance.

Since in most cases no external instance is clearly discernible, many theories of responsibility rely on an internal one, which in most cases is the conscience. While the conscience can be seen as an expression of the human ability to reflect upon oneself (Ropohl, 1994b, p. 113), most authors agree that it is also an internalised version of exterior instances. The human conscience can perform the function of a court of law; it is the internal acceptance of social rules and standards (Walzer, 1994, p. 396). The conscience has something to do with moral and legal rules (Feinberg, 1980, p. 141) and the way they are realised in a society. It can also be seen as God's representation in humans or, in philosophical terms, as a representation of something higher or transcendent (Lenk, 1998, p. 161). Unlike the external instances, however, the conscience is not completely rational. It contains a measure of emotions and of intuitive recognition of right and wrong. This intuitional knowledge of the right or good is then supposed to motivate the subject to act right (Kohlberg, 1995, p. 289). The conscience also disposes of the most important property that an instance of responsibility must possess; it can attribute sanctions. The so-called pangs of conscience or remorse about something one did are the internalised sanctions that are triggered by the conscience (Mill, 1976, p. 50).

The conscience as an instance of responsibility overcomes some of the problems of external instances, but it also runs into some problems of its own. First of all it is too uncertain a phenomenon to base a general theory on. Even though the structure of the conscience seems to be an anthropological fact, the content of that structure depends on circumstances. It can contain all sorts of normative contents, even the worst kind (Tugendhat, 1990a, p. 12). The interpersonal differences between consciences are too great to guarantee a halfway equal distribution of responsibilities. Even though responsibility is recognised, the conscience as instance cuts off public debate and relegates responsibility to the status of something purely private (Höffe, 1995, p. 26). This contradicts the social nature of responsibility. Wuneburger (1993, p. 58) points out that the conscience as the internalised form of social roles is also a kind of psychological group pressure that can be used to ensure the individual's reliance on the group.

Furthermore, we do not know whether all of the subjects of responsibility discussed so far in fact have a conscience. It is an open question whether, for example, corporations can have a conscience. If one says that corporations are morally responsible and that the conscience is the instance of responsibility, then one may be driven to the doubtful conclusion that "a corporation can and should have a conscience" (Goodpaster & Matthews, 1982, p. 133). Most philosophically minded authors, however, tend to locate the conscience in the individual human being (Etchegoyen, 1993, p. 177). Finally, despite all of the recognition and personal experience of the existence of our conscience, there is no more a proof of its existence than there is a proof of God (Wehowsky, 1999, p. 86).

Since neither external nor internal instance are without serious problems, another solution to the problem of the instance is some form of process. The idea here is that the effectiveness of responsibility ascriptions should not be made dependent on any entities, but on the process of ascription itself. One version of this idea is offered by Ulrich (1997), who builds on discourse ethics and tries to see how responsibility can be realised in social settings. In this model one acts responsibly by confronting all the considerations and claims by all of those who are affected and by recognising the legitimate claims. In this case it would be explicitly immoral to "escape" to the excuse of the individual conscience. Discourse ethics is seen as an expression of the universal moral point of view. Realising a discourse by discussing all of the relevant validity claims with everybody concerned in the absence of power, and under conditions as close to the ideal discourse as possible, will lead to the morally best outcome. While this model seems plausible and might even be convincing to other moral theories apart from discourse ethics, it has to deal with the problem of theory and practice. Real discourses will never be held under the legitimising conditions of the ideal discourse, and in the absence of these ideal conditions it is doubtful whether and in what way the results of discourses really can lay a claim to moral validity.

A morally less ambitious process for the realisation of responsibility is therefore necessary. One suggestion, put forward by H. Schmidt (1992, p. 170), aims specifically at the problem of responsibility in the technological age. Schmidt refers to the complexity, the rapidity, and the risks of technological development. His suggestion is to start a fundamental democratic process that would bring together the drivers of the development and its victims in order to facilitate a mediation between the two groups. This idea is based on morality's task of avoiding violence and arbitrating between conflicting parties that we have seen as the cornerstone of the French tradition of moral philosophy. In practice it would probably look very similar to Ulrich's discourses, but the theoretical goals are more modest and therefore more realistic. These different processual approaches are easily combined with the idea of the future as an instance. If there are neither transcendent nor internal instances, what is left as a basis for the ascription of responsibility? One possible answer is that it is the future (Kissling, 1995, p. 424), something we have already encountered as an object of responsibility as well. But how are we supposed to cater for future needs? According to which rules should we design ascription processes and what are the criteria for a successful ascription?

These questions are addressed by another group of theories which diverge from the approach chosen so far in that they do not posit the necessity of an instance at all but concentrate instead on the normative background of responsibility. Instead of the three basic dimensions discussed so far, one can also find the description of responsibility as a relation between an object, the qualification that makes it an object, and the good that was affected (Trigeaud, 1999, p. 92). This directs the attention away from the entities that play a role in the ascription toward the normative background. In fact, some of the more traditional approaches to responsibility move away from the instance as a necessary ingredient and replace it with a "system of standards of judgment" (Bayertz, 1995b, p. 15f).

It is also important to note that responsibility as a procedural notion is devoid of a clear content if the normative background is not defined. Responsibility does not produce values or moral statements, it can only transport them. It is based on moral valuations that it cannot justify by itself. This is meta-ethically relevant because it shows that responsibility cannot be identical with a moral theory and is necessarily subordinated to a moral theory (Bayertz, 1995b, p. 65f). Therefore subjects can only be responsible if they have rules or norms to which they can refer (Ilting, 1994b, p. 96). In this sense it may be sufficient for a responsibility ascription if the moral principles that it relies upon are known (Hartmann, 1991, p. 99) and the question of whether there must be an instance may be irrelevant.

But even if a theory of responsibility refrains from relying on an instance, the next question would be whether an instance would not be necessary to determine which moral norms and rules are acceptable. Another problem is that of morality and ethics in the sense of the German tradition. Do we need a material morality for responsibility or rather an abstract ethics or both? And whichever way this question is decided, neither a morality nor an ethics that is universally acceptable is discernible right now. So, coming back to responsibility for technology or for business information technology, we face the problem that there is no generally accepted instance and there is not even a generally accepted set of rules according to which responsibility might be ascribed. This may be one of the reasons for the apparent shift of relevance away from ethics toward the law. Legal responsibility disposes of clear rules, at least within nation-states, and is therefore attributable and sanctionable. For moral responsibility this seems to be much less the case. If this is so, then the attempt to find a framework for responsibility in relation to IS seems a rather hopeless endeavour.

Thus far we have seen that in the case of each of the three basic dimensions of responsibility, one quickly runs into problems when attempting to simply describe them. Questions like who is responsible for IS; in IS, what is he responsible for; and before whom is he responsible, are difficult to answer. This is not only caused by the difficulties that the idea of business information technology itself contains, but even more because of principal problems of the concept of responsibility. However, the problems are not confined to the basic dimension of subject, object, and instance. Apart from the three basic dimensions, there are several other facts and determinants that also have to be taken into account for a comprehensive picture of responsibility.

Types of Responsibility

So far we have made several allusions to different types of responsibility. A complete theory of responsibility has taken into account that there are different sorts of responsibility that in some cases are similar and in other cases seem to be disparate or even contradictory. A lack of clarity concerning the type of responsibility can therefore result in theoretical confusion and practical inapplicability. While most authors in the field of responsibility would agree to this statement, it has not led to a generally accepted classification of different types of responsibility. Depending on the author, one can find between four (Hart, 1968, p. 211f; Johnson, 2001, p. 174) or five (Baier, 1972, p. 56) and up to ten (Lenk, 1998, p. 265f) different types. Typical candidates for types of responsibility that can be found in most of the texts are causal responsibility, task responsibility, role responsibility, legal responsibility, and moral responsibility.

Since causal responsibility was discussed earlier on, we will concentrate on the types of responsibility that are typically ascribed to agents. Most closely linked to agency is task responsibility, where the subject is held responsible for the fulfilling of a specific task (Ricoeur, 1994, p. 30). The subject of action needs to fulfil several conditions that are similar to the ones that the subject of responsibility has to fulfil, which is the reason why task responsibility seems to be a natural first step in the development of responsibility.

Closely related to task responsibility is the responsibility for recurrent tasks that are linked to the roles a subject plays. Whatever these roles may be and however the subject may have acquired them, it is a unifying feature of most different roles that they entail responsibilities. Whether the subject be a policeman, a mother, a CEO, or a computer programmer, all of these roles lead to certain expectations from the environment and to the ascription of responsibility. Role responsibility "is interchangeable with duty and refers to what individuals are expected to do in virtue of one of their social roles" (Johnson, 2001, p. 174). Those responsibilities that result from the subject's fulfilling a certain role are clearly recognisable and in daily life are probably the ones that can most often be felt. The problem with role responsibility is that it refers to other types of responsibility, mostly to legal and moral responsibility (Hart, 1968, p. 215) without being either one of them.

> *"...role responsibility is a limited concept useful for describing certain social and institutional obligations, but not useful as an absolute criterion for making ethical judgments."* (Werhane, 1985, p. 106)

Role responsibility is the basis of professional ethics, an approach frequently suggested for dealing with ethical problems of IS.

The two most widely recognised and most frequently discussed types of responsibility are legal and moral responsibility. Legal responsibility is the origin of the concept of responsibility, and it has the advantage of being most easily discernible and having the clearest structure. The entire notion of responsibility often seems to be fixed in its legal usage, where the ascription takes place between accused, plaintiff/prosecutor, and judge, and results in compensation or punishment (cf. Ricoeur, 1995a, p. 41). "Responsibility is often thought of as primarily a legal concept" (Long, 1999, p. 118).

However, responsibility is mostly used—even in legal circumstances—with at least an implicit reference to morality. Legal and moral responsibility are clearly related, but the exact nature of this relationship is not clear. Some theories state that legal responsibility, in order to be efficient, must be based on moral responsibility. A legal punishment that does not reflect the moral consensus of a society is not acceptable. On the other hand severe moral offences often seem to require a legal punishment (Neuberg, 1997, p. 3; Downy, 1972, p. 67). In the case of the most serious of moral misdemeanours such as murder, assault, rape, etc., this seems to be plausible, but it should not be understood to mean that moral and legal responsibility are fundamentally the same.

One difference between the two is that moral responsibility aims at reasons and causes, whereas legal responsibility is concerned with the results of actions (Vossenkuhl, 1991, p. 52). Another difference can be found in the sanctions that in the legal case are formally institutionalised, but in the moral case tend to be less clear (Collste, 2000c, 1 p. 26; Lenk & Maring, 1990, p. 98). This is also the reason for the ridicule that moral responsibility is sometimes subjected to due to its apparent powerlessness and its function as an excuse in those cases where the legal institutions fail (Lübbe, 1998, p. 155).

What then is moral responsibility? It is a type of ascription that is characterised by certain facts. First of all its moral nature implies something like a universal validity. It is equally effective for everybody regardless of particular circumstances. It not only applies to the roles that humans fulfil, but it applies to humans per se or to persons (Lenk, 1991a, p. 67; 1994, p. 128). This universality, in the German tradition usually defended by reference to the universal properties of reason, is also a weakness of moral responsibility because it often does not allow the development of sufficiently clear rules of ascription (Krawietz, 1995, p. 197). Moral responsibility is based on moral norms and rules, and it therefore can only accept potentially moral entities as subjects. One of the reasons for this is the instance which in the case of moral responsibility is often understood to be the individual conscience (Kreikebaum, 1996, p. 180; Sänger, 1991, p. 36). The person or group that ascribes responsibility to the subject must extend a certain sort of emotion toward the subject. This is usually described using the word "blame." Moral responsibility entails an element of blameworthiness (Johnson, 2001, p. 175; French, 1992, p. 80; Wallace, 1996, p. 56). Most authors see moral responsibility as one of a multitude of different sorts. Depending on the definition of ethics and morality, however, the scope and scale of moral responsibility differs greatly. If one follows the definitions of morality given earlier on as anything that affects human coexistence, anything that has to do with the way people interact, and especially with conflicts and their peaceful resolution, then every responsibility ascription is moral. Responsibility can then be classified as moral, independent of whether it is at the same time of a legal, political, institutional, or any other nature.

Apart from these distinctions, one can also find others in the literature. Corresponding to causality, responsibility can be seen as direct or indirect (Ladd, 1992, p. 293). Responsibility can be negative or positive, which corresponds to the distinction between action and omission discussed earlier on (Velasquez, 1991, p. 111). Some authors see a difference between natural and contractual responsibility, where natural responsibility is usually taken to originate from a non-negotiable role or position. As a prototype for natural responsibility, the example of parental responsibility is often given (Etchegoyen, 1993). If the definition of responsibility as a construct of ascription is accepted, however, then there is no such thing as natural responsibility. A last type of responsibility that one can find in the literature is meta-responsibility, which stands for the responsibility for the conditions of the possibility of responsibility. This idea is the basis of Jonas' (1984) theory of responsibility, and it can claim a certain plausibility. The problem, however, is that it is not accessible from within any theory of responsibility. The responsibility for the possibility of responsibility is similar to the final foundation of morality or to the question: Why be moral? This is a question that does not seem to be answerable from within moral theory. We will therefore not discuss it here, but start at the point where the subjects assume or are ascribed responsibility without considering the final reason for that.

But there are still a few distinctions concerning responsibility left that need to be mentioned in order to supply something like a comprehensive overview of the existing theories.

The Temporal Aspect of Responsibility

Ethics has something to do with time, and the same is true for responsibility. What the relationship between time and responsibility is depends on the definition of time and the theory of responsibility. For Jonas, responsibility is the moral complement of our human ontological state as temporal beings (Jonas, 1984, p. 198). This existentialist idea refers to Jonas' attempt to give a final foundation of responsibility that we just discussed. The problem with discussing questions concerning time is that it is one of the most complex issues philosophy has ever addressed. Agustinus (Confessiones X, 27, quoted in Bourdil, 1996, p. 28) said that whenever nobody asks him about time, he clearly knows what it is, but as soon as he wants to answer a question about it, he no longer knows. The same problem still applies today. Is time something objective or subjective? Does it exist or is it just a category of perception? These are open questions we will not discuss here. There seems to be enough of an interpersonal understanding of time for us to coexist and to coordinate our actions. In this sense one can say that time is objective and this objective time is of relevance for responsibility ascriptions.

Such an objective time is usually divided into past, present, and future. With the present being only the infinitesimal border between past and future, we are left with responsibility aiming either in the direction of the past (responsibility *ex post*) or in the direction of the future (responsibility *ex ante*). Depending on the temporal direction of responsibility, the concept is filled with differing contents. Classically, responsibility means that the subject has to answer for damages, injustices, and errors that it committed (Ricoeur, 1991b, p. 282). Accordingly, responsibility *ex post* aims at negative events and looks for their human initiator. These negative events, being in the past, can be clearly described and used for the purpose of imputing punishment. Most of the responsibility theories aiming at sanctions imply that the deeds for which punishment is meted out are in the past (Wallace, 1996, p. 56; Hart, 1968, p. 160). Since legal responsibility has as one of its objectives to impose punishments, there is a close link between legal responsibility and responsibility *ex post*. "Retrospective responsibility is thought to be crucial to legal judgment, primarily because the defendant's responsibility, or lack thereof, for committing an offence is thought to determine whether, and to what extent, it is permissible to inflict legal sanction or punishment" (Long, 1999, p. 125).

While backward-looking responsibility is usually clearly defined and has a relatively long history, many authors today share the perception that forward-looking responsibility is gaining in importance (Birnbacher, 1995, p. 146; Ricoeur, 1990a, p. 341; Jonas, 1984). In this case, the object of responsibility is either in the future or at least it will extend into the future. Responsibility *ex ante* is characterised by several facts or common interpretations that distinguish it from *ex post*. Firstly, it is positive rather than negative with regard to the object. While the subject is usually punished *ex post* for a misdeed, the object *ex ante* is often a positive state. That can either be the avoidance of damages or the production of something desirable (Bayertz, 1995b, p. 45). The desirable future state and the corresponding positive sanctions are meant to serve as a (positive) motivation to the subject rather than the deterrent *ex post* (Schlick, 1930, p. 33; Neuberg, 1997, p. 9). Accordingly, the duties resulting from responsibility *ex ante* are generally duties relating to action rather than duties of omission (Birnbacher, 1995, p. 151). The inherent uncertainty of future development demands less reliance on external supervision and instead a higher degree of internal identification with the object. "...internalise responsibility when we take responsibility for the future" (Schmidtz, 1998, p. 10). Finally, where responsibility *ex post* seems to point towards legal proceedings, responsibility *ex ante* is clearly closer to ethics and morality. If the subject has to give an answer concerning the object, that means it must think about it beforehand. This at least implies that the subject accepts its obligation to consider the other as a person and show its respect by giving her a reason for the action. Also, the horizon of the future points most clearly toward the general moral good (Ricoeur, 1990a, p. 341). Morality contains the element of duty, and duty as something one has to do directs the attention towards the future (Etchegoyen, 1993, p. 22).

The two temporal aspects have a close connection. While "being held responsible" often hints at the past and at legal sanctions, the purpose of this is usually to be found in results it will produce in the future. Most of the purposes of responsibility *ex post* can best be justified by their capacity to influence future developments. The "economy of threats," for example, punishes past deeds with the explicit aim of deterring future perpetrators. Thus responsibility *ex post* forces us to assume responsibility *ex ante* (cf. French, 1992, p. 15; Vanberg, 1990, p. 94; Schmidtz, 1998, p. 11; Ricoeur, 1991a, p. 282; Goodin, 1998, p. 150). Beu & Buckley (2001, p. 62) express the same idea by saying: "Knowing you will be held to account in this way for what you have done, in the past, may well make you do better, in [the] future." Some authors therefore believe that the main function of any sort of liability is prospective (Seebass, 2001, p. 89).

On the other hand there is also a reverse relationship. If the knowledge of sanctions forces the subject to assume responsibility *ex ante,* then it is in many cases hard to see how responsibility can be ascribed *ex post* if the subject had no knowledge of it *ex ante* (Birnbacher, 1995, p. 145). This refers to some of the conditions of responsibility, namely knowledge and power. These imply that the subject must at least be aware of the fact that its actions may lead to a responsibility ascription.

The prospective aspect of responsibility also refers to another problem which has led to the prominence of responsibility, to the problem of risk. Risk is an *ex ante* concept which expresses the degree of uncertainty of possible events (Holzheu, 1993, p. 265). The relationship between risk and responsibility has several aspects. Firstly, responsibility for future events is always uncertain and therefore risky (Richardson, 1999, p. 221). Secondly, the future is the realm of the possible where the idea of freedom makes sense (Picht, 1991, p. 28). Thirdly, the interplay between the two temporal directions and the corresponding relationship between the two types of responsibility finds its analogy in risk as well. From a personal perspective, risk is what lies in the future, what is to come. Systemically, risk is something that has to be dealt with after it happened, thus *ex post*. Society has to decide not only how to deal with risks that will come, but also how to distribute the damages of past risks. Again, the two aspects refer to one another (Bonß, 1995, p. 31).

Depending on the type and temporal direction of responsibility, there are different mechanisms of ascribing responsibility that also need to be explained for the concept to make sense.

Reflective and Transitive Ascription

There are two ways in which responsibility can be ascribed—reflexively and transitively. Transitive ascription stands for the process of someone or some group ascribing responsibility to the subject, whereas reflexively, the subject ascribes responsibility to itself. Traditionally and in the legal sense, responsibility is usually called for and ascribed transitively by a person or group that was affected by the subject's action. The subject may have a chance to defend itself, but the eventual sanctions are imposed despite and often against its will.

Modernity, complexity, uncertainty, risk, and all the other developments that led to the development of responsibility keep such transitive ascription from being comprehensive, and one can see a development towards the self-ascription by the subject. Responsibility then becomes the functional equivalent of traditional norms in situations where the traditional instruments of normative control no longer work (Kaufmann, 1990, p. 71). In this sense responsibility can be seen as a correlative to human freedom, and it turns into a self-obligation of the subject (Kaufmann, 1992, p. 41; 1995, p. 80).

This self-ascribed responsibility constitutes the centre of the approaches of moral philosophy that are sometimes called ethics of responsibility (Weber, 1992, p. 71). Since in this case subject and object are identical, the instance is usually thought to be an internal one, usually the personal conscience (Sänger, 1991, p. 36; Lenk, 1998, p. 177). The fact that the conscience is the instance of self-ascribed responsibility also means that the sort of rules applying to it must be moral instead of legal. The absence of external instances and sanctions also requires some of the classical characteristics of moral personhood such as freedom and autonomy (von Foerster, 2001, p. 58). The moral and voluntary nature of self-ascribed responsibility has led some authors to believe that it is of a higher order than transitively ascribed legal responsibility (van Luijk, 1990, p. 42).

Excuses and Exemptions

One last aspect of responsibility that any theory must incorporate consists of the limits of the concept. There must be clear rules outlining under what circumstances responsibility is applicable and when it is no longer valid. These limits are usually called excuses or exemptions. Generally, responsibility can or should not be ascribed if the subject does not fulfil the conditions discussed earlier. This lack of fulfilment of conditions is called "excuse" if it is temporary; it is called "exemption" if the subject is not able to meet the conditions for a longer time or ever. Put differently, there are "excuses, which function locally (examples include physical constraint or coercion); and exemptions, which operate more globally (such as insanity, childhood, or perhaps addiction)" (Wallace, 1996, p. 118). However, the question whether a subject can be responsible is usually not black or white. There are many different shades of grey that often have something to do with possible excuses. De George distinguishes three different categories of excusing conditions: "those conditions that preclude the possibility of the action, those conditions that preclude or diminish the required knowledge, and those conditions that preclude or diminish the required freedom" (De George, 1999, p. 112). Accordingly, a subject is excused from moral responsibility if the action in question is impossible to perform, if the subject does not have the required ability, if the subject does not have the opportunity to perform the action, or if the circumstances are beyond the subject's control.

Excuses or exemptions can be analysed in a more detailed way by looking at each of the conditions of responsibility. Each of the conditions discussed above can pose a problem if it is not fulfilled or if it is impossible to discern whether it is fulfilled. If there is no causal relationship between subject and object, responsibility is impossible to ascribe. The same is true in the case of a clear absence of freedom, power, or the necessary personal properties of the subject. In many cases the problem is to find out whether or not the subject lacked the conditions completely or partly.

This problem of clearly discerning whether a subject can be held responsible or whether it has a valid excuse is probably the most serious threat to the functioning of a valid theory and practice of responsibility. The problem is fundamental for any theory of responsibility because it is caused by the very reasons of the importance of the concept. Uncertainty, contingency, risk, and the modern perception of life as being unpredictable have been major factors in bringing about the success of the concept of responsibility. At the same time they now threaten its applicability.

Two Sorts of Responsibility in Information Systems and Their Resulting Problems

Looking at the different dimensions and determinants of responsibility, it becomes clear that there is an almost infinite number of combinations, each of which will lead to its own questions and problems. It is not possible to discuss all of them here. However, there are two typical configurations of responsibility whose impact on IS we will take a look at. The first one is based on clearly defined formal—mostly legal—norms, is addressed at individuals, and refers to an object that is also clear and in the past. The ascription happens transitively and from an external point of view. The second one is based on moral norms, ascribed most likely by the subject itself for an object that lies in the future and is unclear and uncertain. The subject does not have to be an individual, it can be a group or an organisation. We will later refer to these two poles as "responsibility because of IS" and "responsibility for IS" (Chapter 6). Between these two poles most responsibility ascriptions can be found.

Let us go back to the beginning of the section titled "Problems of Responsibility and Information Systtems", where several examples of responsibility in IS were enumerated. The first two of them fit the distinction between the two types quite well. The programmer who is ascribed responsibility for the programming bug has to answer for something that is in the past that may lead to serious external sanctions such as dismissal. The CIO on the other hand is responsible for the future working of the information infrastructure of the company, which is an object that is much harder to grasp with formal norms. The object is at the same time shrouded in uncertainty. Basically, we are looking at two examples of what responsibility can mean in the business use of information technology. Both examples are too brief to allow any meaningful analysis of the situation, but they can serve as typical illustrations of our topic. At the same time they also serve as a reminder of how difficult it is to realise responsibility. In both cases it is very easy to find excuses even without knowing the details of the example.

The programmer may be causally responsible for the bug in the program, but that is usually hard to determine. Modern programs are simply too complex to be understood by any one human being, including our programmer. She can therefore claim a lack of knowledge of the problem. Also, in all likelihood she will not have been the only programmer working on the program, and thus the complexity rises. The programming bug may have happened due to unclear program specification or a lack of communication that the programmer herself was not responsible for. But even if the causal link were clearly established, it is still possible that the programmer can excuse herself with a lack of freedom. She may have seen the problem coming but had to follow the customer's specification. On the other hand she may not have had the freedom to want to program better because she may not have been aware of programming standards because of a lack of education. Maybe she is just not the right person for the job and lacks the mental capacity to live up to it. Generally, she may not have been aware of the potential problem beforehand and much less of the fact that she might be held responsible for it later on. It is easy to see that there may be others who potentially share the responsibility for the programming fault: the colleague who did not tell her the specifications, the supervisor who neglected to check on her, the company that had no adequate standardised procedures, the computer profession that did not develop a sufficient curriculum, the industry that failed to regulate procedures, the society that did not take action, or the state that did not pass laws. One can see that it is easy to find quite a few excuses even in a case that is potentially as clear-cut as this one.

The second example of the CIO who is responsible for the information systems of her company leads to a number of different problems that are by no means easier to handle. The CIO's responsibilities are uncertain because they are mainly in the future. The definition of her responsibilities—the development and functioning of the company's information systems—is already so wide that it is hard to fill it with life. Additionally, the CIO can usually not realise all of this by herself. She depends on her staff for the fulfilment of the tasks that she cannot handle herself. This means that she has to deal with all of the problems of future responsibility on the one hand and of collective responsibility of the other hand. Future causalities can at best be estimated; there can be no knowledge about the future, and the individual's powers to influence it are clearly limited.

Furthermore, in the case of organisational responsibility that the CIO has to rely on, there are problems concerning the organisation and distribution of responsibility. One would have to ask whether there is the possibility of one individual being responsible for the actions of another and what that means. In addition, both examples show the mix of different types of responsibility. The programmer's as well as the CIO's responsibilities are clearly role responsibilities. At the same time both have a moral aspect and a legal aspect. Even though one may be directed into the past and the other into the future, it is clear that they contain both temporal dimensions. Both also mix transitive and reflexive ascription, and due to the mix of components, it is not clear who or what might be the instance deciding about the final outcome of the ascription.

Having spent this much time on the discussion of responsibility and IS, the result of this analysis of the concept seems to be that there is no coherent theory that would allow an unequivocal ascription. Even though the different theories of responsibility discussed so far agree in a great number of points, this agreement is not far-reaching enough to allow for an undisputed ascription. There are several conclusions one can draw from this. First, one can simply refrain from discussing moral or normative questions in terms of responsibility. This is not a good idea because one would at the same time lose the practical advantages that the term has, namely its general familiarity and the positive reception it is usually greeted with. Also, it might be hard to find another concept that allows the discussion of the different ethical and moral theories that were introduced as the German and French tradition.

Another solution would be to narrow the term down more specifically and return to one of the theories introduced earlier on. One could for example concentrate solely on the moral or the legal aspect of responsibility, and in both cases it might be possible to come up with clearer rules of ascription and the resulting consequences such as sanctions or rewards. While this is certainly a manageable way of dealing with responsibility, the disadvantage would be that it would have to shield out the relationships between the different sorts of responsibility.

For these reasons we will try a different approach to responsibility in IS. Instead of allowing the multitude of facts and theories about responsibility to ruin the applicability of the term, we will attempt to clarify it by applying it reflexively in the hope that this will allow the determination of the theoretical heart and the practical consequences. We will therefore in the next chapter introduce and discuss the idea of reflective responsibility, and after that we will apply it to the normative problems of business information technology.

Chapter V

Reflective Responsibility

What is "reflective responsibility"? The idea behind it is to see whether the concept as discussed so far is applicable to itself and what consequences result from the self-application. It is an attempt to clarify the notion by referring to the term itself without using any other theories. The self-application of concepts is an old tool used by philosophers for centuries, sometimes with great success. The probably best-known example which demonstrates that reflexivity can be highly successful and plausible is the refutation of scepticism. Scepticism, understood as the doctrine that there is no truth, has been part of the philosophical discourse ever since humans started discussing truth. Given the difficulties of defining truth and the obvious fallibility of our knowledge, it is an attractive position that allows the speaker to avoid many pitfalls. However, scepticism has one big problem, which becomes obvious as soon as one applies the idea onto itself. If scepticism is true and consequently there is no truth, then scepticism cannot be true. Scepticism can thus be shown to be self-contradictory. Self-reference on the other hand is also a dangerous game to play because it can create serious logical and practical problems. One example is the mathematical class of all classes that contain themselves. This has led to logical problems that have kept the mathematicians in work for a greater part of the 20th century. A rather practical problem is that of self-fulfilling prophecies. These are created by applying a theory to itself, and they can have a considerable social impact (cf. Watzlawik, 2001b).

In the case of reflective responsibility, what we want to do is firstly try to distil some features of responsibility that are shared by most of the theories. In a second step we will then reflectively apply the features to the theories discussed so far. Finally, we will analyse the theoretical and especially practical consequences that arise from these observations.

COMMON FEATURES OF RESPONSIBILITY

There are three fundamental features that most of the theories of responsibility discussed so far share: openness, affinity to action, and consequentialism. These three features are well-suited to act as the foundation of the reflective use of responsibility. Before the reflexivity of responsibility is explored, however, the three features should be described and their relevance to responsibility should be highlighted.

The first feature is openness. We have seen that responsibility is a moral term that stands in competition with other moral terms. Some of the contents of responsibility can be expressed in terms of duty, for example, or of virtue. Unlike these traditional moral concepts, however, responsibility is less clearly suited for the prescription of certain acts or characteristics of agents. Responsibility is open in the sense that it contains something like a "surplus" that precludes its clear determination (cf. Picht, 1991, p. 28). This uncertainty of the concept, the openness in the sense that it leaves open what exactly is the right or necessary thing to do, is the reason why it has gained relevance in those areas where the traditional means of behavioural control fail: in the case of risky tasks, this can only be solved by high competence and flexibility (Bayertz, 1995b, p. 46; Kaufmann, 1995, p. 88). This may explain why we tend to call those positions "responsible" that require a high measure of openness, that are characterised by tasks which are not always foreseeable and programmable. Examples might be leading positions in the economy or administration such as CEOs, judges, or politicians. In these roles the agents are unable to know and often even to estimate what will happen, and they therefore need certain personality traits which are not shared by everybody.

Openness of responsibility is a characteristic that most, if not all sorts of responsibility share. There may be different amounts of openness in different sorts of responsibility, but it still pervades all of the applications. In the case of legal responsibility, the amount of openness is certainly less than in moral responsibility simply because the law is written and there are clear and calculable traditions of interpreting it. Nevertheless, a judge always has the freedom to take certain facts into consideration or refrain from doing so. She may even under the same circumstances come to different conclusions in different cases. If one compares moral responsibility with other moral theories, it is also plain to see that openness is a feature not shared by most of them. A deontological system in which the only good thing is the good will, which in turn is only good when it is motivated by duty, has a different perception. The good in this case is determined whether it is done or not. Utilitarianism is another example for this. If it is good to do what will lead to the greatest good (happiness, pleasure,…) for the greatest number, then that means there is one good thing to do or at least several things that are equally good. Of course the realisation of any ethical rule or norm will in most cases also require judgment and thus a certain amount of openness. The Kantian ethicist or the Utilitarian will both have to use their faculties of reason as much as the responsibility ethicist. The difference, however, is that under ideal conditions of full information, complete rationality, knowledge of utility functions, etc., it should be possible to determine the morally good action or response in those cases. In the case of responsibility, this is not even theoretically viable. Responsibility is intrinsically open.

The openness of responsibility has several direct consequences. First of all the "sphere of responsibility" is more extended, in the sense of complexity but also in a temporal sense, than for example duties tend to be (Hart, 1968, p. 213). Secondly, the openness leads to additional characteristics that the subject must possess. The subject must reflect the openness by having an open mind, by being free of prejudices. Responsibility ethics require a process of efficient search for information and a rational evaluation of alternatives, which is necessary because it does not say what the good is in a particular case (Kreikebaum, 1996, p. 185). Thirdly, openness requires flexibility. Being responsible means that one has the ability to react appropriately to unknown future occurrences. This is necessary to cover the central problems of uncertainty, risk, and side effects. Flexibility and the ability to react to the unforeseen, fourthly, presuppose tolerance of errors. For Etchegoyen (1993, p. 112), a society of responsible people is a society that admits a right to errors. This is not a metaphysical principle, but it is caused by the fact that responsibility is always a process of learning in which errors necessarily occur. We will return to the discussion of these points later on.

The second feature that most responsibility ascriptions have in common is their affinity to action, to real and immediate results. Again there are several aspects to this. Some authors define the area of responsibility explicitly as that of action and justice (cf. Kohlberg, 1995). Others see the closeness to action in the fact that responsibility statements aim at the agent's actions instead of her rights (Birnbacher, 1995, p. 147). "When we speak of the responsibility of individuals, philosophers say that we mean…something has to be done…" (Goodpaster & Matthews, 1982, p. 133). Finally, the aspect of action can be contrasted with thought. Responsibility can thus be described as "a behaviouristic concept, because responsibilities are discharged by action, not thought" (Staddon, 1999, p. 173).

This affinity to action applies again to most if not all sorts of responsibility even though there are differences between the degrees of relevance. Retrospective responsibility has a link to action at least in the sense that the subject is responsible for something it did beforehand. Criminal acts, for example, are always more than intentions, thoughts, or contemplations. In order to be held legally responsible, one must have done something specific, or in some cases omitted to do something. The entire discussion concerning omissions should in this sense be understood as a complementary part of action. If responsibility refers to action, then it also refers to non-action, to omission. The link between responsibility and action is even stronger in the case of prospective responsibility. If the subject is held responsible or assumes responsibility for something that is still to come, then the association is automatically that this has something to do with action. Whether it be the politician who says she will be responsible for the well-being of her constituency for the next four years or the programmer who is responsible for the development of a new algorithm, it is automatically clear that the ascription requires the subject to do something.

The third point that all responsibility ascriptions share is their inherent teleology. Teleology is an ethical viewpoint that emphasises the consequences of actions as the relevant factor for their ethical evaluation. In this sense it is similar to consequentialism. Depending on which theory one wants to believe, consequentialism is understood as a sort of teleology or vice versa. Teleology comes from Greek "*telos,*" which means the aim, or target. For our purposes this will include consequentialism, and indeed one can see that the different sorts of responsibility are all consequentialist. This becomes clear when one contrasts this with another ethical theory, with deontology. In deontology a good action is one that adheres to certain rules. These rules will in most cases also consider the eventual outcome; however, the ethical character of the action does not depend directly on the consequences. Another aspect of teleology apart from consequentialism can be described by the "good life." This is where ethical theory comes back in. A consequentialist theory needs some sort of justification of its interpretation of the good life. If the agent is supposed to aim for good consequences, there must be some understanding as to the nature of what constitutes them. Most responsibility ascriptions solve this problem by referring implicitly or explicitly to an underlying idea of the good life (Ropohl, 1987, p. 157). This does not necessarily point to an Aristotelian ethics. It just shows that the social process of responsibility ascription needs a normative background. Furthermore, the good life implies that while there is a need for a normative background, this cannot be supplied in an authoritarian fashion. The good life is something that the group in question has to decide about, which implies that the decision about the content of the good life is part of the process of ascription itself.

Teleology is closely related to the first of the common features of responsibility, to openness and action. Responsibility is a normative construct that has evolved in a world of growing uncertainty. In this world people increasingly realised the importance not only of obeying rules, but of making sure that consequences of actions were acceptable. In a changing and uncertain world, consequences can only be considered by a normative construct that is open to changes and the agent's perception of reality. Given the resulting autonomy of the agent and the original intention of realising beneficial consequences, the emphasis will automatically be on the agent's action.

REFLECTIVE APPLICATION OF THE SHARED FEATURES OF RESPONSIBILITY

What exactly does it mean to apply responsibility reflectively? It can certainly mean many things, not all of which can be analysed here. For our purposes it should be enough to emphasise the three main characteristics of responsibility and check whether the use of the notion does in fact lead to openness, proximity to action, and the consideration of consequences. The leading question for this self-application may be: Can we approve of the use of the term responsibility and its results from the point of view of a theory of responsibility?[14] Another similar question might be: Is it an act of responsibility to speak of responsibility and what does the speaker have to do to make sure it is?

These questions are probably easier to answer with regard to given applications. To give a specific answer, one would need to choose a certain realisation of responsibility and then check whether or not this application adheres to the underlying logic of responsibility. This will be done later on with regard to different aspects of business information technology. In order to do this, however, it is helpful to consider the reflective properties of responsibility from a theoretical perspective first.

The first point, the openness of responsibility, does not seem to pose too much of a problem. Openness of responsibility is almost guaranteed by its communicative nature. As we have seen before, responsibility is by its very definition a concept that relies on the inclusion of the affected parties. The subject, usually the agent responsible for an act, a decision, etc., has to answer to the instance because of what happened or may happen insofar as the rights of others are concerned. This should include the hearing of everybody involved. Otherwise it would be impossible to know exactly what the object of responsibility is and what makes it something that is ascribed to somebody. From a practical point of view, this poses relevant problems, as it may prove impossible to even find out who or what exactly is affected. Even if this is known, it may prove impossible to hear all affected parties. Theoretically, however, the use of the notion of responsibility as an attempt to address moral matters is consistent in this regard since it points in the direction of the openness of the answer. Responsibility goes even further than just a simple discussion of moral questions because it allows the social construction of reality. That means that in the communicative process, which constitutes the ascription of responsibility and the following answer, more than normative rules and morality are discussed and assessed. Communication comprises the agreement concerning reality in a specific case and its relevance to moral questions.

While the use of the term responsibility clearly seems to be responsible in that it conveys a sense of openness, which is characteristic for the term, the reflective application is less clear-cut where it comes to the second feature, the affinity to action. As mentioned, the appeal of the term in many circumstances seems to result from the fact that it promises some kind of stalwart result—that actions be taken as a consequence. In fact, the use of responsibility often seems to lead the other way. Many are the times that the ascription of responsibility—especially the reflective ascription of responsibility as in "I take full responsibility for…"—does not seem to lead anywhere. This observation differs for different sorts of responsibility. There are some forms for which action is a defining feature such as legal responsibility. If a judge or a jury ascribes responsibility, that usually has serious consequences. For moral responsibility on the other hand that seems to be far less certain. It is Lübbe's (1990, p. 206) critique of responsibility that it is nothing but the attempt to hide its own inaction. It can therefore be said that the reflective application of responsibility in the field of its perceived closeness to action leads to ambiguous results. While it is not exactly contradictory to use responsibility, it does not necessarily lead to the realisation of the aims either. A reflected and reflective use of responsibility would therefore have to pay attention to the question of whether or not it leads to results.

Result is the key word that leads us to the last feature of responsibility which we have to take into account. Responsibility is a consequentialist concept, which uses the results of actions as the basis for their moral evaluation. What does this mean for the concept of reflective responsibility? The first point here is that the notion of responsibility must be used under consideration of its consequences. The results of an ascription of responsibility need to be taken into account with regards to their nature and their potential use as feedback for the notion of responsibility itself.

This in turn leads to several problems concerning epistemology, metaphysics, and other philosophical fields. If responsibility is to be used reflectively, the question has to be asked whether the consequences of an action can be taken into consideration at all. In order to answer this question, there are numerous problems that need to be addressed. One is whether the consequences are known and if they can be known at all. This question again has two aspects depending on the temporal dimension of responsibility. For responsibility *ex post,* the problem is the determination of facts and the corresponding evaluations of these facts. Even though this is certainly no easy task, it is the classical problem of morality and therefore can be done in many instances. The assessment of results in the case of responsibility *ex ante* on the other hand is much more complicated, due to the fact that by definition the results in this case are unknown.

One can see that the use of responsibility as a moral notion does not ensure the realisation of consequentialism. Reflective responsibility would therefore have to try to find ways of realizing this consequentialism. This again would require several aspects to be taken into account. Firstly, there is the theoretical aspect. Responsibility ascriptions have to be checked for consistency. That means that one has to ask the question whether a certain ascription is feasible. Reflective responsibility would have to make sure that ascriptions are understandable and can be met. One common criticism of responsibility ascriptions is that they are too general, too broad to be of any use. It is often said that where everybody is responsible for everything, the entire notion loses its usefulness (Lenk, 1998, p. 83). It must therefore be possible to delineate the relevant results and make specific ascriptions.[15]

Another open question with regard to results is: For which results can responsibility be ascribed? A basic problem here is the question of how to decide which results are relevant for the assessment of an action. If we see the world as a nexus of causality, we recognise that every action has an infinite amount of results, most of which we will never know. Therefore the emphasis of responsibility usually lies on intended results. This is not really convincing, however, since we already know that one of the main reasons for the popularity of the notion are the developments and especially the negative effects of technology. It can safely be said that most technological developments aim at some sort of good. Even the most morally ambiguous technologies such as the atomic bomb were originally intended as morally good. So what we are looking at as the main reasons for many of today's moral problems are unintended results. A notion of responsibility that neglects these side effects can therefore not be complete. On the other hand we have seen that it is principally impossible to take all consequences into account since we can never know them all. Reflective responsibility has to consider this and deal with it in an open way. One possible solution is indicated in the communicative construction of responsibility. The process of ascription can comprise the determination of the results that it can be applied to, making it a reflective process itself. This can easily lead to theoretical and practical problems, but it saves responsibility from becoming just another deontological or casuistic concept.

The conclusion to be drawn from this question about the implications of reflective application on responsibility is that the results of an ascription of responsibility must be taken into consideration. A consistent use of the notion of responsibility has to include the question of whether it is a responsible action to speak of responsibility. Consequentialism should take its consequences seriously.

This first overview of the reflective attributes of responsibility shows that they are hard to realise. As a solution to the problem of unmanageable responsibility that seems to demand more of the agents than they are capable of giving it seems to have failed. Instead of making the ascriptions of responsibility easier, it has added a whole new dimension of problems. In short, the mere attempt to completely fulfil all of these requirements is doomed to failure. This realisation, however, if viewed in the context of the features of responsibility, also opens up a new window of opportunity. As a consequentialist concept aiming for the improvement of social or individual life, responsibility has no need to claim perfection. If the ascription of responsibility leaves the affected parties better off than the lack of it, then it is responsible to ascribe it even if the results may not be perfect or uncontroversial. This is another facet of the reflective use of the term. It can be argued that small results are better than no results, and if one can view responsibility as a concept that has no absolute claims, then it can be used to create incrementally better circumstances.

This is probably one of the reasons for the popularity of the concept. It is intrinsically incremental and thereby appeals to many of today's people for whom the all-encompassing philosophies, the great narratives have lost their credibility. In this sense the reflective use of responsibility can be seen in the tradition of moral theories that attempt the improvement of life on a smaller scale with limited objectives. One example of similar approaches might be Ricoeur's ethical theory which aims at the avoidance of violence without even trying to justify that goal. Once the affected parties can agree on this goal, all steps taken in this direction can be described as morally good. Another example is Popper's social technology (cf. Popper, 1992), which attempts to move toward a better society by taking small manageable steps at a time—his piecemeal social technology. This is another idea that may claim a high plausibility because it best describes the way a modern democratic government can try to achieve (moral) goals.

The next step before the application of the concept to IS will be to take a closer look at the consequences that result from the reflective turn.

CONSEQUENCES OF REFLECTIVE RESPONSIBILITY

The reflective use of responsibility will lead to consequences in the way the term is understood and used. This is firstly one of the reflective properties of the term itself—a reflective use of a consequentialist term should produce consequences—and it is secondly a necessary result of the change of the use of the term. If the reflective concept did not lead to other consequences than the original one, then the question would have to be: Why bother? As it turns out, however, there are many aspects of a theoretical as well as a practical nature that are affected.

Theoretical Consequences

Taking the reflective turn of responsibility seriously leads to a number of consequences for the process of ascription and its consequences. First of all, however, the term itself is affected. Making sure that responsibility is an open process, which leads to action, and that it has palpable consequences requires some changes in the theoretical groundwork. The first point here has to do with the clarity of the notion. Responsibility can only fulfil the three criteria if it is clear to everybody involved. This means that it is a central task of every theory of responsibility to clearly say who is responsible for what under which circumstances and with what results. Actually, this can be seen as a condition for all sorts of responsibility (Bayertz, 1995b, p. 66f) and also for most ethical theories, but it acquires a new urgency in the light of reflective responsibility.

Another theoretical consequence of reflective responsibility is a certain kind of pragmatism in the ascription process. Pragmatism can be understood as the doctrine that true is what works. In our context that means less time is spent on the attempt to define exactly the facts of a situation, the duties of the parties involved, the foundation of ethical norms, or other potential fields of thought for philosophers. It should be kept in mind that the successful solution of problems is the quality mark of responsibility. This should not be understood to mean an anti-intellectual process that only tries to produce quick results. However, there may be many cases in which the affected parties agree on the relevant circumstances or norms. In those cases reflective responsibility can display its effectiveness without necessarily having an unassailable theory for everything involved. If, for example, it is a recognised industry standard that programmers document the program development and a specific individual fails to do so despite knowledge of that standard, then an ascription of responsibility may be viable without recurring to the basis of this standard. In other cases the opposite may be true as well, and it can very well be necessary for a successful ascription to determine exactly what its theoretical basis is.

This leads to another philosophical position that must at least be partially accepted when dealing with responsibility, to constructivism. In its radical form constructivism holds that the entire world is nothing but our individual or collective construction. We create the world by perceiving it. In its radical form this position, even though it goes back to Kant's distinction between the thing in itself and the phenomenon, will probably be a bit too harsh for the average person to accept. However, reflective responsibility requires the recognition of the constructive nature of responsibility ascriptions. It is a matter of collective agreement, and thus of collective construction, who is eligible to act as a subject, and what can count as object. But many of the other factors discussed so far are also constructions. Among them we find causality as a precondition or the difference between doing and omitting. Causal chains, as I have tried to demonstrate earlier on, are not given by nature but are human interpretations. It seems a perfectly plausible thing to say that the programmer is responsible for neglecting to check her work for mistakes. But this is only possible on the basis of a shared construction of the world and a person's duties. One could for example excuse the programmer and say that the computer did not have a debugging mechanism, that the keyboard did not work correctly, that she forgot her glasses or was educated by her parents to be a forgetful person. Depending on the circumstances all of these facts could count as excuses. Whether we insist on the responsibility ascription is therefore a question of collective agreement, which shows that responsibility is a collective construct that only works on the basis of other collective constructs such as causality or action.

This may on the one hand seem threatening and relativistic because there are no more final foundations upon which ascriptions must be based. On the other hand it is also an enormous opportunity because it allows the process of ascription to determine who or what is eligible for which role. This can for example be applied to the question of whether collective subjects are admissible, as will be shown later on.

A final theoretical result of reflective responsibility is the acceptance of its inevitability. If moral norms can be translated into responsibility and reflective responsibility stands for the consequences of norm application, then there is no way to escape it. Responsibility can be ascribed for doing as well as for omitting, for physical action, for theoretical action such as writing or speaking. Responsibility is a potential consequence of everything we do. In the modern technological age, responsibility grows with the power we have and with the temporal horizon to which we can follow the results of our action. In this sense one has to agree with Zimmerli (1994a, p. 4) when he says that in technological contexts it is no longer a question whether one accepts responsibility; it is a constant factor. The question is only whether the potential ascription will be realised or not. This refers to risk and uncertainty, both of which are inevitable, which is another reason for the close connection between risk and responsibility.

The theoretical consequences of reflective responsibility are thus to firstly clarify what the term means and to secondly reflect on the conditions of its realisation. Apart from this there are several areas where the realisation of responsibility and the way it is ascribed in practice are affected.

Prudence

Reflective responsibility, with its emphasis on openness, action, and consequences, must solve a problem that other moral systems do not necessarily have. It cannot tell the subjects what to do in which situation, how to behave, and what the right thing would be at any given time. In fact it demands the subjects to reflect on this question and find the right answers for themselves, using their own mental faculties. Reflective responsibility thus does not demand a new morality for new problems, but it first of all demands a new way of critically judging the situation and for that, the subjects need an ability that philosophical literature tended to call *prudentia* or *phronesis*. It also goes by names such as good sense, judiciousness, or prudence.

The idea that good intellectual judgment is closely linked to morality is of course not a new one. Aristotle pointed out that ethical virtues and prudence are linked. For him the foundations of prudence aimed at producing virtue. Virtue on the other hand had to be ordered by prudence. Both have to do with passions and therefore with the whole, with body and soul. This, according to Aristotle, shows that virtues have to do with the whole of man and are therefore deeply human. Felicitousness, the aim of human action, can only be achieved by the combination of virtue and prudence (cf. Aristoteles, 1967, p. 1178a).

While prudence is a venerable ethical concept, it is also of particular importance for responsibility, especially of the reflective kind. Not only openness, uncertainty and risk demand that the subject use its mental capacities. Even at an earlier stage, at the realisation that responsibility is a social construct, it becomes clear that it needs to rely on what it is constituted by, the human mind and its capacities.

But what is prudence, what does the word stand for in concrete terms? For Weil (1998; 1960, p. 127), it is defined as the will to be ready to make a moral decision in any given situation. It depends on and demands the subject to know itself and to know the world. For him there is no contradiction between justice or pure moral intentions and prudence. The two depend on each other and could not exist without one another. Ricoeur (1991c, p. 108) follows a similar path when he defines prudence as the art of integrating the moral, the rational, the historical, and the legal into life. He also calls it the concrete reason in the historical world.

Prudence clearly has something to do with knowledge, with rationality, and with the way it is used in given circumstances. It is more than just intellectual brilliance. It is interesting to compare what it means in other languages. When one translates the English word prudence into German and back, one gets terms such as carefulness, cautiousness, discretion, deliberateness, level-headedness, wisdom, or wiseness. Prudence is an individual virtue which finds its expression in the way the individual leads its life and especially in the way it contributes to society (Aristoteles, 1967, p. 1141b).

Prudence is one possible link between rationality and morality (cf. Hausman & McPherson, 1996, p. 25). In this function it is especially suitable to fulfil the promises of responsibility. For Lipovetski (in Russ 1995, p. 33), responsibility embodies the soul of the post-modern culture. This is so because it keeps up the idea of morality without preaching the abdication of the self on the altar of superior ethical ideals. Responsibility for him is reasonable in the sense that it does not force the realisation of its own imperatives, but attempts to find reconciliation between values and interests. In order to be able to do that, responsibility will have to find mechanisms for this reconciliation and this leads us straight back to the idea of prudence.

Another related idea is that of judgment. If prudence is the application of moral norms in concrete situations, then the most prominent place where it can be demonstrated is the act of judging. Judgments are again closely related to responsibility. The clearest example of judgment can be found in the case of a judge who is required to rule according to the criteria named above. The judge must know the normative background, in this case the law, but she must also take other relevant factors into consideration. Making a legal judgment is not a simple matter of applying a norm to a situation and following some kind of algorithm. It requires common sense and character on the part of the judge which in turn are needed to mediate norms, expectations, morality, and facts.

If responsibility stands for the moral good—some idea of a good life—then its realisation depends not only on the idea of the good life, but requires knowledge of the facts and circumstances. It can only become reality if the relevant parties concretise it using judgment and reason (Berger, 1994, p. 137). In this sense responsibility is also open to other ethical theories that emphasise the importance of judgment, such as newer Aristotelian approaches (Höffe, 1990, p. 561) or virtue ethics (De George, 1999, p. 122).

Prudence is an individual human property that requires its bearer to fulfil some preconditions. One of these is experience. Aristotle (1967, 241, p. 1142a) already points out that prudence requires a knowledge of the relevant things and that this knowledge can only be acquired over time. With experience and the age that requires it comes another characteristic that the prudent individual should have—wisdom. For Ricoeur (1990b, p. 265), a practical wisdom is necessary for solving moral conflicts. It is linked to moral judgment and to the situation in which it is needed.

Another link between responsibility in IS and prudence is that prudence can be linked to economic thinking. Prudence requires the taking into account of all relevant facts, norms, people, and every other aspect that might be of importance. It then leads to a judgment that in turn requires the careful weighing of all these different aspects to come to a wise decision. The inherent aspect of weighing is where Broome (1998, p. 26) sees the relationship to the economy. Weighing is only necessary because of the fact of scarcity. Scarcity comes into every judgment, at least in the sense that judgments must be finished in finite time to make any sense. We have already seen that the mere attempt to find all the causes and results of any one action is potentially infinite. Part of the process of making a prudent judgment therefore has to be when to end the "hearing of evidence" and to make the judgment. This aspect of scarcity relates the judgment on the one hand to economic thinking in general, but on the other hand also to all sorts of business decisions that have to do with the allocation of scarce goods.[16] Information technology is just one among many examples in this respect.

Prudent use of responsibility is useful in dealing with technology for other reasons besides scarcity. In many cases technological developments are not yet objects of responsibility. Ropohl (1996, p. 57) identifies several reasons for this which relate to the weaknesses of responsibility as they have to be addressed by reflective responsibility. These are the neglecting side effects, the realisation that side effects are unacceptable at a time when they are already widespread, the dispersion of responsibility among many individuals, none of whom feels responsible, and the constitution of law and politics as a mere repair service of technology. All of these are critical points that jeopardise classical responsibility ascriptions because they undermine the two features of action and consequentialism. Reflective responsibility will therefore have to address these points. It must take the realisation of responsibility into account. But before discussing this next line of reasoning, we should first take a brief look at the problems of prudence.

Prudence is not an unequivocal algorithm that can give clear instructions to those who seek guidance in a complex decision situation. It is, like responsibility, open and, as we have seen, it is more like an art than like a science. It may be acquired by experience, but experience is no guarantee for prudence. Criticism of prudence could therefore be that it cannot be realised, at least not realised in a universal way that would be adequate for a moral term. Morality is often thought to have some universal character in the sense that everybody to whom it applies should be able to understand it and to live up to it. A morality that the subjects cannot follow will have a difficult time establishing itself as obligatory. If this is so, then prudence could endanger reflective responsibility. The answer to this is that there are different levels of prudence. Prudence as the high art of making judicious judgments in complex situations is something that cannot be expected of everybody. However, there are rules of prudence in the sense of acting carefully that are recognisable to the general public. In fact there are standards of prudence that we all know. If we disrespect these standards, we are guilty of negligence: "...negligence can be understood to be a failure to do something that a reasonable and prudent person would have done" (Johnson, 2001, p. 184).

A prudent judgment requires rare personal characteristics from the person making it. On the other hand it also presupposes the existence of some "objective" facts. It must be clear who has done what, where, why, etc. Reflective responsibility, in order to ascribe generally acceptable results to a recognisable subject in an open process, also requires these same facts. As we have seen, one of the problems threatening responsibility is the lack of such objectivity. It will therefore have to be addressed in this theory of reflective responsibility. Prudence aims in a direction that moral theories classically have not spent a lot of energy on, but which seems of high importance in reflective responsibility. It is the question: Is our moral theory realisable? Reflective responsibility, with its emphasis on the closeness to action and the consequences of ascriptions, cannot afford to ignore these issues. The next section will therefore be dedicated to them.

Realisability

The question whether reflective responsibility is realisable and what relevance that has to the theory in general can be placed in the context of the discussion of theory and practice: What is the purpose of theory? What impact does it have on practice? Is theory not some kind of practice itself? This leads to the philosophy of science and the questions: What is the purpose of science? Why do we research what we research? Why do we teach what we teach? This is a particularly virulent problem in the area of information systems research. IS as partly computer science and partly business studies is often unsure about its academic paradigm. It is torn between a desire to do rigorous research and producing results of relevance to practitioners.[17] It also leads to the problem of theory and practice in moral philosophy, parts of which were already discussed in connection with the German tradition. It is impossible to reflect the different viewpoints adequately. One general critique of academic research is always that it produces nothing of practical relevance. This is expressed by the image of the academic ivory tower. One of the reasons why this is so is that many theories forget to take into consideration the efficacy of the theory (Bourdieu, 1998b, p. 59). Whether and how far that applies to all theories is an open question, but it often rings true in questions of ethics. Moral norms are deeply practical because they determine what we do and, as Hausman and McPherson (1996, p. 54) point out, otherwise they would be of little interest. So the question of theory and practice is pertinent in ethics, and many authors agree that ethical theory has to reflect it. The first step is to ask: Is the ethical theory we are using or developing possible at all? It is hard to disagree with Mendieta's (1999, p. 121) reasoning when he says:

> "...ethics concerns action, what one must do. What cannot be done, is not part of ethics. The question is what can be done? The ethical thus must include an elucidation of what is feasible, attainable."

Weil, following a similar train of thought, concludes that those who want the good without asking how to come by it are the worst enemies of morality, worse than those who do not care about it at all. A good intention is a good thing, but it needs the reflection of what is possible. Briefly: "il faut que toute morale soit practicable" (Weil, 1998; 1960, p. 92).

The question whether morality can be realised again has different aspects. The first one, the one Mendieta speaks about, is the fundamental possibility of a norm. If we found a new ethical norm that satisfied all possible aspects of ethical theory but that would be impossible to realise, it could not claim to be a valid moral norm. However, in most cases the problems are less obvious. Questions concerning whether norms are realisable often revolve around the much more subtle question of their enforceability. A norm that consists solely of an ethical appeal can be called naïve if it fails to take into account the legal, institutional, or political measures that would be needed to support it (Lenk & Maring, 1996b, p. 20).

This question is not only one of common sense but also reflects on the foundation of norms. As Habermas (1998b, p. 567) points out, even well-grounded norms have to be reasonable in the sense that one can only expect people to follow them under the condition that everybody else is acting accordingly. This is so because the reasons for the acceptability of norms are based on their universal observance. This means that the validity of norms depends on their practicability (Priddat, 1994, p. 175; Wieland, 1999, p. 24).

This question of validity due to possibility also brings us back to the business part of IS, because it can be rephrased in terms of costs and thus be translated into the field of economic thinking. One reason why a moral norm might not be applicable could be prohibitively high costs (cf. Wieland, 1999, p. 26; 2001b, p. 26; Birnbacher, 1995, p. 133f). This is of high relevance for reflective responsibility because of the attention it must pay to the consequences of responsibility ascription. It implies that it is not only important that responsibility can produce manifest results, but that some quality of these results, such as their cost, must also be considered. To give a brief example from IS, the discussion of privacy rights must react to this. One solution to the question of privacy is to give complete control over all information to the people to whom it pertains. This might be morally defensible on different grounds such as a property approach to data or the idea of human autonomy. While such an approach might be theoretically acceptable, it would lead to a fundamental change in the way our society deals with data. To implement it would produce considerable costs. We will leave it open at this stage whether these costs would be prohibitive, but it is clear that these costs must play a role in the deliberation of the norms and resulting policies.

A fundamental problem with this sort of argument is that it is always suspect of committing the naturalistic fallacy, of drawing normative conclusions from positive facts. It is generally recognised among philosophers that conclusions from 'is' to 'ought' are not admissible. On the other hand 'is' and 'ought' are related, otherwise the entire enterprise of moral philosophy would seem rather pointless. Without going into this discussion in any greater detail, we believe that the arguments just discussed are valid because they reflect on the conditions of the possibility of ethics. Philosophers have to ask whether their norms are applicable, because otherwise their validity is jeopardised. Another argument looks at the individual as a moral agent. If ethics deals with the consideration of others' interests, then it is a moral imperative that the moral agent's ability to consider them be maintained (Priddat, 1994, p. 104). While the (moral) validity of a norm must not be mixed up with its (factual) efficacy, one must admit that there exists a relationship between the two. A social order (for example the law) is only valid if it is effective (Kelsen, 1987, p. 31) and vice versa (Apel, 1980, p. 239).

This area of the realisation of norms in relation to their normative grounding is of high importance for reflective responsibility for several reasons. Firstly, reflective responsibility reflects on the consequences of consequentialism and therefore must enquire what these consequences are. Secondly, reflective responsibility is understood to aim at concrete results and solutions. Thus, there must be a discussion of these solutions, which should start with the question whether they are possible at all. Thirdly, responsibility is a normative but prima facie empty term which has to rely on the provision of material norms from other sources such as the socially accepted morality. If these underlying norms are jeopardised by a lack of practical relevance, then reflective responsibility must react to that.

This special reliance of responsibility on factual consequences and its weakness in the face of a threat to its realisability has been recognised by several authors. For Etchegoyen (1999), the principle of responsibility is the opposite of a heroic but impotent morality. This is why, for him, the true morality mocks traditional morality which neglects this point (*"La vraie morale se moque de la morale—être responsable"*). Responsibility as the true morality concentrates on consequences and thus especially on its own consequences. That, on the other hand, means that moral excuses, such as that of a good idea that was badly applied, are no longer valid. It is not possible to rely exclusively on the good will.

Lübbe (1990, p. 206) reflects on the conditions of the efficacy of responsibility and mentions some of the points that will be analysed in the next few sections. Among them there are institutions that must enable us to act responsibly, mechanisms of social control and sanctions, personal qualities, and power as the limit of responsibility. His conclusion, however, is rather negative because he uses the analysis to unmask the rhetoric of responsibility as a pathetic moralism used to cover its own practical incapacity.

Reflective responsibility must take the same problems into account, but instead of choosing Lübbe's path and in order to lead to consequences, it should try to develop ways to overcome them. From a reflective point of view, responsibility must be construed in such a way that the entire system of responsibility ascriptions is realistic and efficient, that number and intensity of responsibilities remain such that the actors can live up to them (cf. Birnbacher, 1995, p. 170). The most important ideas discussed in the next few sections—accountability, the role of institutions, and the process of imputation—are meant to support the realisabiltiy of responsibility.

Accountability

Reflective responsibility must not remain a theoretical abstraction if it wants to live up to the second and third characteristics, to the affinity to action and to consequentialism. Reflectivity in this case means that the process of responsibility ascription is analysed with regard to what will happen as a result. If the ascription does not lead to action, does not alleviate the problem, react to the broken norm in question, or leads to some other sort of manifest result, then it misses the point of responsibility. In order to be able to lead to action, however, the relevant parties, causal relationships, and norms have to be clear. Rules have to be understandable and applicable, and the underlying facts must be identifiable. This will only be possible within certain limits, but the attempt to do so is what accountability stands for. In this sense accountability means that the preconditions for the practice of prudent judgments are met. Part of accountability will therefore be the clarification of norms as described above.

Another part addresses epistemological and practical obstacles to responsibility.

Accountability is often used synonymously to responsibility. This leads to some very broad definitions such as that "to say that someone is accountable is to say that the person…is the appropriate agent to respond (i.e., to give an account) for an event or incident or situation" (Johnson, 2001, p. 173). Others see accountability as one possible type or meaning of responsibility (cf. Spinello, 1997, p. 16). This meaning usually encompasses certain types and sanctions of responsibility, mostly those that we so far called moral responsibility. "Accountability refers to the perception of defending or justifying one's conduct to an audience that has reward or sanction authority" (Beu & Buckley, 2001, p. 61). Accountability then stands for questions of blameworthiness and punishment (Weckert & Adeney, 1997, p. 89).

In this text accountability is understood in narrower terms. It stands for the securing of the foundations of responsibility, in order that it can bear consequences. Accountability stands for the part of responsibility that "has to do with tracing the causes of actions and events, of finding out who is answerable in a given situation" (Goodpaster & Matthews, 1982, p. 133). A good definition is suggested by Laudon and Laudon (1999, p. 457):

"Accountability is a feature of systems and social institution: it means that mechanisms are in place to determine who took responsible action, who is responsible. Systems and institutions in which it is impossible to find out who took what action are inherently incapable of ethical analysis or ethical action."

This definition of accountability concentrates on the social side of responsibility which will be discussed later on under the heading "institutions." However, there is also an individual side to it. The task of determining who is responsible for what will in large part have to be shouldered by collective institutions, but that does not mean that there is nothing left for the individual to do. In order for these institutions to work, the individuals have to make sure they work, and for that they have to create the necessary conditions. In the first place that means that they have to develop the ability and the knowledge to be able to constitute institutions and to function within them. This is the least that individuals can be required to do in the context of accountability. Creation of individual accountability as a result of the reflective application of responsibility can in turn be seen as a moral responsibility. "A person has a moral responsibility to understand the station he or she occupies in society at large and in more restricted groups" (French, 1992, p. 78).

Apart from the individual and collective requirements of accountability, an important aspect is the epistemological one, which relates to knowledge as a condition of responsibility. Lack of knowledge is one of the most frequently used excuses, and a theory of responsibility that takes its consequences seriously has to address the problem. In some cases lack of knowledge is irrevocably part of the game, such as in the case of future developments. We will never know what the future holds in stock. This is no excuse, however, for not trying to determine scenarios or probabilities and for not making use of the facilities that are there. Accountability here means that all the tools for forecasting are used in order to allow calculable decisions which will then allow an accurate ascription of responsibility.

Another limit of knowledge and of responsibility are side effects. We have seen the epistemological problem that there is by definition an infinity of incalculable effects that result from every action. It is impossible to consider all of them for responsibility purposes. From the point of view of accountability, this fact has to be acknowledged, but again some of the difficulties can be overcome. The first one is the determination of results for which responsibility is ascribed. Which are the main effects of an action and which are the side effects? This question can be answered by returning to the original intention. Let us take a look at a technological example, at the generation of nuclear energy. It can be said that the main and intended effect of nuclear power plants is the production of energy while the production of nuclear waste is a side effect. Similar observations can be made with regard to computer technology. Computers are mostly bought because they will facilitate some kind of task and it may be easier to do them with a computer. The same is true for the networking of society. These intended main effects do not tell us anything about the side effects. As Weizenbaum (1995, p. 549) points out:

> "...the direct societal effects of any pervasive new technology are as nothing compared to its much more subtle and ultimately much more important side effects. In that sense, the societal impact of the computer has not yet been felt."

Accountability in this context means that the distribution of main and side effects must be questioned, and that responsibility ascriptions are facilitated not only for the intended result but also for non-intentional results, at least for those that were foreseeable.

The determination of which effect is intended and which is a side effect is also at the heart of a discussion that reflective responsibility has to take into account, the discussion of external effects. External effects can be defined as those results of an action that affect others in an unforeseen way (Priddat, 1994,

p. 38; Küng, 1997, p. 317; Galtung, 1998, p. 240), which would correspond to the side effects. The interesting thing about external effects is that they are an increasingly recognised field of economic sciences. Unlike side effects, external effects are accepted as an attributable result of actions. They therefore require the development of attribution instruments which is exactly what the idea of accountability in reflective responsibility demands. The economic dealing with external effects tries to integrate effects that used to be neglected into economic thinking. The natural environment is certainly the most important example of this. For a long time environmental resources were not factored into economic decisions. Air and water, for example, were seen as resources for which the laws of scarcity did not apply. This led to the pollution of air and water, and consequently to the identification of environmental protection as something that the economic system had to take into account. The idea is now to internalise external effects, which in economic terms means to impute a price to them (Hausman & McPherson, 1996, p. 10). The next question would have to be how to do that, and there are presumably no simple answers to this. However, the internalisation of external effects is one approach to the production of accountability as the process of facilitating responsibility ascription.

External effects and accountability problems exist not only in the environment but also in technology and especially in IT. For Weckert and Adeney (1997, p. 98), the reason that accountability is important with regard to IT is that it leads to more care, which is important because of our increasing reliance on it. De George (1998, p. 50) sees accountability as the only way "to provide a break on computers outpacing human beings and on humans blindly relying on computers to do what humans want." Rotenburg (1995, p. 136), then president of Computer Professionals for Social Responsibility, emphasises "individual accountability as the cornerstone of computer ethics." But while there seems to be a general consensus that accountability is necessary and useful in the field of (business) computing, it is also difficult to realise. After doing an analysis of the accountability of computer decision systems designers for outcomes resulting from use of their systems, Johnson and Mulvey (1995, p. 64) concluded that it depends on norms of behaviour in a field where norms are poorly articulated, if at all. Nissenbaum, having done a comprehensive study of accountability in computing, concludes that there are some systematic barriers that are specific to the field. The four that she discusses in detail are:

"1) The problem of 'many hands'—because computer systems are created predominantly in organizational settings, 2) bugs— because bugs not only cause problems but commonly are con-

ceived of as a fact of programming life, 3) the computer as scapegoat—because it can be convenient to blame a computer for harms or injuries, and 4) ownership without liability—because in the clamor to assert rights of ownership over software, the responsibilities of ownership are neglected" (Nissenbaum, 1995, p. 528f)

All of these problems have already been discussed in one form or another under the different conditions and problems of responsibility. A theory of reflective responsibility will have to address all of them, because as long as they impede the accountability of actions and thus the process of ascription, responsibility will be without result and, from the reflective viewpoint, useless.

Institutions

One conclusion that can be drawn from what was said about reflective responsibility so far is that it will certainly have to depend on the support of institutions of one sort or another. This follows from the fact that it must be realisable as well as from the idea of accountability. The discussion of the limits of responsibility has shown that the most important obstacle to the success of the term is that those entities that play the role of subjects in many cases no longer fulfil the requirements that subjects are generally believed to need. Especially the individual agent no longer has the necessary power, knowledge, and other capacities to assume responsibility. From this, one can either conclude that responsibility has become a useless term or one can try to change the circumstances in such a way that it becomes realisable again, which is the idea behind the reflective use of responsibility. In order to achieve this goal, responsibility ascriptions will need to enlist the help of institutions.

If we want to move the burden of rendering responsibility realisable to institutions, the first step will be to define them. For Ricoeur (1991a, p. 242), institutions are the forms of social existence which govern the relationships between human beings in a normative way. As examples he notes the legal systems but also, in a wider sense of the word, politics represents institutions. For the purpose of facilitating responsibility, institutions can be understood in a wide sense such as we find it in institutional economics. For our application of responsibility in business information technology, this holds the added advantage that it refers to the economic side of the problem. From the point of view of institutional economics, institutions are formal or informal rules of the game of societies which govern and limit people's actions (Wieland, 2001a, p. 25). Examples would be codified law or uncodified morality. Wieland (1999, p.

117) emphasises that modern societies are institutional societies as opposed to personal ones. Today's societies are governed by institutions rather than individuals. Again this links in nicely with the problem of responsibility because responsibility is a characteristic feature of modern societies and an answer to the problems that modernity produces. While responsibility requires institutions to be manageable, it seems on the other hand that institutions are sometimes instantiations of responsibility or at least an expression of the wish for responsibility.

This idea is confirmed by Priddat's (1994, p. 167) definition of institutions as collective arrangements of mutual stabilisation of expectations. This mutual stabilisation can be interpreted in terms of responsibility as the mutual duty to answer to one another, which is the etymological root of responsibility. Priddat points out that institutions require a certain amount of consensus as well as trust in their validity in order for them to remain stable over time. Institutions thus have the function of a moral order that they discharge by synchronising the expectancies of their members.

If these characteristics of institutions were indeed valid and viable, then reflective responsibility could use them in order to facilitate individual, collective, or other responsibility ascriptions. This is Grunwald's (1996, p. 200) conclusion when he demands the rational establishment of institutions[18] and it is also the central idea of this chapter.

The idea of institutions as an expression of the willingness to realise responsible responsibility can become clearer when one looks at what they are supposed to achieve. Institutions generally have the purpose of disburdening humans, to free them from having to orient themselves over and over again. This disburdening should facilitate the people's becoming socially active (Lenk, 1998, p. 23). How can people be disburdened? To answer this we should recall what the problems are that impede responsibility ascriptions. The first problem is that of knowledge or the lack of it which is caused by complexity. If the complexity of a situation is greater than what the subject can manage, then responsibility is jeopardised. Institutions therefore have to ensure that complexity is reduced (Spaemann, 1975, p. 331f). One way of doing this is to define intentional and side effects, so that the subject can concentrate on the former. As we have seen, the number of potential side effects is infinite. Determining which ones are the ones that responsibility is ascribed for and which ones are not is a necessary precondition for a successful discharge. This means that the subject becomes free to ignore the side effects, but it also implies that a new responsibility is created, namely the responsibility for what was formerly the side effects. Arguably, the institutions themselves will have to assume this responsibility because there will not be anybody else to do so. A brief example should make this point clear. The responsibilities of a computer programmer tend to be limited to questions of correct performance of her work. This means that there are in fact institutions in place that shield her from having to worry about all other results of her activity. These institutions are our legal system as well as public perception, which allow the programmer to do what she does. This is necessary because it allows her to concentrate on the small area of her expertise.

On the other hand there are countless side effects of computers that now go without anybody's taking responsibility for them. The entire area of social or psychosocial effects that the programmer's work may entail is not taken care of. Following this theory of institutions, the result would be that the institutions themselves would have to assume the responsibility. This is of course no easy task. How could the law or public opinion assume responsibility for things it may not even know about? The answer to this can probably be found in other institutions. Institutions could create institutions with the explicit purpose of facilitating responsibility that would otherwise be forgotten. The legal system, for example, could define institutions—this means laws—that would ensure that foreseeable side effects are taken care of. So, while it might disburden the individual programmers from the task of thinking about the social impacts of her work, it might burden the company or the industry with assuming this exact responsibility. This of course leads back to some of the problems discussed earlier in the context of collective responsibility. Can institutions be responsible? And if so, how? While this is no easy question to answer, the idea of institutions allows one approach that might calm critics by defining collective responsibility in terms of individual responsibility. Institutions could for example determine which individual or individuals are going to suffer the sanctions in case of a collective mistake.

It becomes clear that we have to distinguish between two fundamentally different sorts of institutional responsibility. On the one hand institutions facilitate responsibility by defining it in such a clear and precise way that the individual regains his ability to assume it. On the other hand institutions must in this process assume responsibility themselves as collective agents. These two types of institutional responsibility are closely linked. Institutions can only facilitate individual responsibility by assuming their own collective responsibility. Yet, collective institutional responsibility will in most cases only lead to tangible results if it is retranslated into individual responsibility. Institutions must shape the individual's reality in such a way that he or she feels capable of living up to the normative standards that define responsibility. As we have seen this includes the definition of intended versus side effects and thus the definition of the object. It includes the definition of acceptable conditions in terms of knowledge, complexity, causality, freedom, etc. Responsibility is a social construct, and institutions play an important role in constructing this social reality. They act as mediators between different realities, norms, and perceptions with the aim of allowing responsibility ascriptions to come to fruition. To borrow an expression from Preuss (1999, p. 408), there are boundaries beyond which individual ethics have to be reinforced with institutional ethics. Institutions make sure that the individual's capacities for moral action are not overstretched as they would be if they had to continually keep in mind the well-being of society.

Institutions are thus part of reflective responsibility because they give an answer to the question of how responsibility can be realised. They do this by disburdening the individual and by helping to construct the social realities that constitute responsibility. They also play a role in establishing accountability. Institutions can be used as a means for the end of imputation. This is part of the social construct, but it is a part that deserves special attention. One of the reasons why responsibility in modern technological contexts often seems misplaced is that there seems to be no way to establish a relationship between subject and object, that there is no plausible imputation possible between the two. Institutions can and must be created that overcome this problem if responsibility is to be viable. An example might be the software faults or "bugs" that are a normal part of computer life and that every computer user knows better than they would like. The reasons why there is no bug-free software are manifold, but it seems that bugs are intrinsic to software as we know it. These bugs can have high moral relevance. A crashing business system or the failure of a safety critical device can have serious consequences. But who is responsible? According to a classical theory of responsibility, one would have to establish a causal relationship to an individual and then impute blame and punishment to this person. However, this is usually impossible due to the complexity of the software and the different tasks in developing it which are held by different persons. Responsibility ascriptions thus do not take place; this leads to a situation where a normative problem is not addressed. In this situation institutions allowing the creation of imputation would be helpful and they are therefore what reflective responsibility would require. An example for an institution that might alleviate the situation is the idea of strict liability as we know it from the American legal system. It allows the imputation of responsibility in complex cases by disregarding some of the classical conditions such as clear causality and takes the pragmatic standpoint that effectiveness in these cases is more important than theoretical stringency.

The development of institutions of imputation is necessary to let individuals know what they should or should not do, and it is necessary to facilitate responsibility ascriptions (Lübbe, 1998, p. 153). It is also necessary to change seemingly natural processes to controlled processes, or, to return to the beginning of the book, to change uncertainty to risk, for which responsibility can be taken.

Good institutions, to summarise this section, are characterised by the fact that they enable responsibility (Hastedt, 1994, p. 262). Some authors go so far as to say that responsible action is only possible in an institutional context (Priddat, 1994, p. 244). One of the reasons for this is that responsibility depends on some continuity. The subject must realise that it is responsible and that this is a state of a certain temporal duration (cf. French, 1992, p. 19). This can again be explained by the moral nature of responsibility, by the fact that it takes others' moral rights into account, that it is a form of answering to the other. As long as the subject is in the position where it has to answer, responsibility remains in place. It can therefore be interpreted as a sort of self-institutionalisation of the moral intention (Priddat, 1994, p. 244).

Another area where institutions are of crucial importance for responsibility ascriptions is the final result—the sanction or the punishment. The ascription of sanctions and the subsequent enforcement is also something that in most cases must be institutionalised in order to be effective (Lübbe, 1990, p. 206). This is obviously true for legal responsibility where the courts of law, the police, and the penitentiary system work together. It is also true for other, "softer" forms of responsibility. Moral responsibility also needs institutions that can enforce sanctions such as the revocation of reputation, even if these institutions are less clear-cut than their legal counterparts.

Even though institutions play a central role in reflective responsibility, they are no panacea and they produce some problems of their own. Institutional responsibility in the sense of collective responsibility can produce all of the problems discussed earlier. As soon as individuals feel they are not held responsible individually but collectively, there often develops the phenomenon of the "risky shift," the fact that groups are willing to take higher risks than individuals (Böhret, 1987, p. 9). Another problem is that responsibility can become a routine organisational matter, and the actual moral duty to answer is neglected. An important problem is the replacement of the individual. Institutional responsibility can be used as an excuse by individuals for not living up to their responsibility or even as a reason for the general abolition of individual responsibility. Again, this is a problem that was already discussed in the chapter about collective responsibility. The solution is to realise that collective, institutional, and individual responsibility are not to be interpreted as contradicting alternatives but as mutually supportive. Responsibility must be facilitated by institutions and in institutions (Hastedt, 1994, p. 262). One should also realise that the apparent alternative between individual and institutional responsibility is a false one because the two sorts of responsibility are categorically different. Institutional responsibility refers to the possibilities of individual action whereas individual responsibility refers to the actions themselves (Hubig, 1994, p. 157).

There is another categorical problem with institutional responsibility. If we see institutions as a necessary condition of individual responsibility, then the next question is: Who is responsible for the institutions? Who maintains them and before all, who creates them? In some cases individuals can probably be credited with erecting an institution, but in most cases the task would be to great for any single human being. This brings us back to the start: who is responsible for institutions is a question that apparently can only be answered by institutions. That means a society would need something like institutions of a second order which in turn would be responsible for the creation of institutions. In fact, in democratic societies the elected representatives and parliaments can be interpreted as just such second-order institutions charged with building institutions. Philosophical completeness would now demand to know who is responsible for the second-order institutions; a possible answer might be: third-order institutions. This obviously leads to an infinite regress, which is why we will leave it here, with the idea of political systems as institutions of a second order. This idea also has some plausibility because democratic governments link the institutional responsibility back to the constituents and thus back to individual responsibility. The entire topic is presumably more complicated than this, but for our context of responsibility and IS, it can be seen as sufficient because IS usually operates within given states and institutions.

The most important institution guaranteeing responsibility is without a doubt the legal system. It is not only the origin of the word responsibility, it is also the best example of how responsibility can be realised with the help of institutions. The law also shows some of the difficulties of responsibility in and through institutions. There is for example the problem of the moral foundation of the normative background of responsibility. It was said earlier that all sorts of responsibility are inherently moral. In the case of legal institutions, this leads to the question of where morality enters the game. In order to answer this question, one would have to give an exhaustive discussion of ethics and law which will not be possible here, but it should suffice to state that the law must have some moral foundation in order to be legitimate. Immoral law would be illegitimate and would be hard to enforce. Whether ethics stands over the law and directs it, or whether it is a procedure that somehow migrates into the law (Habermas, 1998b, p. 568), it is an institution that makes attributions feasible. The law is also a good example for institutions because it contains all of the other aspects of institutions mentioned before. It defines who or what can be a subject, who or what the object might be, and which sorts of objects are not part of the ascription because they could not be considered. The legal institutions state clearly how the process of ascription has to take place, who decides about the consequences, and how they can be enforced. This clarity of the legal system is presumably the reason why the emphasis in normative questions moves from ethics to the law.

Another interesting theory concerning the normative use of institutions which can be interpreted in terms of responsibility is a theory that sees business ethics located in the economic framework. This theory that in Germany is closely linked to the name Karl Homann states that in the economic system, individuals have to act according to the rules of the system. The single person may be morally motivated, but this motivation will not come to fruition if it contravenes against the imperatives that govern the economy. The idea is that if the individual has to adhere to economic rules, that is if she has to act on her preferences under given constraints, then the institutional setting must be modified in such a way that the preferences reflect what is morally desirable. Homann calls this an incentive ethics (*Anreizethik*) (Homann, 1997, p. 16). Homann's approach to business ethics therefore asks whether conflicts can be retraced to institutional causes (Homann & Blome-Drees, 1992, p. 188). If this is so, then the change of the institutions is a much more promising approach to solving the conflicts than any sort of moralising might be. Moral norms in Homann's theory can only be effective if they are beneficial to individuals. "Homann thus propagates an economic theory of morality, which studies how proposed moral norms can be made beneficial and immoral behaviour disadvantageous" (Preuss, 1999, p. 410). As Pies (2001, p. 196) puts it, the theoretical alternative is to either implement ethics against or through economic incentives. This idea that ethics must be realised by institutions refers mostly to those situations where classical morality does not seem to work any more. These are typically the situations where big and anonymous groups are concerned. In these cases where individuals do not know each other, moral rules may be unknown, and even if they are known, the temptation of free riding is great. The institutional ethics approach would then try to change the environment in such a way that individual and collective utility coincide (cf. Scheuch, 1990, p. 92; Kliemt, 1990, p. 74).

Interestingly, this approach can lead to the elimination of ethics out of the ethical theory. If one follows the idea that institutions can and must be modelled in order to allow the individual's interests to coincide with the greater good, then the question becomes a rather technical one. Do the institutions live up to their promises and do they facilitate the desired behaviour? Asking these questions means that one interprets institutions as mechanisms that regulate actions. Such mechanisms can best be judged in terms of means of ends (Grunwald, 1996, p. 200), in terms of economic rationality. The question of what this greater good is, this morality that they are supposed to protect or to facilitate, is not necessarily a part of such a theory. The proponents of this approach therefore have to rely on other theories to provide them with the ethical content that they then try to implement. Wieland (1999) simply proposes that society has a reservoir or morality that can be used for this purpose. Whether this is true is doubtful, and the main criticism of the idea of institutionalising ethics in social systems is therefore that it is not an ethical theory at all but rather an economic theory. For our purposes, namely the idea of reflective responsibility, this does not appear to be too serious a problem because, as was stated earlier, reflective responsibility has to reflect on its normative foundations in the context of the theoretical clarity of the notion. For theoretical purposes we can therefore suppose that the ethical background is clarified or at least that the lack of clarity is clear.

Where does this leave us in terms of responsibility and IS? A first answer to this question is that a reflective use of responsibility in IS must take institutions into account. If responsibility is to play a role in this area at all, it must be supported and facilitated by institutions. Many of the current approaches to computer or information ethics rely heavily on individual responsibility. Marc Rotenberg, president of the influential Computer Professionals for Social Responsibility, for example emphasises "individual accountability as the cornerstone of computer ethics" (Rotenberg, 1995, p. 136). In light of what was said so far, this sort of approach must be seriously reconsidered. Even if individual responsibility remains the centrepiece of the normative setting, it must be recognised that first of all the necessary institutions, organisations, or procedures must be created that will facilitate this responsibility. In this sense the use of information technology within or outside of the realm of business is only one example of the fact that modern technology raises moral problems and that it is generally realised that institutions must play a central role if we are to address these problems successfully (cf. Hubig, 1995, p. 122; Schmidt, 1992, p. 170; Ropohl, 1987, p. 170; Hastedt, 1994, p. 262).

A difficult question with no general answer is what these institutions should look like. If they have the purpose of reducing complexity for the individual in such a way that the individual is able to grasp the situation and to assume responsibility, then the form of the institution depends very much on the situation as well as on the individual in question. One sort of institutional arrangement that is frequently discussed in relation to the use of computers and IT is that of professional codes of conduct. These can indeed be interpreted as ways of institutionalising individual responsibility (cf. Eckard & Löffler, 1991, p. 286; De George, 1999, p. 205). In this sense they would be an expression of reflective responsibility. On the other hand codes of ethics or codes of conduct produce their own problems and dynamics.

As a last aspect of reflective responsibility before we come to the more specific problems of IS, the process of imputation deserves a closer look. Institutions are meant to allow imputation of responsibility and therefore it makes sense to ask how this can be done in a fashion that would maximise its utility.

Imputation

The last general consequence resulting from the reflective use of responsibility that we will discuss here concerns the process of imputation or ascription itself. We have seen that responsibility is defined as the process of imputation, and it is of interest whether and in what way the three characteristics of openness, affinity to action, and consequentialism affect the nature of the process. The starting point for reflective responsibility must be to ask how the ascription can be realised in a way that it facilitates the three characteristics. How can one ascribe responsibility in such a way that it is open, that it leads to action, and that the consequences of the actions as well as the ascription itself are taken into account?

Given that there is a virtual infinity of ways of ascribing and this virtual infinity can be applied to the actual infinity of cases where responsibility can play a role, an easy answer to the question is not to be expected. However, there are two prominent theories of business ethics that seem to point in the direction that responsibility has to take if it wants to be open, active, and consequentialist. These two are the discourse ethics and stakeholder approaches. The decisive feature that the two share and that will lead to a fulfilment of the requirements of reflective ascription is that they both try to maximise the participation in the imputation process.

The discursive approach is based on discourse ethics as developed by Apel and Habermas (cf. Apel, 1980, 1988; Habermas, 1983, 1991). Discourse ethics is based on the idea that within every speech act, there lie several validity claims without which the speech act would be meaningless. Whatever a speaker says, she claims truth, (normative) correctness, and veracity or authenticity. This does not mean that these claims are fulfilled, only that we have to assume them if we are to communicate meaningfully. These validity claims can be doubted, in which case they have to be defended in a rational discussion in front of all of the affected people, in a discourse. The discourse is a counterfactual construct where the discourse community can theoretically discuss every argument in a power-free environment until the reasoning leads to a consensus. Even though this sort of discourse will never happen, it is the regulative idea that guides our real-life discourses. Discourse ethics understands itself explicitly as an expression of an ethics of reason in the succession of Kant. At the same time it can be interpreted as an expression of a responsibility viewpoint, due to the fact that the answer, the response is the central idea of discourses.

This concept can be used fruitfully for all sorts of different applications of responsibility. Despite the fact that it is rather abstract and refers to a counterfactual ideal situation, it can be interpreted to give us clear rules of action. For Ulrich (1997, p. 90), responsibility in the economic system can be demonstrated using discourse ethics when people try to live up to the conditions of discourses. To act responsibly the subject must face up to the criticism and claims of all of the affected persons, and it must take these positions into account when acting. That means that the view of responsibility as a lonely decision in front of one's own conscience is not acceptable.

It is a difficult question whether discourse ethics is applicable at all. Both Apel and Habermas emphasise the importance of real discourses, well knowing that these will never fulfil the legitimising conditions of the ideal discourse. The result of real discourses is thus always fallible, and it is hard to determine under what circumstances it is binding and under which ones it requires a new discourse. Another problem would be that it is often impossible to lead real discourses because of time constraints or because the affected parties are not available. Since real discourses are the instantiation of discourse ethics, it can be argued that the weaknesses of real discourses endanger the moral foundation of the entire theory. Fortunately for our purposes of reflective responsibility, these objections are not of the highest importance. We can stick with the idea that the attempt to realise discourses is an expression of responsibility. This attempt may be fallible, like the entire construct of responsibility, but as we have seen before, reflective responsibility is a modest concept. Its inherent consequentialism demands that the consequences of ascriptions be good, but they do not have to be perfect. In this sense the use of discourses as a tool is possible in responsibility settings, as long as it can be shown that it is better to have them than not to have them. And this seems to be a rather simple task.

There are a few advantages to discourses from the point of view of responsibility that do not depend on the theoretical background. First of all discourses are necessary to define the normative basis. What is the morality, what are the rules that the community in question believes in? Without an answer to this, responsibility makes no sense. At the same time discourses never exclusively concentrate on normative questions, but they always consider questions of facts and truth as well. This means that the question of who or what can be a subject or an object can be discussed at the same time. Discourses can even be interpreted as the instance of ascription, because they determine the accusation as well as a potential punishment. Another advantage of discourses is that they maximise the knowledge base. Asking all of the parties in question is a guarantee for finding out the most about potential and probable consequences of an action or decision. In this sense, discourses are eminently consequentialist. They also promise to maximise awareness of side effects, because as far as these are foreseeable, they will be raised by the interested parties (Habermas, 1983, p. 116). This knowledge allows the determination of those norms, practices, or projects that can be seen as legitimate (Böhler, 1994, p. 269). All of these facts taken together have a great impact on another aspect of reflective responsibility, on the realisability. Given that there is a maximum of knowledge about results, a shared definition of norms and of potential subjects and objects, the probability of an ascription being viable is maximised. All of these points clearly show that holding discourses in the sense of discourse ethics is a sensible procedure in the context of reflective responsibility. The expected results will generally outweigh the costs of such discourses. Despite the theoretical problems of discourse ethics, the more modest idea of reflective responsibility—which does not aim for theoretical perfection, just for practical improvements—will generally be able to profit from discourses.

How would we have to imagine such a discourse? Let us look at an example from IS. Let's say that a manager is thinking about the acquisition of a new human resources information system. The manager wants to act responsibly, but at first sight is hard pressed to say what that means. Following the idea of discourse ethics, there would have to be a discourse in which the validity claims could be checked. Implied validity claims of such an information system might be that it can handle the required tasks better than the system in place right now, that it can save money, that it is more efficient, that it has improved functionality, etc. Apart from these claims of truth, there are normative claims. These might be that the use of the system is good for employees in the HR department because it makes their lives easier. It can be helpful to other employees by providing better information or reacting more quickly. Another normative claim might be that the use of the system does not infringe on anybody's rights. The veracity claim could be the manager's assurance that she really wants to implement these improvements. In order to get a discourse started, the manager would have to identify all of the affected parties. Discourse ethics is different from ideal discourses in that the manager can exert a big influence on the outcome by choosing the representatives in the discourse, but the discourse will have to be started by someone and the initiator of the change is probably a good starting point.

The next problem would be the identification of the participants of the discourse. If the system is to be introduced into a big multinational corporation, then chances are that thousands of employees might be affected. It will be impossible to have all of them participate. Therefore, representatives must be chosen. This is again a step away from the ideal discourse. Apart from the employees, there will be others who have an interest in the process. Those might include management of the company, shareholders, the system supplier, relatives of the employees, trade unions, and special interest groups from all sorts of backgrounds. It is plain to see that realising a discourse that would even try to emulate ideal discourses is hard work and potentially a very costly endeavour. The manager and her superiors might therefore ask: Why bother?

There are different answers to this, but one can try to group them again around the validity claims. The claims of truth are those that have to do with knowledge, risks, and side effects. Even though the initiating manager must have some idea of the objective reality, she runs the risk of having overlooked relevant facts, and that risk is minimised by holding the discourse. It might turn out that the planned system has serious flaws, that it is unable to perform certain relevant tasks, or that there are better comparable systems. The normative claims might also be challenged by pointing out that the new system allows for new sorts of breaches of privacy or that it favours business practices that are not welcome in all of the states where the company operates. Finally the veracity of the manager might be challenged, it might be pointed out that she had a consulting relationship with the supplier or that her motives are clouded by well-known prejudices.

The result of the practical discourse is that the validity claims that emerge from it will look different from the ones it started out with. Given that the discourse itself is by definition flawed, these results can again not claim infallibility. However, they do have the advantage over a mere management decision that, because they are derived using more resources, they are more viable than the starting point. From the point of view of management, this means that the introduction of the new system will have a higher probability of being successful. At the same time the new system will have a higher level of acceptability for all of the parties that participated in the discourse. These results can on the one hand be seen from an economic point of view. Discourses cost resources, but at the other hand they produce a higher probability of a positive outcome. A purely monetary cost-benefit analysis will be hard because many of the factors are intangible. Therefore holding such a discourse is a question of management's judgment. The discourse can also be seen from a moral point of view. It gives an answer to the manger's initial question: If I want to act responsibly, what should I do? The results of the discourse should tell her that and thus allow her to take the course of action with the highest probability of being ethically acceptable.

The discussion of the example of a discourse may have reminded the reader of a different approach to ethical problems that in practice looks very similar, the stakeholder approach. The stakeholder approach first started in 1963 in the Stanford Research Institute and argued that executives needed to understand the needs and concerns of the stakeholder groups in order to fulfil the organisation's objectives (Kujala, 2001, p. 236). It is interesting to note that the original idea was not an explicitly normative one, but was dictated by business interests. In the meantime, however, the concept of stakeholders has been taken up by business ethicists and is used to formulate an ethical viewpoint. Stakeholder management in practice is very similar to the applied discourses just discussed. It requires, as its key attribute:

"...simultaneous attention to the legitimate interests of all appropriate stakeholders, both in the establishment of organizational structures and general policies and in case-by-case decision making" (Donaldson & Preston, 1995, p. 67).

The stakeholder theory is today mostly used as a counterargument to the shareholder value theory of businesses (von Weizsäcker, 1999, p. 41f; Hank, 2000, p. 272). There are fundamental normative and descriptive reasons why the shareholder theory does not seem adequate. The stakeholder view allows the description of a firm as a multi-purpose organisation and not as the institutionalised interest of the shareholders (cf. Koslowski, 2000). A good account of stakeholder thinking is given by Donaldson and Preston (1995). For them the theory has three aspects that are nested within each other. First of all the theory is descriptive and gives a better account of organisations than a one-dimensional theory could. Secondly the theory can be used instrumentally—it helps make predictions and obtain desired results. At the core, however, the theory is normative. Recognising the legitimate claims of stakeholders is what it essentially is all about.

This stakeholder view can be seen as an expression of reflective responsibility because it recognises some of the same fundamental principles. It looks at the questions of reality, what is realisable, but at the same time it has a moral foundation. The underlying assumption of answerability, the equality of all humans is also the implicit reason for the recognition of the legitimacy of stakeholders. In this sense the stakeholder approach can be seen as an expression of reflective responsibility. Realising the stakeholder approach therefore runs into the same problem we have seen in the case of the other expression of responsibility, of applied discourses.

The fundamental difficulties that the stakeholder approach raises are the justification of the theory and the identification of the stakeholders. The answers to the first question can either be the instrumental or the intrinsic value of the approach. From an instrumental point of view, the stakeholder theory can be seen as advantageous because it allows a better description, prediction, and thus control of the company. The intrinsic strength is that it is built upon the perception of humans as free and equal, and therefore is an expression of the humanistic ethical tradition of enlightenment. For our purposes this question is less relevant because using the stakeholder approach as a means for reflective responsibility means that it is morally charged anyway and the two sorts of answers will both apply.

More difficult to answer is the question: Who do we accept as stakeholders and on what grounds? This question corresponds to the problem in discourse ethics concerning the participants in the discourse. The stakeholder literature offers several answers to the problem. One can distinguish between wider and narrower approaches to the question. Donaldson and Preston (1995, p. 85) for example identify stakeholders "through the actual or potential harms and benefits that they experience or anticipate experiencing as a result of the firm's actions or inactions." Another wide definition would be that of "any group or individual that can affect or is affected by the achievement of the firm's objectives" (Kujala, 2001, p. 236). Some authors have tried to bring a little more order in these potentially infinite groups. We find the distinction between primary and secondary stakeholders, based on the view of the firm as a nexus of contracts (Hendry, 2001, p. 225). Here the primary stakeholders are those who have a formal contractual relationship with the company; the secondary ones comprise everybody else who might be affected by the company (Gibson, 2000, p. 245).

All of these attempts to define stakeholders run into problems. A very wide view that sees everybody who can affect the company as a stakeholder would have to include terrorists and extortionists. A narrower view that would be helpful to management because it might be easier to realise runs the risk of losing its ethical foundation because it may exclude relevant groups. One could therefore follow Ulrich (1998, p. 13) when he says that a stakeholder is someone who has legitimate claims towards the firm, but that it is impossible to deduce an *a priori* list of those claims.

For our purposes it is less important to determine who stakeholders are in general than to recognise the close connection of the stakeholder approach to the idea of reflective responsibility. The stakeholder theory is close to responsibility because it is open, it relies on communication, it promises relevant action, and it maximises the chances of realisability by including everybody affected by a decision beforehand, thus maximising the factual as well as the normative knowledge necessary to facilitate the attribution of answerability.

This discussion of some ideas concerning the realisation of responsibility ascriptions finishes the theoretical observations of reflective responsibility. In the next chapter we will apply these ideas to the field of business computing and discuss some practical problems and how they can be viewed from the perspective or reflective responsibility.

Chapter VI

Reflective Responsibility and the Management of Information Systems

Before we start analysing the details of how reflective responsibility impacts on the use of information technology, we should briefly recapitulate what the purpose of the entire enterprise was and where we stand right now. Responsibility has been identified as a central term that is used in the public discussions about normative problems. It has been demonstrated that the core of responsibility is a social process of ascription. An overview of the literature on responsibility, however, has shown that the term is highly complex, consists of a large number of conditions, dimensions, and aspects, which in many cases are contradictory. In order to render the term useful, we have tried to identify common features that can be found in most if not all responsibility ascriptions and that help give meaning to its use. The three shared characteristics that were found are openness, affinity to action, and consequentialism. In a subsequent step it was asked what would happen if responsibility ascriptions were analysed with regard to these three characteristics. The result was a notion of responsibility that was called "reflective responsibility," which was then further investigated with the aim of determining what the consequences of this reflective use of the term was. It was shown that reflective responsibility has theoretical and practical consequences that relate back to some of the ethical theories on which responsibility ascriptions might be based. Reflective responsibility requires the classical virtue of prudence as well as a modern reliance on institutional settings. It can be instantiated by following the ideas of other theories of practical philosophy such as discourse ethics or the stakeholder approach.

Now that we finally have the solid foundation of a theory of responsibility, it will be possible to spell out the impact of responsibility on business information technology. Given everything that was said so far, it is obvious that the potential number of starting points for this discussion is almost infinite. Since this text aims at a readership with a business background as well as philosophical readers, it makes sense to concentrate on a business viewpoint. The salient position that seems predestined for the discussion is that of the manager. Analysing questions of (reflective) responsibility from the point of view of management has several advantages. Firstly, managers are commonly identified or defined as the persons responsible for and in an organisation. They tend to think of themselves as responsible as well and therefore will presumably agree to the approach. Secondly, even though responsibility is never a solipsistic process, managers will in many cases be the best placed to identify potential normative problems and to initiate responsibly ascriptions. Thirdly, they also possess the necessary means to start the process, to identify stakeholders and begin a discourse, and they fourthly have the institutional backing to sanction or reward the subjects.

This, of course, also contains the danger that due to their superiority in power, they might misuse responsibility or misdirect it in a direction favourable to their own ends. This is in itself then a problem of responsibility that will have to be addressed later on. Another problem of the concentration on the managerial viewpoint of responsibility is that many of the relevant issues are not within the power of individual managers. Again, however, for managerial responsibility this is a problem of its own which can be addressed in the responsibility framework. Given the alternative approaches (general responsibility, responsibility of the company, governmental responsibility,...) the emphasis on managerial responsibility is still the best choice because managerial responsibility is characterised by its manifest results. In terms of reflective responsibility, this is a decisive criterion and the choice can thus be justified.

Having come so far, the next question is: Who are the managers whose position is to be analysed? The short answer is that the managers in question are those people who have it in their power to influence the use of IT in business. This is basically everybody from the CEO or CIO downwards to the operational manager or the IT specialist. This is again a rather large group, but since all of these managers or decision makers can influence moral circumstances and they all can be responsible, it seems reasonable to regard them all. The problem with this view is that the responsibility aspects over such a large and heterogeneous group will differ greatly according to scope, scale, and results of their decisions. It will therefore be necessary to concentrate on the fundamental problems that they all have to deal with.

The starting point for the different aspects discussed in this chapter will be the manager's question: "When dealing with information technology in my area of influence, how can I act in a responsible way?" There are two groups of issues that need to be looked at when addressing this question. The first one centres on the question of why the managers in question should want to act responsibly in the first place and what the advantages of our theory of reflective responsibility will be in this situation. Having answered this question, the next problem is: What are the consequences of the decision to act responsibly, and how can responsibility regarding IS be realised in a managerial environment?

There are many possible approaches to this question. Since this chapter is the "application" of the theory developed in the previous parts of the book, it seems appropriate to use examples to clarify the points in question. Again, there are different strategies to do this. One could choose several smaller examples or one larger example that could reflect the complexity of the issues at stake. Since the idea of reflective responsibility finds its justification at least partially in the problem of complexity, it seems to be more appropriate to use one lengthier example. The next question then is what example to choose. It should be one that has direct relevance to managerial practice, that poses difficulties in real life, and that can demonstrate the advantages of reflective responsibility. Again, there are several areas from which to choose such an example. Generally, most of the problems discussed in computer or information ethics could be chosen. Among them one can find the problems of power, access, intellectual property, etc. In this text we will concentrate on the problem of privacy/surveillance. The reason for this is that questions of privacy/surveillance play an increasing role in managerial everyday life, that they are deeply influenced by moral attitudes, that the legal view of them is often unclear, and that there are no recognised international standards of dealing with them.

This chapter will begin by describing the problem of privacy and employee surveillance. It will then proceed to a discussion why management might and should want to assume responsibility for it. The weaknesses of traditional responsibility approaches are briefly described before the advantages and possible ways of realisation of reflective responsibility are illustrated. After this, different aspects of reflective responsibility in this context are given and the discussion is broadened to other problems. In a final step, the focus is shifted from the manager, in order to see what other consequences reflective responsibility might entail with regards to the use of information technology in a business context and what this means for the surrounding society.

AN EXAMPLE: THE PROBLEM OF PRIVACY AND EMPLOYEE SURVEILLANCE

In order to give a convincing account of the reflective responsibility approach to privacy, it is first of all necessary to describe the problems and why it is considered a matter for consideration in a normative context. Privacy is similar to other concepts discussed so far in that it seems quite clear when one thinks about it on a superficial level, but it becomes much more hazy when one tries to define it and understand why it seems worthy of protection (cf. Weckert & Adeney, 1997, p. 76). Historically, privacy is a matter of public interest that can be traced back to the ancient Greeks (cf. Rotenberg, 1998, p. 152). Even though the concept has been part of public discourse ever since and played a role in the U.S., for example, since the founding of the state, its modern formulation only arose toward the end of the 19th century (cf. Sipior & Ward, 1995, p. 50). The first legal definition was given in a seminal article by Warren and Brandeis in the *Harvard Law Review* of 1890. In the article, the authors try to deduce a legal basis for privacy protection, and they argue that it is part of a broader right to be "let alone." For them it is comparable with or an extension of such recognised rights as those not to be killed, assaulted, imprisoned, or harmed (Warren & Brandeis, 1890, p. 205). This definition of privacy as a right to be let alone, sometimes changed to "left alone," is still prevalent today (cf. Britz, 1999, p. 16; Velasquez, 1998, p. 449). While this definition has the advantage of being easily remembered, its disadvantage is that it is too broad and says little about the concrete content of the term. As Gavison (1995, p. 334) points out, the status of privacy is generally unclear, whether it is a situation, a right, a claim, a form of control, or a value. Also, it is not obvious whether it refers to information, to autonomy, to personal identity, or to physical access. More specific definitions therefore suggest that privacy exists when an individual can control social interaction, make autonomous decisions, and control the release and circulation of personal information (Culnan, 1993, p. 344). Another useful distinction is that between psychological and physical privacy— one referring to the inner life such as thoughts, plans, beliefs, feelings, etc., and the other to the exterior physical world (Velasquez, 1998, p. 450).

What is clear, however, is that the attempts to protect privacy result from a tendency not to respect it. There are many different incentives for infringing on other people's privacy, which traditionally seem to have been curiosity or even voyeurism (cf. Gumpert & Drucker, 2000, p. 180). While these motives tended to be either of a private or political nature, the character of the threats to privacy is changing. Increasingly, the incentives to breach other people's privacy are set by economic imperatives. Another reason for the increasing importance of the topic is technology, especially information technology, which facilitates breaches of privacy on a new scale. The combination of these reasons renders the issue relevant to managers, especially managers of information technology in commercial companies which warrants lengthy discussion here.

While IT poses some obvious threats to privacy that will be discussed shortly, it is interesting to note that technology has always played a role in the development of the modern concept of privacy. In fact, the possibility of having pictures taken against one's will was one of the reasons for Warren and Brandeis' development of the legal notion of privacy (Warren & Brandeis, 1890, p. 211). Information technology is generally recognised as having a great potential for breaching privacy, and therefore the concern with privacy has been part of computer ethics from the development of this discipline. There are many different ways in which IT can be used to produce information that the persons to whom it pertains might want to keep secret. The huge amount of data that is stored about everyone of us in databases, and the ease with which it can be extracted and compiled is one of the reasons (Mason, 1986, p. 7). At the same time more and more communication is transmitted by IT and can be automatically recorded and evaluated.

An image that captures this development quite well is that computers "grease" data (cf. Moor, 2000). The image of the greased data can help visualise how data and information, which in principle has always been around, all of a sudden acquire a new meaning. Like a machine that runs more smoothly when greased, the greased information helps find new applications for the collected information. And like grease in a machine, the information is hard to contain, hard to hold on to. Grease gets everywhere, especially if the machine runs hot, and if it gets somewhere where it is not supposed to go, it is hard to get rid of. These technical factors are one of the reasons why as long as 10 years ago many people considered the invasion of privacy "their greatest fear about the misuse of computer technology" (Straub & Collins, 1990, p. 150).

The new technological opportunities combine business interests to form a new dimension in the threats to privacy. Again, this development is not really new and was foreseen by Warren and Brandeis (1890, p. 195), who see "recent inventions and business methods" as the reason for their development of a right of privacy. However, the technological development not only facilitates new ways of collecting data, but also provides new ways of translating the data into business value. Data mining, direct marketing, automated customer checks, e-commerce, and others are examples for the business interest in data. The manifest business interests in computer-generated information and the resulting incentive to breach privacy have led to a change of paradigm with regards to the threats to privacy. While state and government used to be viewed as the classical threat to privacy, this perception has changed and one can increasingly find statements such as: "In developed countries, at least in peacetime, business is a greater menace to privacy than the government tends to be" (Himanen, 2001, p. 99; similar: Tavani, 2000, p. 74). This shift in the perception of threat is interesting from a social perspective, because in some ways it mirrors the political discussion between liberal individualists and communitarian collectivists about personal freedom versus social needs (cf. van den Hoven, 1999, p. 140). Furthermore it raises interesting questions about the place of business in a society and thus about the moral foundation of business (Johnson, 2001, p. 125). In order to understand how these ideas are to be judged and also to see the basis of managerial decisions with regards to privacy, it is helpful to take a look at the discourse concerning the justification of privacy. This will also lay the groundwork for the following discussion of responsibility regarding privacy.

As a general starting point, one can state that there are different paradigms used for the defence of privacy protection. These can be divided into absolute and relative positions. Proponents of the absolute approach view privacy as a non-negotiable right or obligation similar or equal to human rights such as the right to life (cf. Spinello, 1997, p. 5). The relative viewpoint sees privacy as one among many goods that is worth protecting but that has to be seen in the perspective of the other rights that also require protection. A similar differentiation is sometimes made between privacy as an intrinsic or instrumental right or value (cf. Tavani, 2000, p. 70; Moor, 2000, p. 203). Intrinsic values need no further justification, they are justified in themselves, whereas instrumental values are values only with regard to some other value that they protect or promote. Whichever view is taken, it is generally recognised that a right to privacy has limits. One can easily see that a society with an absolute right to privacy, understood as the right to control the information concerning oneself, would not function. Civic duties such as taxes, military service, and administration in general could not work in this sort of environment. In order to determine where exactly the limits of a right to privacy are, it is imperative that one understands its foundation. Here one can distinguish between an ethical defence of privacy and a legal one. Some authors see privacy as a moral hypernorm in the sense of Donaldson and Dunfee's (1999) integrated social contract theory (Milberg, Burke, Smith, & Kallman, 1995, p. 73), whereas others limit their arguments to legal and constitutional arguments (Shattuck, 1995, p. 306).

Among the answers to the question why privacy is important, one can again distinguish between two great groups: one sees privacy as important because of the effects on the individual, the other emphasises the social utility of the concept. The first group of answers tends to posit privacy as a precondition for personal development. It is viewed as necessary to become an independent individual. "Privacy, or personal freedom, is the basis for self-determination, which is the basis for self-identity as we understand it in American society" (Severson, 1997, p. 65). The protection of privacy can be seen as important for the development of abilities that enable the individual to function correctly within society, to develop its potential, to develop self-consciousness, etc. (cf. Rachels, 1995; Introna, 2000). At the same time a Kantian argument can be used that sees privacy protection as an expression of the recognition of a person's autonomy (Spinello, 1997, p. 5). This group of arguments that emphasises the importance of privacy for the individual gradually leads over to the utilitarian arguments that emphasise its importance for social groups (Elgesiem, 1996, p. 54). Privacy, by allowing the individual to develop to its full potential, also allows it to develop those character traits that are necessary to interact. One important fact that is frequently named is that of trust. People apparently need some private space that enables them to build a trusting relationship to others (cf. Koehn, 2001; Johnson, 2001, p. 120). A similar idea can be found in the argument that a sense of privacy is needed to feel secure, which in turn is a precondition for the development of a stable self (Brown, 2000, p. 63).

If these arguments are correct, they lead to the conclusion that privacy protection is necessary for a functioning society because it is a condition for the development of individuals who can collaborate to build such a society. Especially those forms of social organisation that are based on strong participation of the individuals will therefore be keen on the protection of privacy. Therefore one can frequently find arguments that privacy is of essential importance to democracy (Johnson, 2001; Gavison, 1995).

So far it seems as if privacy were a universally recognised right or value. Therefore the question could be: Why worry about it; if everybody agrees that it is important, where is the problem? One of the problems is that despite the principal agreement to privacy protection, there is a multitude of attempts to realise it that are not necessarily coherent. On the one hand there is the international confusion about privacy. Some countries enact a strong approach by putting the fundamental right to a person's data in the control of that person. Germany, for example, recognises a constitutional right to informational self-determination (Hoffmann-Riem, 2001). The U.S./American approach, on the other hand, is to emphasise the protection of the individual from the state, but other than that it only recognises a right to privacy where there is an expectation of privacy (Tavani, 2000, p. 86). In practice this means that the individual's protection from breaches of privacy is much weaker in the U.S. This is not only a matter of different national interpretation, it even threatens the transatlantic trade relations because the European Union requires equal protection of privacy from its trading partners under the threat of an end to data exchange (Langford, 1999a, p. 124; Culnan, 1993, p. 343). And these are only the differences between democratic states that stress the importance of the individual as their common basis. The problems become even worse in those areas where traditionally the individual is seen as less important *vis-à-vis* the community.

Another problem is posed by the different definitions of the limits of privacy. We have already seen that privacy is generally recognised as a limited right. Unlimited protection of privacy would also protect the "dark forces in society" (Levy, 1995, p. 652). Those limits cannot be clearly defined *a priori*. One will have to agree with Introna (2000, p. 190) that the appropriate protection of privacy in a concrete situation is a matter of judgment. This leads us back from the general description of privacy to our question of how the use of information technology can be managed in a responsible manner. As we have seen, the reflective use of responsibility also requires a measure of judgment and prudence. Before we come to the question of responsibility with regards to dealing with privacy and IT, however, it will be necessary to narrow down the problem a little bit more in order to be able to discuss it somewhat coherently.

Within the area of problems concerning privacy caused or aggravated by technological advances and business interests, one can distinguish between consumer privacy and employee privacy (Rogerson, 1998, p. 22). For our discussion of the application of reflective responsibility to privacy, the problem of employee surveillance seems more interesting because some of the moral features are clearer. We will therefore leave aside for the moment the question of how management should deal with customer data and concentrate on the problem of data concerning employees.

Surveillance can be defined as the "possibility of being observed by other members of an organization" (Beu & Buckley, 2001, p. 65). While surveillance in the morally relevant sense of the term is included in this definition, it usually stands for a very specific way of observing and being observed in the organisation, for the observation of employees by employers or superiors with the purpose of checking the employees' behaviour during work and sometimes even outside of work. This practice, while again not new, has become more widespread due to the use of computers and IT. An employee's behaviour online is easily followed by looking at log files and other data that is routinely produced. Additionally, there is by now a multitude of software with the express purpose of recording and directing employees' behaviour. Special software can be used to determine exactly how many keys an employee strikes or how much time she spends on the Internet and at what sites. Other software can be used to restrict the Internet access, to automatically check email messages, or to filter out certain types of attachments. Another technological means of surveillance that is increasingly used in organisations is video cameras that control the physical location and activities of employees.

While it is hard to determine exactly how many employees are subject to surveillance, which is partly caused by the lack of clear definition of the term, it is obvious that it is a substantial number. Already in 1988 the U.S. Office of Technology Assessment estimated that ten million American workers were subjects to concealed video and computer monitoring. From 1985 to 1988 the number of surveillance systems sold to business firms tripled to 70,000 (Bowie, 1999, p. 85). A survey conducted in 1996 by the Society for Human Resource Management found that 36 percent of responding companies searched employee messages regularly and 70 percent said that employers should reserve the right to do so (Schulman, 2000, p. 155). Other sources state that more than 30 million workers were subject to workplace monitoring in 2000, up from 8 million in 1991 (Hartman, 2001, p. 12). These partly contradicting numbers show that it is difficult to get reliable information about employee surveillance, but at the same time they also show that it is a widespread phenomenon that is still growing. Given the fact that there seems to be general agreement that privacy is worthy of protection and that at first sight employee surveillance constitutes a breach of privacy, one can ask why it is done at all.

There are several arguments defending employee surveillance. The most frequently named one is that employees' use of ICT for non-business purposes produces huge losses for corporations and that therefore surveillance of employees is something like self-defence. There are estimates saying that U.S. corporations alone lose more than $54 billion a year because of non-work-related employee use of the Internet. Apart from the waste paid-for employee time, this misuse also uses up other scarce resources such as bandwidth and productivity (Boncella, 2001, p. 12). Another strong argument used predominantly in American arguments is the legal importance of surveillance. Given the strong litigation culture in the U.S., many companies feel obliged to check on their employee behaviour in order to avoid lawsuits on the grounds of harassment (Koehn, 2001), negligent hiring, negligent retention, or negligent supervision (Brown, 2000). Employee surveillance can even be framed in our terms of responsibility by describing it as a measure that enforces accountability. The underlying thought is that people who have nothing to hide have nothing to fear from being surveyed. In fact, few would doubt that employers have some right to know what their employees are doing and employees have a duty to disclose the truth about them (cf. Posner, 1995, p. 361).

Some of the arguments against employee surveillance are based on the fundamental reasons for the protection of privacy discussed earlier. If it is true that privacy is a necessary precondition for humans to develop those characteristics that enable them to come to their full potential and to interact in society, then employee surveillance might endanger this development. "Given the transparency of the worker's life to employer inquiries, one can legitimately raise the question if the level of employer inquiry now impinges on the inner self of workers" (Brown, 2000, p. 62). Another view that also relies on human nature stresses the power aspect of surveillance. Surveillance in this sense can be interpreted as a means to project power, specifically as a way to stabilise hierarchical relationships between a powerful centre and a weak periphery (Rule et al., 1995, p. 322). Also, the constant surveillance can be seen as a realisation of Bentham's Panopticon, which Foucault (1975) has used as a model for the description of power relations in society. Computerisation is the perfect tool to spread surveillance in the Panopticon and thus to be used as a power tool (Yoon, 1996). On a less abstract plane, one can also argue that surveillance is a sign of bad labour relations. Surveillance of employees can be seen to undermine trust between mangers and employees and "it also indicates great scepticism about the ability of people to behave morally" (Bowie, 1999, p. 85; cf. Weisband & Reinig, 1995, p. 44). Furthermore, it can be argued that surveillance undermines the aim of instituting accountability. Accountability requires autonomy and trust. If a sense of privacy is necessary to develop these properties, then accountability is based on some measure of privacy (Introna, 2000, p. 195).

Why Assume Responsibility Concerning Privacy?

The description of privacy, its justifications and limits, was supposed to serve as a background for an exemplary analysis of the role that reflective responsibility can play in IS. What should have become clear is that privacy is a complex social problem that touches on moral and ethical questions; that affects people, groups, and organisations; that has a legal as well as a moral side; and that clearly does not lend itself to simple solutions. In this sense privacy can serve as an example for many other problems resulting from the use of ICT in business. It is therefore going to be used as an example to demonstrate the application of the theory of reflective responsibility developed so far. Before we come to the advantages and the application of reflective responsibility, however, it makes sense to briefly look at the alternatives. The question now is: How else can one react to the challenges of IS, what else could or should be done apart from trying to act responsible in a reflective way? This question comprises the question why one should act responsibly at all. As was mentioned earlier on, there is no final answer to this question. If people are not interested in acting morally, it is probably a doomed enterprise to try and force them to do so by using normative theories. However, there are reasons why even from a non-moral point of view it seems advantageous to act responsibly. We will try to show now that responding responsibly to privacy considerations will lead to positive results from a moral point of view, as well as from a self-interested, economically rational point of view.

This demonstration is probably most easily realised by looking at the alternatives to responsibility. The first one would be not to react at all. In order to see what effects this would have, we must become more specific than the discussion of privacy has been so far. The refusal to be responsible requires a subject just like responsibility itself. For the sake of the argument, we will now pick a subject that can play a role in privacy matters: the individual manager, say the CIO of a business enterprise. The CIO as possible subject could simply decide to ignore the problem. This would be a possible course of action where responsibility does not seem to play a role. Furthermore, it is a course of action that is practically possible and that one can even find quite frequently in practice. The problem, however, is that even this deliberate ignoring of responsibility matters does not really help the subject evade responsibility ascriptions. The CIO who fails to take privacy matters into consideration will have to deal with ascriptions of responsibility if, due to her inaction, employees lose motivation, leave the company, or if the corporate culture suffers or other results of her inaction are seen as objects of responsibility ascription. If privacy is indeed as serious a concern as was suggested in the discussion of the term, then it seems that responsibility will be ascribed no matter whether the potential subjects realise this or not. In a sense this leads us back to the problem of doing and omitting. Failing to assume or accept responsibility is an action in itself that is again an object of responsibility ascriptions. Responsibility simply seems inevitable. Therefore the option of refusing responsibility is not really an option. Furthermore such a failure to accept responsibility would run counter to the image of managers who usually tend to take pride in being called responsible. Similar arguments could be made for other possible subjects of responsibility ascriptions in privacy protection, ranging from the government that sets legal standards to the individual technician who installs a CCTV camera. Refusal of responsibility will generally not be possible. There is no opt-out option. The example of legal responsibility shows us that ascriptions can be successful despite the subjects' willingness to accept them. The conclusion is that responsibility will play a role in normative questions such as that of privacy protection.

Problems of Traditional Responsibility Concerning Privacy

However, the area of privacy protection and surveillance at the same time shows us that even when and if responsibility is accepted and ascribed, the process of ascription runs into other problems if it follows a classical model of responsibility. If we say that privacy protection is the object of responsibility, then in the classical model we would have to determine all of the dimensions, conditions, and determinants in order to build a case for the ascription. Unfortunately this seems impossible to do. It starts with the question of who or what the subject should be. In the brief example above, we just posited an individual manager, the CIO, as responsible. However, it is plain to see that there are others who might be considered the subject with the same amount of justification. One could either see the CEO as the person representing the entire organisation as the subject, or the line-manager who does surveillance, or the technician who installs it. Another argument might be that it is not in fact a single individual who is responsible, but the corporation as such because of its corporate culture, or a part of the organisation, or maybe the industry where surveillance is accepted standard. Finally, one could see the state, government or legislature, society, or international entities as subject because they set the rules or fail to regulate surveillance.

The discussion of the problems of the traditional idea of responsibility runs into similar problems caused by a lack of clarity with regards to the other dimensions as well. Who or what is going to be the authority that decides about the acceptability of an ascription and about the sanctions? Who enforces the decision and on what normative grounds is it to be taken? What type of responsibility are we talking about, what is the temporal horizon, is it ascribed reflexively or transitively? And what exactly is the object? Even in the narrowed-down area of privacy and surveillance, there are a multitude of potential objects that one might be responsible for.

Of course not all of these questions have to be addressed by everybody. In most situations the answers to many of them are predetermined by circumstances. Unfortunately in most cases this will still not be sufficient to determine a full and viable set of dimensions for a responsibility ascription. Let us go back to the example started earlier, the responsibility of the CIO for privacy protection in a specific organisation. Let us further assume that the decision in question has been boiled down to the question of whether or not to install an Internet tracking and email checking software that would allow managers to check the use of Internet resources by the employees in their department. That means that the subject, the CIO, is clear, as well as the object. One could hope that this would allow us to describe the responsibility settings of the case. However, it turns out that there is still a multitude of potential sets of responsibility that could play a role here.

First of all there is the object. While at first sight it is the decision to install the software or not to do so, there is in fact a huge number of objects that hide behind this one. The question is: What is the aim of the decision? Is it to streamline workflow, to save company resources, to exert control over employees? And what is the ultimate rationale behind these objects? Is it to improve the corporate culture, to help employees live up to their full potential, or is the final aim just to make profits? But even if profit is what management, represented by the CIO, is aiming at, how can it best be achieved? Corresponding to the many sub-objects, there are many different instances. While the CEO or the shareholder might judge the profitability of the decision, the employees would judge some of the social results, a judge might judge the conformity to legal standards, and the CIO's own conscience might judge the adherence of the decision to her own moral standards. Accordingly, we have a mix of moral, legal, role, and other responsibilities that can point to the future or the past, which can be aiming at ascription of blame, guilt, or at promotion or a bonus. At the same time these different sorts of responsibility of the CIO may lead to contradicting behaviour and lead her to a multitude of dilemmas.

What is worse, even if we accept this confusion as the given reality of responsibility, we still do not know whether these different ascriptions are possible or acceptable at all. This is where we need to come back to the conditions of responsibility. The question then is whether the CIO fulfils the conditions that traditional theories of responsibility prescribe for their subjects. While one can argue that the CIO makes the decision and therefore is part of the causal chain that leads to the different results, the opposite view might hold that the decision would have come about without the CIO as well and that she is therefore not causally responsible. One could argue that it is part of the corporate culture, of the industry standards, that the board clearly voiced its preferences and that therefore the CIO had no choice. This then leads to the problem of freedom and power, where one could argue that the CIO herself was nothing but an instrument. But even if she had the power to freely decide, we still run into the problem of limited knowledge. It is impossible for the CIO to foresee all of the results of her decision, especially if there is no temporal limit to those results that are considered objects. This makes it impossible for her even to concentrate on profit maximisation as her exclusive object of responsibility, because maximising profits next month or in ten years may require different sorts of action. Also, this traditional approach to responsibility predetermines that a discussion of the kind that was just demonstrated is artificially limited to certain types of responsibility, for example to individual subjects.

This brief review of the problems of traditional responsibility with a view to managerial responsibility for employee privacy protection was supposed to serve as the background of the following discussion of the contribution of reflective responsibility. For the rest of the chapter, we will discuss some of the relevant aspects of reflective responsibility and IS with the aim of demonstrating why the reflective turn may render the concept useful where the traditional approach fails.

In this situation there may arise a multitude of questions, and we will use the theory of reflexive responsibility to identify the most important ones and to answer them as far as possible. In order to give structure to the problems, we will go back to the dimensions of responsibility and analyse how these are affected by the reflective use of responsibility in IS. After that we will take a look at different aspects of responsibility and IS, namely at responsibility because of IT, responsibility for IT, and responsibility through IT. Finally we will leave the immediate business surrounding and ask what problems of the framework of responsibility might be relevant for managers which will lead to a brief discussion of fundamental philosophical problems arising from responsibility questions in IT. At the end of the chapter, we will summarise the content in a sort of "checklist" in order to give an overview and allow people faced with immediate responsibility problems to quickly identify them more easily.

DIMENSIONS OF REFLECTIVE RESPONSIBILITY AND IT

As we have seen already, the first and arguably most important step in any responsibility ascription is the identification of the dimensions. One needs to answer the question: Who is responsible for what, and before whom? More specifically the question now is: Does the reflective turn of responsibility change anything about the dimensions with regard to their function in IS?

Subject

In order to live up to the theory of reflective responsibility, the subject must be chosen in such a way that the ascription is viable and open to scrutiny. The process of imputation must show results and aim at the improvement of the circumstances of the involved parties. That means that some of the traditional problems of the subject of responsibility as discussed earlier appear less severe.

The traditional subject, the individual human being, is certainly still the central player in reflective responsibility. In our example, that means that the manager deciding about surveillance, the technician who installs it, or the company itself are still candidates. Reflective responsibility, however, demands more than just an easy identification, it requires checking whether the subject is capable of discharging its responsibility. At this point reflective responsibility may make matters even more complicated than traditional approaches. It is no longer enough to determine who or what is responsible; it is now required to ascertain that the responsibility in question is realisable. In the case of our example, that means that it is not enough to hold the CIO, the technician, or the firm responsible. These potential subjects must now be analysed with regard to their ability to live up to the expectation. Especially in the case of classical individual responsibility, this may lead to problems.

On the other hand reflective responsibility also offers advantages for any sort of subject. The emphasis on results and the recognition of the fallibility of the concept combine to facilitate ascriptions even in those cases that so far were problematic due to a lack of the fulfilment of conditions. Reflective responsibility recognises that even in the modern world, there is no alternative to the traditional system of the control of individual behaviour (cf. Seebass, 2001, p.

98). In those cases where individual conduct can make a difference and individuals are aware of this and able to act, the ascription of responsibility makes sense. In this sense the reflective idea of responsibility is in agreement with those approaches to the ethics of business information technology that emphasise the importance of the individual (cf. Langford, 1999a, p. 73).

However, reflective responsibility must take into account that there are limits to what the individual can do and that there are vast areas of ethically relevant problems where the limitation to individual responsibility is counter-productive because it leads to the oversight of important alternatives. This is the area of collective responsibility where the idea of reflective responsibility shows some of its strengths.

The main problem of collective responsibility in traditional moral philosophy, as we have seen, is that collectives are not recognised as moral subjects. They do not fulfil the conditions of knowledge or self-consciousness. They have neither conscience nor body, they know no moral feeling and no compassion. They are not persons. While these objections may be valid for many ethical theories, they weigh far less with regard to reflective responsibility. The main questions here are: Is the ascription open, does it have consequences, and does it improve our collective life? If this is so, then the ascription makes sense. It is clear that in many cases these questions can be answered in the affirmative for collective subjects and therefore collectives can be accepted as subjects.

Of course collectives such as corporations have been recognised as responsibility subjects in some areas such as, for example, the law for some time. Moral philosophers might therefore object to the idea that corporations are responsible, that this has nothing to do with ethics, and that their point that collectives are not suitable subjects is not touched by these deliberations. A theory of reflective responsibility would reply that the determination of the normative foundation on which ascriptions are made is part of the process of ascription. Therefore, philosophers who rule out collectives as moral subjects and thus conclude that there cannot be collective subjects create the very situation they describe. They generate self-fulfilling prophecies or tautologies. In the cases where these are accepted as the normative basis in a given group or society, this would mean that no collective could act as a subject. However, if a group or society does not adhere to this normative basis, there is no prima facie argument against collective responsibility. In fact this point of view allows the use of moral ascriptions that go beyond what is admissible for human beings. One can for example use responsibility ascriptions for the purpose of stigmatising companies for unwanted behaviour that is usually deemed to be inappropriate behaviour if applied to humans (cf. Maring, 2001, p. 139).

While corporative collective responsibility does not pose any fundamental challenges to reflective responsibility, things become more difficult in the case of group responsibility. Here the problem is that there is no unified subject of action, and consequently it is hard to define a responsibility subject. A theoretician of reflective responsibility would first have to ask whether it is possible to assign responsibility in this setting in such a fashion that consequences become noticeable. In order for this sort of ascription to become viable, there will usually have to be institutions and mechanisms for accountability which allow the ascriptions to become viable and potential sanctions to be effective. This means that for example the anonymous user of a car realises the costs and damages he produces and is made liable for them. Similarly, the user of a computer or a certain program might be held responsible for the cumulative results that the use produces. Possible candidates for our example of privacy are those groups that set the tone of the discussion. This might be the group of CIOs in a particular industry or even the group of all business users who have to contend with or decide about surveillance. This is of course much more easily said than done, and even if it were possible in any given case, the question remains whether such an attribution of responsibility to the single individual of a group has anything to do with collective responsibility. However, from the point of view of reflective responsibility, this is a secondary problem. The distinction between the different types of responsibility is an artificial one anyway since they overlap in most cases. Reflective responsibility needs to ensure that the subject is identified and accepted, that it is capable of living up to the expectation, that the ascription is open, that it has results, and that it leads to an improvement of conditions in a general way. This is clearly ethically relevant in itself. Other than that, the question whether it is an ethical ascription, a legal one, or any other sort of responsibility is of secondary importance. Reflective responsibility thus solves the problem of collective responsibility by assigning a low importance to the traditionally contentious points and by concentrating on its own criteria. For our example that means that it might be reasonable to hold a heterogeneous group responsible such as a specific industry that has developed specific ways of dealing with privacy. If there is something like a collective approach to employee surveillance in, say, call centres, then it might make sense to ascribe responsibility for this practice to the call centre industry, regardless of whether it can have the status of subject in any other environment.

In the same manner the reflective approach addresses the difficult question of what the relationship between individual and collective responsibility is. All theories of collective responsibility as we have seen agree on the fact that they are not meant to replace individual responsibility. Collective responsibility is seen as a complement or an enhancement of individual responsibility. It is meant to facilitate individual responsibility or to cover different areas. In all of these cases, however, it has some kind of bearing on the individual aspect. Collectives are constituted by individuals, and therefore collective responsibility will usually have results for individuals. They will lead to individual responsibility. A software company for example may decide to monitor its employees without notifying them. The employees can sue the company and it will then be held responsible by having to pay compensation. This may translate into individual responsibility when the manager who made the decision is fired or all of the employees get a financial compensation. But even in less clear-cut cases, collective responsibility will have individual consequences, which can be interpreted as individual responsibility. Just like individual responsibility can lead to or result from other individual responsibility, the same can be said for individual and collective responsibility.

One of the typical arguments against collective responsibility is based on the difficulty of distinguishing between individual and collective aspects of the ascription. Again, reflective responsibility has a relatively simple theoretical answer to this. Among the results of the reflective turn of responsibility, we have seen that it typically postulates the introduction of institutions with the purpose of rendering ascriptions viable. Also, it emphasises the importance of accountability and underlines the relevance of institutional and organisational factors for the establishment of accountability. The trick is therefore to find institutions and organisational arrangements that will allow the distribution of individual and collective responsibility. One example for such an institution that seems well suited for the realisation of the combination of the two aspects are codes of ethics or codes of conduct (cf. Eckard & Löffler, 1991, p. 286). This is of course only one possible approach. But again the important part is that the responsibility ascription is viable, that it is open, that it has consequences, and that it improves social life. Therefore the theoretical problem of untangling joint responsibility may be less important from the reflective viewpoint. Even though it is complicated at first sight, it is also manageable. In fact, as Schmitz (1998, p. 10) points out, it is a matter of daily routine in any court of law and therefore not a fundamental threat to responsibility.

There is one last point of interest with regard to responsibility subjects in IT. The question is whether computers or information systems can themselves acquire the status of subjects.[19] There are two extreme answers to the question. The first is yes, computers can be responsible because they make decisions, consequentially are subjects of action, and thus can be subjects of responsibility. On the other hand one can argue that computers are not moral subjects, that they do not fulfil any of the conditions, that they have no knowledge, no feelings, no judgment, no body, no mind, nothing that traditionally characterises moral subjects or persons.

From a reflective viewpoint one can again concentrate on other factors, namely on the questions of whether the ascription to a computer would be viable, whether it would have consequences that might further the underlying normative order. In this sense it might make sense to ascribe responsibility to computers in cases where further causal relationships are not discernible. An information system might be held responsible because it is known to be faulty. False and morally negative decisions made on the grounds of such a system may be attributed to the system. In some sense we all know this sort of reasoning when we hear: "I could not do it because the computer crashed." Often this sort of reasoning is used as an excuse to render responsibility inapplicable. In these cases the use of computer responsibility would be against the spirit of reflective responsibility. However, it is conceivable that the ascription of responsibility to computers could make sense. In cases where it is no longer determinable which individual caused a certain behaviour of the computer, it may be a helpful construct to say the computer is responsible. The next question would then have to be what the results of such an ascription might be. If it were possible to build institutions that could translate computer responsibility into a form having to do with humans, then the ascription could fulfil its purpose. What we have in mind is a situation like this: An information system is recognised to deduce wrong conclusions from the given data. If this were known it could be said that the system is responsible for these conclusions. In a next step one could then say that humans or organisations dealing with this system are responsible for using it and will therefore be attributed the actions that result from the wrong conclusions.

Critics might object that this is not really a case of the computer being the subject of responsibility, but rather personal responsibility hidden under a new name. This is correct in the sense that the end result would be personal responsibility. However, the computer would still play the part as the subject in an irreducible part of the chain of ascriptions. Also, it could be argued that this has nothing to do with moral responsibility, and again the answer would be that the analytic distinction between the types of responsibility is not really important. In the end the ascription would affect how people act, and it would therefore have moral repercussions.

Where does this discussion of the subject of responsibility leave us with regards to our example of privacy and employee surveillance? We have seen earlier on that the problem of the traditional approach to responsibility for privacy was that it rules out some subjects such as collectives while the subjects it admits, individual human beings, do not fulfil the conditions of causality, knowledge, power, etc. By concentrating on the three main points—on openness, consequentialism, and the good life—the reflective approach can neglect some of the theoretical problems and the need for complete stringency and coherence of every type of ascription. What is important is whether ascriptions are open and thus acceptable, whether they improve our living together, and whether they refer to factual or expected results. This facilitates the ascription to subjects that so far did not play a role in responsibility such as corporations or even information systems. Of course the advantages of reflective responsibility go further than just admitting new promising subjects to the ascription process. In order for the ascription to be successful, there must be objects that correspond to the subjects, objects whose being ascribed to the subjects makes sense and is acceptable to those who are party to the ascription.

Object

There is a close link between the subject and the object of responsibility. Most of the conditions of responsibility discussed earlier refer to this relationship. The subject must have knowledge of the object, it must have a causal relationship and a certain amount of power over it. The subject must have a choice of whether to realise the object, or it should at least have the chance to avoid it. We have seen that these traditional conditions run into a number of problems. Firstly, there is complexity, which obscures the knowledge of causal chains as much as that of rules. Secondly, the objects in question may be out of the reach of available subjects. Some objects are cumulative; others do not appear to be caused by any subject at all. Thirdly, there is an apparent lack of intention in many of the technological problems. Fourthly there is the problem of side effects, and fifthly there is the huge problem of doing and omitting, the problem that apparently one does not have a chance of discharging all of one's responsibilities without running straight into new ones.

Let us take a brief look at the example from the beginning of this chapter. Possible objects of responsibility that were identified with regards to privacy and surveillance included the well-being of employees, profit generation of the company, the technical functioning of surveillance software, social acceptability of company practice, the image of the company, etc. If we again concentrate on the CIO as responsible subject, we quickly find that she has huge difficulties with being responsible for, say, the decision to install a monitoring system. The CIO will never be able to consider all of the results of this decision. While there may be good reasons to suppose that it will lead to an increase of turnover as well as an improvement of business processes, the totality of the results will only be determinable in hindsight. Maybe a certain group of employees will not get used to the new system and leave the company. Maybe it will offer a new weakness in security and allow hackers to destroy essential data. Maybe it will change business processes in such a way that the company all of a sudden discovers completely new services that it could provide. Similar uncertainties can be constructed for each and every possible object of responsibility.

What use can reflective responsibility be with regard to the object of responsibility in IS? Again, as in the case of the subject, the criteria of reflective responsibility help setting priorities, which in turn allows realising ascriptions. Openness and the corresponding discursive nature of ascriptions should help identify the relevant objects in the first place. In order to render the ascription practically relevant, reflective responsibility has to make sure that the object is clearly defined and delimited. These definitions cannot be produced by the subject itself. They always depend in some degree on the subject's environment. Depending on the situation and the scope of the ascription, this may mean the creation of large institutions or maybe just contractual agreements. There is a social side to it which is needed to define the temporal range and the question of side effects. Society and public administration must make it clear up to which point in time the results of actions have to be considered and how much care must be taken with side effects. In fact, it is constitutive of the notion of action itself that the agent has to limit the range of results in question (Spaemann, 1980, p. 189f). These are obviously difficult issues that determine much of the current discussion about technology. We are unable to consider all of the results of our actions, but we must be required to consider some of them. The limit is subject to debate, and it is one of the challenges for people who want to live in a responsible society to ensure that this limit is set and accepted. The debates about nuclear energy or biotechnology are examples for the relevance of these questions. But also the business use of computers will need this sort of guidance. As we have seen, the central problem of privacy is exactly that of its limits. Not the idea itself is contentious, but the question where it must yield to other interests or values.

Apart from this social scale of things, the same need for clarity and limitation of objects is also needed on an operational or managerial level. If someone is to be ascribed an object, then that object must be discernible. In our example this could mean that the CIO who is responsible for the surveillance system looks only at the immediate business implications of her actions. Of course she may be held responsible for more than that. Therefore, she must be willing to listen to the other stakeholders and take their opinions into consideration. A definition of the object that is too narrow may hold the advantage of being manageable, but may also run into the problem that it backfires later on. If the CIO accepts responsibility from the board of directors for improving discipline in the organisation by installing a surveillance system, then there is a good possibility that this responsibility can be discharged as planned. The example makes it clear at the same time, however, that there are more objects of responsibility that can be ascribed because of this action. Employees can feel insecure or customers may object to the fact that their emails are read for purposes other than intended. The CIO must be aware of this fact and act accordingly. This means that she must keep an open mind with regards to possible subjects and that she should follow open and discursive procedures in order to determine what these may be. Acting responsibly in a reflective fashion for our CIO means that she communicates with those people or groups whom she knows will be affected before making the decision. In the case of surveillance, there are some obvious candidates such as employees, but also management, customers, or other departments. The communicative nature of responsibility forces her to hear these opinions. As we have seen, responsibility ascriptions will follow morally relevant decisions anyway. The question therefore is: How can the CIO react to this knowledge? The two alternatives that we tried to develop here were:

1. Follow a traditional model by being responsible in her role for the fulfilment of her task, and
2. Being reflectively responsible by having the affected parties participate. The advantages and disadvantages of both courses of action are obvious. Action 1 is easier to handle, clearer to manage, and success/failure can easily be determined. On the other hand this action runs the serious danger of overlooking relevant factors that management is not aware of or does not consider important. This sort of behaviour goes a long way toward explaining the estimated 40% of failures of information system investments. Action 2 has the clear disadvantage of being more complex, more difficult to handle, more lengthy, and more expensive. On the other hand having the stakeholders participate in a decision is the best guarantee possible for finding out problems at an early stage, for maximising knowledge and prognosis in the future. The probability of success in determining relevant objects of responsibility is greatly increased by this sort of action. Consequentially, it can be argued that it makes economic as well as moral sense to choose this sort of action.

Summarising the problem of the object of reflective responsibility in IS, one can say that the fundamental problems discussed in the general theory of responsibility are not really changed. However, reflective responsibility can put aside some of the fundamental difficulties and concentrate on the realisability of an ascription. This will not solve all of the difficulties, and again most of the resulting ascriptions will be less than perfect and subject to justified criticism. Nevertheless, there is still the plausible case that the attempts of realising responsibility will leave the affected parties better off and therefore, given the procedural nature of reflective responsibility, it will be justified. The attitude that would result from reflective responsibility could be summarised as saying that an imperfect ascription of responsibility is better than none. The reflective turn of responsibility might help constituting such imperfect ascriptions where the traditional theory would fail.

Instance

The last of the three classical dimensions of responsibility is that of the instance or authority that determines the result of an ascription. As we have seen earlier, the instance is the most contentious dimension because many doubt its very existence. Some of the deciding authorities, however, are beyond any doubt. The legal authority of the judge is clearly recognisable in its power and tasks. Others such as God can no longer claim universal acceptability. We have also seen that some authors doubt the necessity of an instance and instead postulate that the recognition of and agreement to a set of rules is all that matters. This complete renouncement of the instance seems to go a little too far. The legal instances are a good sign for the fact that even in cases where the rules are known and accepted, there needs to be someone who can determine their fitting interpretation for a given case. Furthermore, one of the defining characteristics of responsibility is that it leads to consequences, often to sanctions. These sanctions will in most cases be against the will of the individual in question, and they will therefore have to be enforced against resistance. An effective ascription therefore needs someone who shapes the rules to a given case and who also has the power to enforce this interpretation. The specific weakness of moral responsibility is in many cases that this instance is nowhere to be seen.

What can reflective responsibility offer as a solution? The three functions of the instance, the identification of valid rules, their contextual interpretation, and their enforcement will all have to be integrated in the process of ascription. Let us recall the characteristics of the process of ascription from the point of view of reflective responsibility. In order to obtain validity and to be open and lead to consequences, all of the affected parties—as far as possible—must be included in the process. The discussion or discourse between all of these parties will have to address all of the relevant matters. This means that factual questions of truth and the relevant reality are as much an object as are questions of norms. We can see that the first task of the instance, the identification of the normative background, is always a part of responsibility ascriptions. Reflexive responsibility cannot take a particular set of norms or rules for granted, but always has to ascertain them.

This leaves us with the interpretation and the enforcement of the rules. Both of them are also addressed during ascription. The identification of and agreement on certain rules will usually happen with regard to a specific case, and it will therefore include the question of the appropriate interpretation. At the same time this question of the appropriate interpretation will tend to include or at least touch on the problem of enforcement. Reflective responsibility thus allows the addressing of all of the issues classically connected with the subject of responsibility without having to postulate the existence of any sort of physical or theoretical authority. This of course does not rule out that such an entity exists, but it does not presuppose its existence either.

Let us turn once more to the example. If the CIO wants to act responsibly in introducing the new surveillance system, then she will in a first step have to do a stakeholder analysis and try to find out who will be affected. These individuals or groups will then have to be given space and time to voice their opinions concerning the project. In this discussion (we call it discussion instead of discourse because the conditions of an ideal discourse will be far from fulfilled), subject, object, and instance of responsibility will be determined. Possible objects might be job security, ease of use, economic considerations, or many other things that depend on the specific case. These objects will then be attributed to the subject. That means that in all probability, more subjects than just the CIO will be identified. The responsibility ascription will most probably end in a web of responsibilities rather than in a single case. However, for our main subject in question, for the CIO, the result will be that the objects that she must pay attention to should be clearer. At the beginning of the project, the responsibilities will usually be prospective or *ex ante*. As the project progresses she will have to live up to and discharge her responsibilities as they appear. The responsibilities will then turn from *ex ante* to *ex post,* which means that the CIO will later on be judged on her performance with regard to the issues she knew in advance.

It is plain to see that this sort of process will be rather messy and error prone in real life. Every step of the way may lead down a dead end or may have to be repeated. The identification of stakeholders may overlook a relevant interest group, or the resulting discussion may be too dominated by any one group to be of value. But even under perfect discourse conditions, all of the affected parties may overlook a relevant issue. Furthermore there can be a lack of agreement on the norms and rules or on their application. The subject may not agree to the ascription, thinking someone else should be responsible. The persons holding specific roles could change and the successor may not know about expectations. Finally, the enforcement of rules may not work and people can use power positions to avoid sanctions. At the same time the mere attempt to organise such a responsibility discourse is costly and time intensive. From the point of view of the manager, the question is important: Why bother at all?

As we have already seen in the last section dealing with the object, there are two possible answers to this question: a business and a moral answer, both of which argue similarly. The tenor of the answer is that despite the costs, the attempt to realise responsibility is worth the effort because the benefits are potentially high. From the business point of view, the process can serve as a procedure to minimise the failure of an investment. Empirical research suggests that around 40 percent of the investments in information systems fail. Of those, only 10 percent fail because of technical difficulties, and the majority of failures are attributed to human and organisational problems (Forester & Morrison, 1994, p. 226). Given the immense value of technology investment in today's economy, the complex and expensive process of responsibility ascription would be economically justified if it could prevent just a relatively small percentage of these bad investments. Another typical problem with new technologies is that they tend to be implemented in a cultural gap. Those who are charged with implementing them tend to have a technical background, whereas the users and top management will look at issues of usability and profitability (Ward & Peppard, 1996). This culture gap is another reason for the failure of investments and again it might be overcome, at least in some cases, if the responsibility process as suggested here were realised.

A similar argument can be made from the ethical point of view. If the CIO wants to act morally, wants to accept ethical responsibility, then the stakeholder-and-discussion-based approach offers a high probability of achieving this. A solipsistic ethical approach, where an individual tries to identify the ethical issues and to find the answer to them all by herself, may work just as well. However, there is a high probability that the individual does not know all of the relevant facts or overlooks some of the important perspectives. As we have seen some of the reasons for the rise to importance of the ethical concept of responsibility were the limitations of the individual, its lack of knowledge, power, or perception. The process as described above can help overcome these problems.

However, it should be stated clearly that there is no guarantee that this approach will work and that its results will indeed be better than those that would come about without it. This refers to the economic as well as the ethical side of it. The entire process of identifying and realising responsibility can be very costly, time consuming, and still not have a satisfactory result. Worse still, it may itself become a reason for the failure of a particular project that would have worked fine without it. Ethically, too, it may turn out that the responsibilities identified in the process are not the ones that matter in the end, or that they are not viable or that the results are more immoral than what would have happened without them. This lack of certainty and trustworthiness in an ethical process would seriously jeopardise it in many cases. A Kantian ethicist could probably not suggest something as uncertain with a good conscience. However, it is one of the features of reflective responsibility that it realises and takes into account its own fallibility and builds on it. There are many good reasons why the process as described has a relatively high probability of being successful. It therefore stands to reason that instituting it will have positive results, that it will lead to consequences even if those are just incrementally better than what would happen without them. The intrinsic modesty of reflective responsibility with regards to its goals therefore allows the conclusion that the attempt is justified because of a positive expected outcome, even if there is no guarantee for it.

Another advantage of the reflective and discursive approach with regards to the instance is that the discourse may be able to identify a possible instance. If we see the ascription as a contest in which ascribers and ascribed try to sort out the acceptability of their claim, if we see responsibility as a conflict, then there is one characteristic that the instance must have: impartiality. Just as we assume that a judge is impartial in a court of law, any instance deciding about ascriptions and sanctions must be impartial. In the constructivist world of reflective responsibility, however, it is impossible to define who or what is impartial because there is no neutral ground. On the other hand any instance that is acceptable to the parties of the ascription and who is determined beforehand will be able to claim acceptability when enforcing its decision afterwards. This determination of the instance must therefore be part of the stakeholder process. It is also a good example for the mix of validity claims that are the basis of responsibility. The question of the instance will be answered by mix of normative, factual, and personal arguments that cannot be clearly distinguished.

REALISATION OF RESPONSIBILITY IN INFORMATION SYSTEMS

Having seen that reflective responsibility allows the identification of the three basic dimensions of responsibility, the next sections will deal with the specifics of the relationship between reflective responsibility and the business use of information technology. We will now take a look at the realisation of responsibility in IS. For analytical purposes it makes sense to distinguish between different viewpoints here. We will therefore differentiate between reflective responsibility **because of** IS, **for** IS, and **through** IS. The idea behind this distinction is to demonstrate the difference between prospective and retrospective responsibility, and to show how the use of IT can affect the basis of responsibility ascription by influencing communication.

Reflective Responsibility Because of Information Systems

Of the different possible relationships between responsibility and IS, the one that comes to mind first is responsibility because of IS. This stands for all those situations that are caused by the use of IS in which responsibility could or should be ascribed. The emphasis here is on *ex post* ascriptions for objects that have already happened. Computers and information technology and especially their business use can affect rules and behaviour in many different ways. A prominent example is the one already discussed in some detail earlier on, the question of privacy and surveillance. Here, the use of IT is recognised as a moral problem that will lead to the ascription of responsibility *ex post*. The corporation, the CIO, the technician, they all can be held responsible for their action and their use of IT. Possible consequences of this can include legal sanctions, moral sanctions, but also economic or social rewards.

Similar problems of responsibility because of IS can be found in other areas of what is usually referred to as computer ethics. One of the problems most frequently discussed is that of power. We all know Bacon's dictum that knowledge is power. This in itself can mean different things. It can mean the actualisation of potentialities of the human mind as well as control over information commodities. It can be seen as an intrinsic good or a means to something (Stichler, 1998, p. 175). The reason why power is often cited as the number one ethical problem in computers and information is usually that it is quite obvious that these systems can serve as means of power.

"The giving, orchestrating, and taking of information is a basic use of power. Power is capability, the ability to get things done that one wants done." (Mason et al., 1995, p. 40)

"...information systems are one of the crucial media on which organizational power rests: power is based on organizational positions that provide access to the IS, and on the special skills for using and interpreting IS outputs." (Lyytinen & Hirschheim, 1988, p. 23)

Laudon and Laudon (1999, p. 453) point out that information systems change the distribution of power, money, rights, and obligations.

While it is clear to the observer that information systems change tasks, jobs, and obligations, and consequently also power relationships, it is less clear that this must be a bad thing. In fact some authors point out that it is not power itself that is the ethical problem, but its misuse (Langford, 1999b, p. 9). Furthermore power in a formal sense not only does not have to be negative, it even has the status of a basic value. It is a condition for the actualisation of different life plans (Höffe, 1995, p. 146). Power should therefore be understood to be morally ambivalent (Gethmann & Gethmann-Siefert, 1996, p. X). It can be used for the good or the bad.

In a business setting it is important for managers to recognise this ambivalent moral status of power produced by information systems. Managers should also be aware that the use of information technology affects power distributions on all different levels of society. It has a lot to do with the business environment that managers find today. Globalisation and multi-national corporations that dominate international trade would not be possible in their current form without the capabilities of transmitting information (cf. Castells, 2000, p. 136f). Furthermore, the use of IT changes the political landscape in other ways. There is a drive towards international harmonisation of the global social, economic, and political world (Johnson, 2000, p. 22). Also, IT is gaining a more dominant role in the democratic process of power distribution.[20] Managers need to be aware of these developments because they play a part in them. The increasing use of IT in business sets the tone and prepares employees as users for the further spread of technology. A digital democracy, if we ever achieve it, will in large part build on competences that the citizens pick up at work.

Of more immediate importance to managers is how power distributions are changed on the meso-level of the firm. IT plays a role in and facilitates many changes in the way business is done. Looking at the management fads of the last few decades, one finds that most of them are based on an increased use of information and knowledge provided by technology. Many of these management fashions, if realised, result in severe organisational changes. Examples would be management theories such as just-in-time production and transport, or, more recently, business process reengineering (cf. Currie, 2000). Both lead to a restructuring of work processes and also of decision processes. They change how much power some members of an organisation hold over others. In IS literature, one therefore frequently finds the assumption that the introduction of IS is a destructive and creative process à la Schumpeter. That means that by introducing new technologies, one destroys old structures and processes, and replaces them with newer and presumably better ones. Especially business process reengineering (BPR) is often described as the reinvention of the business from scratch, and it is usually facilitated by the use of IT.

However, there is also the opposite view of the use of IT in organisations. While the introduction of new technologies may change the way things are done, it also has the capacity of preserving old structures that would be doomed without it. It can be argued that the old hierarchical production structure that we inherited from Ford and Taylor would be obsolete nowadays because it would not be able to process the required information if it were not for information technology. It can be argued that "computer and information technology has entrenched the pre-existing employer-employee relationship" (Johnson, 2001, For a more detailed discussion of the ethical impacts of IT on democracy see Stahl (2001b 203). What is true for the company can also be extended to the state. A modern welfare state requires and processes a huge amount of information, and it would probably cease to function without technology. This is why Weizenbaum (1976, For a more detailed discussion of the ethical impacts of IT on democracy see Stahl (2001b 250) could say that the computer is "an instrument pressed into the service of rationalizing, supporting, and sustaining the most conservative, indeed, reactionary, ideological components of the current Zeitgeist"—a comment that still rings true today.

Finally, the use of information technology and the developments just described also affect the use and distribution of power on the micro level. The individual may become empowered by IT or she may also be alienated by it. New processes can require greater autonomy and thus give employees the chance to make relevant decisions without supervision. On the other hand employees can be degraded to mere means of feeding data into computers.

There are certainly more aspects of the relationship between the business use of computers and power. However, for our purposes it suffices that several points have become clear. Firstly, the use of computers and the subsequent change in the distribution of power can be morally relevant, but it is morally ambiguous. Therefore, secondly, power issues related to computer use in business can be a reason for the ascription of responsibility. Management should at least be aware of that possibility. In fact it is plain to see that questions of power play a role in most other normative problems of IS. Thirdly, there are some points which are specifically relevant to reflective responsibility. Questions of power are a good example of the close relationship of facts and norms. If a manager wants to act responsibly in the face of power changes, then one of the challenges is the clarification of the issues. Questions like: who used to have what power, what changed, why did it change, who or what caused that change, etc., must be asked. The clarification of the problem will require the cooperation of the affected parties who may not wish to cooperate. An added difficulty is that these power changes will in many cases be implicit and informal. Therefore there is also the challenge of finding means or institutions which will clarify the situation and support accountability. At the same time this sort of unclear situation will also require some space for prudent decisions and therefore some openness.

There is one last item with regard to power that managers must take into account when they want to exercise reflective responsibility. This is the basic problem that power endangers the legitimacy of discourses. Our argument so far was that reflective responsibility requires the participation of everybody involved, and that in this sense it can be seen as something like the realisation of a Habermasian discourse. There is a great amount of philosophical problems with the realisation of discourses, because real discourses will always miss some of the relevant ideas that provide the idea of discourses with its legitimacy. So far we have argued that reflective responsibility can accept sub-optimal solutions such as a necessarily imperfect real discourse because it aims at the improvement of circumstances and not at ethically perfect solutions. This argument will remain the basis for discursive responsibility, but one danger is that real-life power differences are so great or so detrimental to real discourses that they destroy their legitimacy. This is an area where management should become active. Usually management will hold an important position of power in responsibility discourses, and they should use this position not to press their own positions, but to facilitate a maximum of equality within discourses. This is of course easier said than done, and it will often be counter-intuitive because managers acquire their power in the first place to promote their causes. However, if they are serious about acting responsibly, then this use of power for the decrease of power differences will facilitate a successful approach. And there is one last issue in this context. In order to facilitate a discourse, to make it an instrument of legitimate ascriptions, thus to move it close to the conditions of an ideal discourse, managers will need a capacity of judgment and they will need to use it prudently. This prudence will then be used to provide structures of accountability which in turn will often be institutions that allow ascription. One can thus see that the problem of power raised by IS touches on all of the characteristics of reflective responsibility as developed above.

Next to privacy and power as an object of responsibility because of IS, another problematic area is that of intellectual property. The western market economy is based on the assumption of property. The idea usually is that individuals as well as collectives can own property and that they can do with it as they like. They especially have the right to exchange it against other property—they can buy and sell it. On the other hand much of the criticism of this system such as Marxism is also based on property and its negative effects. There is a great amount of literature on property and its justification and its role in society. Most of this, however, has been written with the example of physical goods in mind. In the computer and information age, the emphasis is shifting toward intellectual property. Unfortunately the entire field of intellectual property is ill defined and hard to navigate. There are definitions of intellectual property such as the World Intellectual Property Organisation (WIPO), which sees it as the right to, among other things, the results of intellectual activity in the industrial, scientific, literary, or artistic field (cf. Forester & Morrison, 1994, p. 57). On the other hand it has to be objected that the term does not have a clear definition. But not only that, it can be said to be very misleading because it suggests that one can own ideas or ways of thinking about things, which in fact is not protected by any current approach to intellectual property (Snapper, 1995, p. 181). The use of the term also suggests that there is a coherent set of laws and rules governing the topic, when in fact there is a complex mix of legal and moral traditions, which are not only not coherent but sometimes even contradictory.

It is clear, however, that the area of intellectual property is steadily gaining in importance; this is mostly due to technological advances that are based on knowledge, information, and ideas rather than on physical goods. These technological advances can frequently be translated into services, goods, or business models which in turn generate huge profits. The prototypical example for this is software. Computer software can be sold as a good, and in fact some of the world's largest companies such as Microsoft, Oracle, and SAP do just that. Microsoft's CEO has become the richest person on the world just by doing so.

While intellectual property gains in importance, it also produces problems because the established rules governing property often do not apply to it. Property is a traditional concept originally based on physical manifestation (Barlow, 1995), and it can therefore not apply equally in the world of computers and cyberspace. In order to understand the specifics, it helps to contrast intellectual and traditional property. One difference is that one can trade manifestations of ideas such as images, books, or software CDs whose content nevertheless still belongs to the author (Weckert & Adeney, 1997, p. 65). This means that the acquisition of intellectual property follows different rules from those that apply to the acquisition of traditional property. The most striking examples are again software programs where one usually has to agree to a licensing agreement before being allowed to install them on a computer. This leads to differences in the characteristics of property that many users are not aware of or do not understand. If a user has property in a car, then she can do with it as she likes. She can for example lend it to a friend, change the interior, or sell it to someone else. If she bought software instead, then the same activities would in most cases be considered illegal.

The rules that lead to these results are usually justified by quoting the necessities of the production of intellectual property. It often is extremely costly to produce one specific piece of information, to produce one piece of intellectual property (Mason, 1986). A large software program can contain thousands of man years of work and be worth millions of dollars. Once this first copy has been produced, however, further copies can be made with very little expense. This reproducibility is a characteristic of property items having to do with computers (Johnson, 2001, p. 93). It has been facilitated and spread even further by the Internet, where files can be stored and downloaded by any interested party. The copies will then be useable without any decrease in usability or quality. At the same time the original is not affected by the copying at all. This means that there is another big difference between traditional and intellectual property, which is the issue of theft. While theft deprives the owner of traditional property of her possession and thus decreases her utility, the same does not apply to intellectual property. Kuflik lists three senses in which a person who gets an idea from me need not be taking it away from me: "(1) I can still think it; (2) I can still enjoy whatever praise or admiration others might be disposed to give to me as the person who thought of it first; and (3) I can still use it, to all the same personal advantage, in my own personal life" (Kuflik, 1995, p. 173).

As we can see, intellectual goods are fundamentally different from goods for which the institution of property was originally developed. Also, computer data and computer programs do not fit the established rules for intellectual property (Moor, 1985). At the same time one can see numerous attempts to strengthen intellectual property rules and to extend the reach of those rules, especially to include computer readable data and programmes. In order to evaluate these efforts, it is helpful to take a brief look at the arguments for and against the protection of intellectual property.

There are several different arguments for intellectual property in general and for its application to IT in particular. First of all, there is the theory of property in the tradition of natural rights whose most influential protagonist was John Locke (cf. Johnson, 2001). His idea is that we originally own ourselves, our bodies, and therefore everything that we produce. One acquires ownership in something by mixing one's labour with it. This theory can run into a lot of problems in the physical world, but for intellectual property it is deeply plausible. If you write a programme or collect data, then you create something that would simply not be there without you. Locke further discusses a proviso, which can be interpreted to mean that acquisition of property must not lead to anyone being worse off for it (cf. Nozick, 1974; Gauthier, 1986). This, too, seems to be the case for intellectual property, unlike for many examples of traditional property. Another natural rights approach would be that a program could be understood as an extension of the programmer to which she could again claim ownership (Nissenbaum, 1995, p. 206).

The second group of arguments in favour of intellectual property are teleological ones. According to these arguments, intellectual property should be protected because of the positive effects it has (cf. Weckert & Adeney, 1997, p. 61). The institution of private property can be interpreted as a device encouraging parsimonious yet efficient use of resources (Donaldson & Dunfee, 1999, p. 128). This can of course be transferred to intellectual property. More frequently one can hear the argument that the protection of intellectual property is a necessary prerequisite for the production of software. Innovation and development of new software are seen as positive goods, which can only be guaranteed if the developers have the right to profit from their work. If copying software were legitimate and companies could not profit from their investments, then they would simply cease to invest. This argument is applied to corporations as well as to the individuals who produce intellectual property. Stallman (1995, p. 191) pointedly paraphrases the individual argument as follows:

"I want to get rich (usually described inaccurately as 'making a living') and if you don't allow me to get rich by programming,

*then I won't program. Everyone else is like me, so nobody will
ever program. And then you'll be stuck with no programs at all!"*

The two most important legal means for the protection of property rights
in the area of computers and IT are copyright and patents. There is no space
to discuss the intricacies of these here, but it should be noted that they are in
fact temporal monopolies. Both ensure the exclusive rights of use to their
holders for a limited period of time, and both effectively exclude competition.
Given that the usual defence of competition is that it is to serve the common
good, it is surprising that the limiting of competition is also justified with the same
argument. The question whether intellectual property rights should be granted
or not thus boils down to the empirical problem of which course of action will
actually promote the common good in a greater degree (cf. Kuflik, 1995).

This last point opens a first counter-argument against the protection of
intellectual property. Questions of illegal copying of software, but also of other
intellectual property, are at the forefront of international trade agreements, and
they are heavily emphasised in international trade relations. The World Intellectual Property Organisation or the agreement as part of the WTO treaties are
just two examples. In fact these treaties aim at the international recognition of
national standards. Apart from problems of implementation, enforcement, and
international legal issues, this area has become a target for the opponents of
globalisation. Some opponents argue that the monopolies that are erected in the
name of intellectual property threaten the diversity of culture and only benefit
some of the big corporations (Smiers, 2001). While this sort of argument refers
mainly to other forms of intellectual property such as music, films, and literature,
it can easily be extended to the realm of computers as well. The quasi-
monopoly that the Microsoft Corporation holds in the area of PC system
software is a good example.

Another argument against strong protection of intellectual property in the
computing area involves the specific characteristics of software. The most
important aspect is that the "theft" of software or data by copying does not
necessarily affect the original owner. When someone steals my bicycle, then the
fact that makes this hardest to bear is that I am deprived of its use. It can be
argued that this is in fact the reason why we find theft immoral, and why moral
and legal institutions were built to avoid it. If this is so, then there are no good
arguments why the same moral and legal standards should apply if the basis is
not applicable (cf. Johnson, 2001, p. 156; Weckert & Adeney, 1997, p. 70).
This can be interpreted as the attempt to invalidate the Lockean natural rights
argument. Even if one follows Locke by agreeing that putting work into

something will lead to the acquisition of property, it does not necessarily follow that intellectual property rights as we see them today are justified by this premise. The probable purpose of Locke's argument that people should not be deprived of the enjoyment of the fruits of their labour is not necessarily touched by allowing copies of software and data.

There is also an argument against the teleological defence of intellectual property. The assumption that the producers of software are individual profit maximisers who would cease to work if they did not make a large amount of money from their work is quite weak. Artists, scientists, or academics produce their work usually without the hope of financial rewards (Weckert & Adeney, 1997, p. 62). Some authors (cf. Stallman, 1995) have argued that programming, for example, is a highly satisfying activity that provides people with enough intrinsic motivation to be independent of financial rewards. If this is true, the argument that no more software would be written if we were to drop the protection of intellectual property is wrong. It stands to reason, however, that fewer people would do it and spend less time on it. This disadvantage would have to be weighed against potential advantages. There are some conceivable advantages, which have been listed by Stallman (1995). Chief among them is the increased productivity. Even though less software might be produced, more people could use it because it would be free. Furthermore, existing programs could more easily be adapted because source code would be known; programmers could get a better education for the same reason. Finally, duplicate efforts might be avoided.

In fact, the origins of today's success of computer technology took place in an environment of free access to intellectual property. However, business interests were opposed to this, and they carried the day with legislators on an international scale (De George, 1998, p. 53). This is ironic because the current economic success is based on the set of intellectual property rules which, had they been in place earlier, would most probably have stunted the development of the Internet (Schiller, 1999, p. 10) and presumably most of the other developments in IT as well. Furthermore, it can be argued that the economic success of high technology is only possible because companies could draw on publicly funded and owned research. The capitalist success of IT thus depends on the communist approach to knowledge that is generally adopted by academia (Himanen, 2001, p. 60).

This contradictory theoretical background of intellectual property does not make it any easier for management to deal with it. Managers who want to act responsibly in questions of intellectual property in relation to computers and IT will often find one general rule: act legally. It is a common assumption that following the law will in most cases lead to ethical behaviour and that it is thus the sensible thing to do (cf. De George, 1998, p. 53f). A big advantage of this stance is that it avoids the tricky questions of morality and property. As we have seen, there are some quite strong moral arguments that reject the institution of intellectual property. Solutions like Johnson's (2001, p. 41)—"I argue that it is wrong to make a copy because it is illegal, but not because there is some prelegal immorality involved in the act"—simply circumvent having to find a solution to moral questions. In this sense they follow Montaigne's moralism by simply endorsing common practices independent of its justification.

However, this solution is often not really helpful because the legal positions are not clear either. This is the case in situations where more than one country is involved and therefore national law does not apply, or where it is unclear which law applies. Even though there is an increasing number of international agreements with the purpose of unifying the legal framework of intellectual property, many questions are still open. Furthermore, intellectual property rights are subject to intensive modifications, and it can be argued that some of the basic assumptions are being changed because of the specific questions arising in IT. One pertinent example is the change of interpretation of patent law and whether it is applicable to software. Up until the 1980s, American courts held that computer programs were mathematical algorithms and therefore not subject to patent law. This interpretation has changed in the last few years, and now patents are granted for software on a regular basis. Without being able to discuss the background of such changes and their potential results, it is clear that managers must find orientations in their dealing with intellectual property that go beyond a simple adherence to the law. This is where the question of responsibility enters the arena and where the concept of reflective responsibility can prove helpful.

If a manager faces a potential normative problem with intellectual property, the solution in the spirit of reflective responsibility will be similar to what was suggested in the case of privacy. First of all the pertinent reality must be established. That means that subject, object, and norms should be discovered. This in turn implies that the stakeholders must be identified and their claims should be discussed. Potential stakeholders here, apart from the usual suspects such as managers, employees, and stockholders, will probably include authors and programmers, users and customers, but also the political system and the general public. Again management will run into the problem that this process, which is modelled on the idea of a discourse, will not be possible to the point where it could create universal legitimacy. And again the answer to this objection would be that the mere attempt to have a stakeholder discourse promises advantages that can outweigh the disadvantages. But there is no guarantee that this will be so.

But even if a real stakeholder discourse is impossible, the theoretical background of reflective responsibility offers some hints as to the interpretation of intellectual property. First, property in general can be seen as an institution that guarantees accountability. It is generally assumed that owners must take responsibility for what is theirs, be it their thoughts, their houses, or the product of their work. Thus understood, property is an institution that facilitates the ascription of responsibility and therefore promises to improve its realisability. In this sense a strong protection of intellectual property is to be welcomed. However, while this argument is a strong support for the institution of property in general, it seems to continually lose weight in the area of IT-related intellectual property. That is because it relies on the assumption that rights imply duties, specifically that the right to property implies the duty to take responsibility for it. Anybody who has ever installed a commercially distributed programme on his or her computer knows that at the start of the installation, they must agree to a licensing agreement. These licensing agreements tend to explicitly contradict what was just said about rights and duties. The producers usually reserve all rights to the program, but they categorically rule out any responsibility (cf. De George, 1998, p. 54f; Nissenbaum, 1995, p. 534). In any other area apart from software, this sort of agreement would run counter to our beliefs. It stands to reason that the identification of the underlying norms of a responsibility ascription would identify this as a contradiction, and that most potential stakeholders would not accept it (even though factually we accept it because we see no alternative). The conclusion is that a responsible manager who wants to claim the rights to intellectual property should also accept the duties that come with it.

Furthermore, there are genuinely social questions caused by the business use of IT. Computers change not only the business organisation of work, but also the social ways of doing things. On the one hand it allows new industries to develop and it has produced unknown riches in some parts of the world. At the same time it leads to rationalisation and loss of employment in other parts. Business and IT combined are the driving force behind the modern form of globalisation, which is one of the clearest examples for a generally perceived need for responsibility (even though it is completely unclear who could be responsible for what and how).[21] IT and business interests also increasingly colonise other areas of society where they played a much smaller part up until now. A good example here is that of education. Under the heading of e-teaching or e-learning, we see a large number of initiatives of moving IT into the educational process at all different levels. This development is right now becoming a fact that most educational institutions have to accept, and at the same time it is also becoming a multi-billion-dollar market.

Questions of privacy, power, and property are of immediate interest to managers because they make decisions based on these or decisions that change the status quo. What most of the problems from this area have in common is that they are within what is frequently called the "sphere of responsibility" of the manager anyway. Mangers would consider themselves or be considered by employees and superiors to be responsible for solving these problems. In these cases it is therefore plausible that the idea of reflective responsibility would be attractive for managers trying to understand how they can discharge their responsibilities. We have tried to show how reflective responsibility offers an approach to these problems that allows managers to discharge their responsibility.

There are on the other hand also moral problems caused by the business use of IT that are no longer within the sphere of influence of individual managers. These problems can still have a severe impact on the way the economy in general and a company in particular is run. Also, they can lead to individual responsibilities of individual managers. It is therefore necessary for managers to remember this higher level in order to be aware of potential conflicts or requirements. The actual list of changes in society and the way it is organised that are due to the use of IT is again potentially infinite and impossible to discuss comprehensively. Also, there is the problem of ambiguity of most changes. Whatever new technology is introduced, some people will welcome it and some people will object to it (Schwartz & Gibb, 1999).

The first and most general observation is that IT is increasingly becoming an agent of change. The way we act and interact seems to change because of the use of technology. Some of the buzzwords of business theory of the last few years are closely linked to IT. One example would be business process reengineering/redesign, which proposes that businesses should reinvent themselves and redesign their processes according to technical possibilities (cf. Turner, 1998). Another example is the idea of the "virtual organisation," where the borders between and within classical organisations dissolve, and organisational units are created for certain tasks and only exist for the duration of the task (cf. Pennings, 1998).

Critics of these ideas might point out that they are just intellectual fashions and often do not live up to their promises. This is not the place to weigh these claims. However, it is clear that these ideas, whether well-grounded or just fads, do have a real impact on the way the economy is organised. Spectacular examples such as the French Vivendi, a gas and water supplier turned media conglomerate (and now going bankrupt), the German Mannesmann, a steel producer turned biggest German mobile phone operator (before it was sold to Vodafone), or the American Enron, an energy supplier turned virtual market-place (before it went bankrupt), prove that the changes are real enough. Technology and organisation are closely intertwined, not only on the meso level of the organisation, but also on the macro level of the economy. Even though the dot.com bubble has burst and most of the hype has gone, e-commerce and e-business are here to stay. The advantages of reduced transaction and agency cost, combined with a high degree of customer convenience and service potential, make sure that many markets will continue to develop in the direction of e-commerce. Since every organisational change has the potential to affect someone's moral rights and obligations, it can also be seen as an object of responsibility. Among the specific problems one can count the change in the nature of work, unemployment caused by rationalisation, the power shifts discussed above, and many more. The social changes that ICT engenders on all levels of the economy must therefore be counted among the reasons for responsibility because of IS.

The changes caused by IS are not confined to the area of economic activity in a narrow sense. Another area that has the potential to change many of our institutions and the way society is organised is the use of IT in state, government, and administration. This field, which is usually discussed under the heading of "e-government," deals with the way societies use new technologies in their processes of government and administration. Many governments from national to municipal now offer some of their services on the Internet or are at least considering doing so. In many Western states, for example, citizens can file their tax returns or receive information electronically. This can obviously lead to new problems:

- How can the state guarantee the privacy of the data it receives?
- For which purposes can the state use the data?
- Can information given for tax purposes be used to find parents who do not pay alimony or who at the same time get social welfare payments?
- How does the state authenticate the users of the new services?

Apart from these rather technical questions, there are also some issues involving the very legitimacy of the state. Here, the use of IT can be described as having positive as well as negative effects. On the one hand the widespread use of IT and especially the Internet promises new possibilities of participation in government that so far were impossible. Groups of interested citizens can be included in decision processes, they can create national and international special interest groups, and generally a new dimension in the flow of information can be realised. On the other hand there is the danger that those parts of society that are excluded from the new technologies will be further marginalised or that a technical bias in the perception of reality could influence what topics are considered relevant.[22] Again, businesses and managers are not the only stakeholders in the process, but they need to be aware of them because they are among the stakeholders. Furthermore, commercial interests are increasingly shaping the development of technology, which in turn can have repercussions on the legitimacy of e-government.

This section was meant to demonstrate that there is a multitude of ways in which IS can become the reason for the ascription of responsibility. A manager confronted with this list of issues and with the normative problems that build its background might feel overburdened. How is any one human being expected to take the multitude of problems into account and react responsibly? This is exactly the problem of the traditional approach to responsibility, and it is where the reflective approach can offer some directions. One of the strengths of reflective responsibility as it was introduced here is that the manager trying to act responsibly does not have to be aware of all of the aspects that are relevant to the decision or action in question. In order to act responsibly, the manager must answer to those who are affected. This implies that the manager tries to identify those parties and is willing to communicate with them and consider their viewpoints. All of the details that were discussed so far will then emerge insofar as they are relevant to the specific situation. This also facilitates dealing with the problem that the issues we have discussed tend to be related among each other.

As an example of the relationship between different normative questions in IS, let us return to privacy/surveillance. While privacy is a multi-faceted problem in its own right, it is also closely related to other problems, not least of all to those problems that were discussed in this section. Privacy, for example, can be framed in terms of power, intellectual property, or social issues. The invasion of employee privacy by the employer is very clearly a use of power, which can be interpreted quite well in Foucauldian terms. Surveillance of employee Internet access or email use, especially when the employee is not certain whether she is being monitored, is a good example for the interpretation of Foucault in IS. Feeling watched permanently with the possibility of being punished for infraction of rules is the definition of the Panopticon. Of course other questions of power also play a role: Who has the power to start surveillance? What power do employees have to stop it or to monitor the monitors? Similarly, privacy is related to intellectual property. If we take a strong approach to intellectual property, then the result can be that everybody owns all information concerning themselves. This would translate into people's right to control who can use what information about them for what purpose. For an employer wanting to monitor his employees, this would mean that it would be an infringement of property rights to use information about them without their consent. Therefore, a company using technical means of surveillance on its employees could be said to act in a self-contradictory fashion if it insists on a strong protection of its intellectual property rights in other respects. And finally, privacy can of course also be seen in the light of the social repercussions it produces. The way a society deals with privacy is an expression of its values, but it can also change its values.

Coming back to our example of the CIO who has to make the decision whether or not to introduce surveillance software, we see that this is not a decision where the responsibilities that may result from it can easily be estimated in advance. This is why a traditional approach is bound to fail. Trying to realise a reflective approach, however, does not have to deal with this problem because it is by definition open and able to accommodate differing views. The discourse between the stakeholders allows the determination of the relevant subjects, the corresponding objects and instances, as well as the other determinants. Initiating a responsibility discourse therefore requires, first of all, the willingness to go ahead with it and then to accept the results. It is important to note that such a responsibility discourse may produce more than just one ascription. In our example the immediately affected parties would be the CIO herself, the employees, and higher management. Additionally one could see as affected the shareholders, customers, regulatory bodies, and many more. Starting a discourse with the immediately affected persons might lead to several ascriptions. The CIO, for example, might be held responsible for the technical proficiency of the surveillance measures and for making sure that it is done according to rules. Management could be held responsible for the supervision, while a new body or institution could be created charged with the task of creating rules for acceptable surveillance. The CIO might now be held responsible for assembling this new body and chairing it. It is easy to see that we could continue this imaginary case study further. What is important to understand is that these ascriptions, while they may be plausible, might happen this way, but they might also look completely different. It is impossible to foresee the material form of the resulting ascription.

What also becomes clear is that despite the effort involved in initiating the process of ascription and despite the possibility of failure, this reflective approach to responsibility is not only viable, it is in many situations the only recourse someone who wants to act responsibly has. Discursive participation of stakeholders offers the biggest possible resource of knowledge and expertise, thereby overcoming as far as possible the limitations of knowledge, power, and causality of traditional ascription. It thereby relieves the individual to the point that it regains its ability to act. In this sense responsibility is in fact the answer to the normative problems of modernity because it allows addressing the normative problems caused by risk and complexity without requiring the strong standards of most other ethical theories. The formal idea of reflective responsibility can therefore offer a promising approach with regard to normative problems caused by IS, where other approaches fail. Having shown this, we will shift our emphasis toward the future aspect of responsibility under the heading of responsibility for IS.

Reflective Responsibility for Information Systems

Responsibility for IS differs from responsibility because of the fact that it relates to intentional activity with regard to IS—it is prospective rather than retrospective. That means that responsibility for IS looks at what managers would think of first when asked about their responsibility. How is a system designed, how is it maintained, how do business processes link in with technology, and who are the persons to whom all of these things are ascribed? The distinction between responsibility because of and responsibility for IS is slightly artificial because the limit is unclear. If responsibility for a system is not properly discharged, that can lead to responsibility because of the results of this negligence. On the other hand the experience of being ascribed responsibility because of IS will in many cases lead to decisions that aim at institutionalising responsibility for it.

The difference between the two aspects runs roughly analogous to the distinction between prospective and retrospective responsibility, which was discussed in general terms in Section 5.2.6. Accordingly, there is also the difference between transitive and reflexive ascription. While responsibility because of IS as discussed in the last chapter tends to focus on things that have happened and tries to establish a responsibility relationship to third parties, responsibility for IS focuses on the future and will therefore have to rely in a higher degree on the voluntary assumption of the responsibility in question. Again, it is important to stress that these two aspects tend to go hand in hand and that they are mutually dependent. Nevertheless, the analytical distinction makes sense because it allows the identification of implications that become clearer when one concentrates only on one aspect.

The field of responsibility for IS is related to or contains many aspects that cannot be discussed here. There is, for example, the entire question of political responsibility for IS. States and governments make decisions that determine how technological development will progress or what sort of technology is likely to succeed. These decisions are made under a great deal of uncertainty because technological development is hard to estimate for more than a short time span. There is a whole field of science that deals with this sort of decision influencing technological development, not only IT development, which goes under the name of technology assessment.

For the purposes of the text, however, we will concentrate on the intermediate range of technology use in organisations and thus on the mangers' view. Managers' responsibility for IT in business can be divided according to several criteria. One could distinguish internal from external responsibility or look at the temporal horizon. Responsibility for IS in the short-term sense is just one example of responsibility for certain fields or areas of business. In this sense every line manager is responsible for the correct working and adequate servicing of the systems in his or her area. More interesting is the long-term responsibility for IS, because this is where the reflective approach can help matters most.

The prospective aspect of responsibility for IS can be most usefully applied at those stages where the actual manifestation of information systems is still unclear and where, therefore, considerations of responsibility can affect the greatest changes. This is in the early stages of the systems analysis, design, or development. If a decision has to be made about the use of IT, about the acquisition of new systems, the upgrading, or any other change, then it is a direct consequence of the theory of reflective responsibility that the ethical and social consequences must be considered as early as possible. Rogerson (1998, p. 16) names the deskilling of jobs, redundancy, and the break-up of social groupings as examples of what project management should think of early on. There are again the same two arguments for this prospective action that we have encountered before. On the one hand it is in the business interest of any organisation to make sure that its investments have a high probability of success. On the other hand it is an imperative, resulting from the idea of responsibility that the process of answering to those who are affected by a decision to be taken as early as possible. Since the first argument comes natural to businesses, we will put more stress on the second one. The early stages of systems analysis and design should not be misunderstood as pure technicalities where ethics enters only in the form of externally determined specifications, if at all. General managers and IT managers who hold positions of responsibility for system design must be aware that this responsibility expressly also covers an ethical angle. That means that they have to be aware of the fact that a good and appropriate systems analysis and recommendations for design makes it "far less likely that there will be either practical or ethical problems with the resultant system" (Langford, 1999b, p. 68). At least as important is that they recognise the fact that the process of analysis and design is already value-laden before it begins. This refers partly to the last section, to the relationship of IT and fundamental philosophical questions. The questions that are asked before and during the design process, which naturally determine which answers can be given, depend on the worldview of the persons involved. They therefore necessarily imprint this worldview or life-world on the answer that can be given to them. The myth of amoral computing must therefore be destroyed before the planning process can start properly. Managers and technicians must be aware that "design often involves ethical decisions based on social context and social values, and the technology transmits or embodies the value decisions (and assumptions) made during the design process" (Huff & Martin, 1995, p. 82).

If this is realised, then it also becomes clear that solitary design by individuals or small groups of experts will run the risk of idiosyncrasy. The ideas that were presented earlier as models for reflective responsibility, namely Habermasian discourse or the stakeholder approach, will then automatically enter the picture as viable alternatives. In order to overcome one-sided views and conceptions, the affected parties should participate and they should do so as early as possible.

The discussion of reflective responsibility for IS must necessarily remain on a rather abstract level because by its very nature, the fact that it concerns future developments, it cannot go into details. However, there are two areas about which one can make observations from this general point of view. These concern the reliability of computers and the resulting necessity to design systems for fault tolerance on the one hand, and questions of the framework in which responsibility can be realised on the other hand. These will now be discussed under the headings of reliability and fault tolerance.

Many of the moral problems produced by computers and information systems are caused by their not functioning as intended. Examples range from the computer crash that wipes out a day's work or more, to incorrect data in FBI files, to failing security features in nuclear power plants. Business examples could include proprietary databases whose integrity is breached by hackers or lack of order fulfilment caused by faulty customer files. This sort of problem is an object of reflective responsibility for IS because it can at least be partly addressed by forward-looking use of technology. Some solutions can be found in the design of information systems, but in order to account for them, the subject of responsibility first has to be aware of them.

A first question to ask is therefore how reliable information systems are. It turns out that this relatively simple question is not simple to answer. For many other potentially safety-critical technologies, we have clear rules for the evaluation and judgment concerning reliability. The engineer responsible for the development of a bridge, for example, would be able to clearly state how much weight that bridge can carry, for how long it is designed to last, and other factors of reliability. The same sort of exactness is rarely if ever achieved for computers. The reasons for this are manifold. One of them is a lack of a clear and agreed-upon language for the communication about the subject. Risks of software or hardware can often best be expressed in statistical terms, and these are frequently translated in misleading or false statements of a non-statistical nature (cf. Corbato, 1995).

Another problem leading to fundamental problems with the reliability of computers and information systems is their systemic nature and the resulting complexity (Littlewood & Stringy, 1995). One reason for the complexity of computers is the interaction of hardware and software. Reasons for failure can be found in either one and also in a lack of compatibility of the two. An added difficulty can also be human error such as incorrect equipment, operation, or maintenance. System failure can be caused by unusual combinations of problems from several of these categories (Borning, 1995). Accidents are usually caused by complex interaction between various components and activities, and it is mostly a mistake to try to attribute them to a single cause (Leveson & Turner, 1995).

There are many other reasons for a lack of reliability of software caused by complexity. One human-centred problem is the cooperation of people from different functional areas with different backgrounds. This sort of inter-disciplinary collaboration can lead to misunderstandings that influence systems design and can only be detected in later stages (Rogerson, 1998). A more technical cause of problems is that traditional laws of engineering do not necessarily apply to software. Software is not linear, and a reliability test cannot rely on the interpolation of testing results. Therefore, if one wanted to be certain to exclude faults completely, one would have to test every single combination of input and output and check whether the results are correct. This sort of check is impossible even for relatively small programs, because the permutation of inputs and outputs are astronomical and a complete check for most programs would be impossible even if one used the combined power of all computers. What makes matters worse is that even if one could check a program completely, the identification of errors and their rectification would most likely introduce new errors so that after every cycle of checking and correcting, one would have to start it over again. For programs with between 100,000 and 2 million lines of code, "the chances of introducing a severe error during the correction of original errors is so large that only a small fraction of the original errors should be corrected" (Forester & Morrison, 1994, p. 121).

An added problem is that even if one could solve all of these problems, the guaranteed correctness of the program would only refer to the relationship between the underlying model and program. Whether the underlying model is correct and adequate is a question that cannot even be addressed by these measures. Some of the most spectacular malfunctions of computer systems were caused by faulty models. In 1960, for example, a newly installed early warning system used by NATO to detect Warsaw Pact attacks indicated that the United States was under nuclear attack by Soviet missiles with a probability of 99.9%. The reason for this wrong report turned out to be the rising moon, which the Ballistic Missile Early Warning System had misinterpreted (cf. Borning, 1995). This sort of mistake is impossible to completely rule out by prior testing because the malfunction was not caused by faulty programming, but by an inadequate model of reality. Users and managers of IS must therefore be aware of the fact that even by using new technologies such as program verification, programs can never be "proven correct"; in other words, one cannot be sure that they will do what is intended (Smith, 1995).

Reflective responsibility for information systems will have to accept the fact that absolute reliability of computers is impossible to guarantee. The reflexivity requires that expected results of actions be considered and that the realisability of a responsibility ascription be part of the ascription process. A simplistic statement requiring managers to take responsibility for the full functionality of information systems could. in the light of the difficulties with ensuring functionality. not count as reflectively responsible. Reflective and prospective responsibility for IS will therefore have to accept the reality of systems faults and try to find a way to deal with them. One way to do this is to design fault tolerance into systems. There are different definitions and realisations of fault tolerance. On the one hand there are technical definitions. These tend to stress that the functionality of systems must be retained even in cases where parts fail (Kornwachs, 1996). For information systems this is a relevant viewpoint because it takes into account the nature of the systems. A technical way of achieving this is to build in redundancy. One can have different design teams develop several versions of a program in the hope that the teams will not make the same errors (Littlewood & Stringy, 1995). Another way to achieve fault tolerance is to limit the criticality of any one part. That means that critical parts of a system should be constructed with as little complexity as possible, that backup systems are still less complex, and that main and backup systems operate completely independently.

While such methods are certainly necessary and it appears to be highly desirable that they be implemented in safety-critical systems such as control systems of nuclear power plants, airplanes, or military hardware, users and managers should be aware of their limitations. No formal proof can guarantee the reliability of systems, and even the best laid-out improvements of safety features can fail. In fact, the continuous attempts to improve safety can themselves become liabilities (Borning, 1995).

An important point for managers and technicians to realise is that the reliance on technology and the belief in its infallibility can have dire consequences. Human beings are unable to supervise and control dynamic systems without mistakes. Therefore, the hope that mistakes in complex systems can be ruled out by human supervision is doomed to failure (Bergmann, 1996). It is doubtful whether the distinction between technical and human errors makes any sense at all. One can argue that most if not all faults are caused by human action (De George, 1998; Leveson & Turner, 1995). The attempts of exculpation of technical and socio-technical systems on the ground of singular human errors, which one can usually hear after technological catastrophes, make little sense in this light.

What is necessary is the acceptance of the old wisdom of *errare humanum est*. If decision makers go so far and accept their fallibility, which as we have seen is another characteristic of reflective responsibility, then the question is: How do we deal with the risks and lack of reliability of all technical systems and especially of information systems? There is clearly no easy answer to this, but the idea of reflective responsibility can suggest an approach. The first step is to identify the moral question of the use of risky technology as such. References to technology, to fault tolerance, and to specific problems can be used to conceal the moral nature of the question. If technology is used and if it has the potential of affecting people's lives and rights, then this is a moral issue. It has to be recognised and treated as such. Reflective responsibility is helpful in this regard because the first step in ascribing it is the identification of the relevant reality. That means that the fact of the matter must be addressed as well as the normative foundations. The next point where the theory of reflective responsibility is helpful in dealing with technical systems is its emphasis on the participation of the affected parties. Solipsistic decisions concerning complex systems are likely to fail because they tend to neglect relevant aspects. Using a participatory approach as suggested by reflective responsibility can overcome the problem. Finally, reflective responsibility is aware of its own fallibility, which is another important aspect. It indicates that even under ideal circumstances, the entire process of ascription may fail, which in the case of prospective responsibility for technological systems can mean that the system fails and that unforeseen results appear. This realisation leads on to another level of responsibility ascription, namely to the question of who is responsible for the distribution of responsibilities. What that means is that in view of the fallibility of responsibility, it must be ruled out that responsibility can be assumed merely on the grounds of personal interest. There must be institutions that ensure that responsibility can only be assumed or ascribed by parties that are competent to do so. Of course we are surrounded by such institutions. A middle manager of an electricity supplier cannot take responsibility for building a nuclear power plant. In the case of business information technology, however, such meta-responsibilities are not yet established. Who is responsible for the way technical development will go? Who makes steering and controlling decisions and on what grounds? Right now there seems to be an implicit consensus in the industrialised world that market interests should shape the future development of information technology and its use. It is unclear up to what point these forces have the legitimate right to control where social, political, or legal limits are or should be. This responsibility of a higher order is something managers of IS must be aware of, and in order to act responsibly, they have to assume their role in it as experts and decision makers.

Responsibility as a social construction needs to take more into account than just the nature of its object, which was just discussed as the fallibility of information systems. It also needs to take into account its own social nature. Managers who have responsibilities for the use of computers and information technology must ensure that the ascription process can be realised, that it has consequences, and that it follows the agreed-upon rules. We are not going to dwell on this point for too long because it is mostly the specific application to IS of the general directions that resulted from the analysis of the concept of reflective responsibility in Chapter 6. It does seem useful, however, to recall what these consequences are and how they apply to IS.

Before one can discuss the framework of responsibility for IS, one must recognise its nature. That means its characteristics as an ascription must be established and, as a result, its social nature must be accepted. If this is the case and the manager or group in question agrees to accept responsibility for IS, then there is a multitude of aspects that need to be covered. These start with external factors for which managers have no direct responsibility, but which can be partly ascribed to them. This refers to the social framework as it is provided by society and the state. Many of the questions regarding responsibility matters in IS are regulated or can at least be subject to official regulation. Questions of health, security, ergonomic design, etc., are regulated by law in most societies. For reflective responsibility this means that there is a normative basis for ascriptions. The first step of clarifying the issues can in many cases be greatly facilitated by such official social rules. While these rules will in most cases be part of the responsibility environment that the actors have to adapt to, they are at the same time an object of responsibility from the reflective point of view. If official regulations can clarify the ascription, then reflective responsibility demands that these regulations be realised. For the individual manager, this can mean that from her primary responsibility for IS, a secondary responsibility for the collaboration in the development of social rules can arise. An example might be a manager responsible for the implementation of a new system who finds that safety standards of a certain type of device are insufficient or do not exist. In this case a new sort of moral responsibility for the development and implementation of adequate safety standards can flourish. That can mean that the manager provides means to professional bodies that define such standards, that she collaborates as an expert on the development, or that she uses her role as a citizen in a democracy to effect similar change. The framework of responsibility, when viewed from the reflective viewpoint, therefore also becomes an object of responsibility.

This responsibility for the framework, for the realisability of responsibility, of course goes beyond the social and political frameworks. There are a great number of issues that could be counted under the heading of "framework" which are placed within the classical areas of responsibility of management. That means that managers are aware of them or at least could be aware of them, and that they have the power to influence them. Included Among are those areas where morality and economic reasoning coincide such as the question of efficiency. Efficiency is an economic good, which on a business level usually stands for the adherence to the economic principle of minimisation or maximisation. Either way, the amount of input is to be optimised with regard to the amount of output. This is not only an economic aim, but it is also a moral good (cf. Donaldson & Dunfee, 1999). Efficiency is morally relevant because it is the basis of wealth. The ethical defence of capitalism usually emphasises this aspect, the fact that markets produce the maximum welfare which can in turn be seen as the basis of a moral life.

While efficiency as management's responsibility is probably hardly contentious because it clearly benefits everybody involved (even though it can of course come into conflict with other values such as employment), there are other framework issues where management needs to become active. We have seen before that one of the conclusions to be drawn from the idea of reflective responsibility is that it has to consider the viability of ascriptions and that this in many cases will require the introduction or maintenance of institutions. These institutions should ensure that the ascription of responsibility stands a chance of being realisable and acceptable. In other words, they should help to increase the viability of responsibility. This can be done by improving the clarity of all of the dimensions involved. An important aspect of this will be the improvement of accountability. Accountability is of high importance in information systems because their systemic nature—the problem of the "many hands" that design and use them, and the combination of hardware, software, and people—often make it hard to determine which person or group caused which result. Institutions of accountability are meant to overcome this problem by establishing clear guidelines for the determination of causalities. It is hard to say what these institutions would look like in any particular circumstances, but examples are easy to imagine. They can range from organisational measures such as clear job descriptions, and understandable outlines of tasks over technical measures such as well-defined levels of access to broader questions of organisational culture, which determines whether accountability is taken serious at all. Also, accountability should be recognised as something that is not an end in itself and not an absolute entity, but something that itself can only survive in a social environment and under norms that are conducive to its development (Johnson & Mulvey, 1995). Accountability and responsibility in the sense the words are used here are therefore mutually dependent.

A last important aspect with regards to the framework of responsibility for IS and accountability are side effects. These pose a serious problem for responsibility ascriptions because they complicate the process due to the lack of intention that is inherent to them. Traditionally, in law as well as in ethics, the subject of responsibility had to show an intention, it had to fulfil the *mens rea* requirement in order to be held responsible. Side effects are defined by their not being intended, and therefore responsibility ascriptions for them tend to be difficult. There are basically two ways of dealing with this problem. On the one hand one can define responsibility without intention. This is what the legal doctrine of strict liability does. In strict liability, producers of goods are held liable for damage caused by these goods, independent of their knowledge of defects or their intention of selling them defectively. On the other hand one can attempt to realise responsibility by removing side effects from their obscurity and by explicitly making them objects of responsibility. The two approaches are clearly related. The doctrine of strict liability aims at improving the responsibility of producers for side effects and thus implies that it is possible to move these effects to the centre of attention. Managers trying to anticipate responsibility for side effects can do so by using different organisational and institutional measures. The most important step is the raising of consciousness that side effects exist and that they are considered to be objects of responsibility. The realisation of responsibility by discursive methods, by stakeholder analysis, or by any other means that includes a considerable number of affected parties is a good way of doing this. The more people who have a chance of participating in discourses about decisions, the higher the probability of something unexpected being detected before it becomes serious. The downside is of course that decision processes become unwieldy and, in a worst-case scenario, do not happen at all any more. It is therefore part of managers' duty to weigh these considerations and decide to which point such discourses can be led. This then brings us to another aspect of reflective responsibility, to the faculty of judgment which is necessary for the successful ascription of responsibility. It becomes clear that managers who want to act responsibly and who are in a position of doing so need this capacity in order be successful.

The aspect of prospective responsibility for computers and information systems in a business environment is by definition highly complex because it deals with developments that are still to come. However, the two points discussed here—the recognition of the fallibility of information systems and the emphasis on framework and institutions—can go some way in helping managers identify areas where they should become active. One important aspect of the framework is that it has to build a bridge to the retrospective view, to responsibility because of IS. Institutions should not only clarify who should look out for what, but they must also make it clear what the consequences for neglecting these institutions are. Institutional and organisational rules put in place should make both of the temporal aspects clear to the affected parties.

Apart from the two temporal aspects of the relationship between responsibility and IS, there is a third aspect which aims less at the establishment of responsibility ascriptions but rather at the impact that IS has on the processes of responsibility itself. This is what will be discussed as "responsibility through IS" in the next section.

Reflective Responsibility Through Information Systems

While the last two sections were used to analyse what it can mean to ascribe responsibility because of and for information technology in a business setting, this one will look at how the use of computers and IT change the nature of these ascriptions. It is obvious that the use of different media of communication can change the character of communication, its moral and informational content, and consequently also the character of responsibility. However, it is less clear what the relevant mechanisms of change are and how they are to be evaluated. The answer to these questions depends on the choice of theory used for the description of communication. In order to demonstrate the effects of IT on communication and responsibility, we will use the Habermasian theory of communication because it is already well introduced in this text and because it has already been demonstrated that it is a useful theory with regards to responsibility due to the structural similarity between the two.

According to Habermas, human beings communicate in order to survive and prosper in the world. Communicative action serves these aims, but it goes beyond that. Communicative action is the highest form of human action (compared to pragmatic and strategic action), because it recognises the others not only as objects of manipulation but as subjects or, to use a Kantian expression, as ends in themselves. We all live in our respective life-worlds which form the horizon of our realities. These life-worlds, however, are not purely idiosyncratic, but they are constructed and modified using communication. That means that our life-worlds are always there as a sort of background conviction which only becomes relevant in that moment where they lead to an impediment to collective action. If two or more life-worlds (more exactly: aspects of life-worlds) collide and thereby change their status from an unconscious background resource to an issue of contention, then we come to the point where discourses become necessary. Discourses in the Habermasian sense are discussions that take place in an ideal speech situation or at least under the conscious effort to produce circumstances that resemble the ideal speech situation as far as possible. In order to achieve an ideal speech situation, the participants should:

> *"endeavour to ensure that (a) all voices in any way relevant can get a hearing, and that (b) the best arguments we have in our present state of knowledge are brought to bear, and that (c) disagreement or agreement on the part of the participants follows only from the force of the better argument and no other force."* (Habermas, quoted in Ess. 1996b, p. 216)

Every statement made in a discourse is implicitly accompanied by three validity claims: truth, rightness, and authenticity.[23] That means that whenever something is said in a discourse (or outside of discourse as well, but in everyday circumstances it may be less obvious), then the speaker implies that the proposition is true, that it is normatively right and acceptable, and that she means what she says, that she is authentic or truthful. It is these three validity claims that necessitated this brief repetition of Habermas' theory because they allow a good insight into how computers and information technology impact on the process of responsibility ascription.

Validity claims in the Habermasian sense are important for responsibility ascriptions because they constitute the first step in conforming with the idea of reflective responsibility, which is clarity of the notion. As was shown in Section 6.3, the first and most important step in ensuring an open and effective ascription of responsibility is to clarify what exactly is involved. That means that the dimensions must be identified as well as the relevant norms and factual circumstances. This is where validity claims enter the picture. The clarification of all of these points is only necessary in those cases where they are controversial. Controversial claims, however, need to be argued for or against. These arguments are based on validity claims. The outcome of the arguments determine how responsibility is ascribed, to whom, with which consequences, etc. It is therefore clear that if IT affects validity claims, it also affects responsibility ascriptions.

The use of computers and IT can affect validity claims in different ways. First of all they change the starting position with regards to claims by affecting our life-world. The shared life-worlds in western industrialised societies nowadays contain entities which 50 years ago would have appeared ridiculous, such as cellular phones or virtual reality. That means that our shared reality, changes, and accordingly our claims to truth, which are based on our reality, change as well. Another way in which computers change claims to truth is by influencing our epistemological criteria. According to Postman (1992, p. 115), the recourse to computers has become the modern-day equivalent to "it is God's will" and has roughly the same consequences, namely immunising statements against criticism.

Another aspect of the changes of validity claims incurred by the use of IT are the anthropological effects discussed earlier. Humans are seen as computers or computers are viewed as humans. Both views affect the basis of our assumptions about humanity. Our view of humanity, on the other hand, is the basis of responsibility ascriptions. This leads back to the conditions that subjects have to fulfill, and it is clear that humans, viewed as information processing systems, will not be considered as free and thus will generally fail to be responsible.

Apart from these fundamental ways in which IT can change responsibility ascriptions by affecting fundamental notions, there are also some effects it can have just by acting as a medium of communication. This thought is easily understood by looking at the two most important innovations in computer-mediated communication—hypertext and email. Email is not equivalent with other means of communication because it crosses the line between several of them. On the one hand it is similar to written communication as we find it in letters or books. On the other hand the rapidity of exchange and the ubiquity of its use lets it appear closer to face-to-face or telephone communication (O'Leary & Brasher, 1996). In some respects the characteristics of emails make it an ideal medium for the exchange of validity claims:

> *"In terms of argument patterns, the rhythm of email and mailing list exchange encourages opposing manifestos and summaries but also quick movement from what you just said to the arguments and presuppositions behind it. Positions get examined from a variety of angles, and there will be demand for backing on specific points. This makes email a good medium for the kind of dialogue that Habermas speaks of, which demands justification for each speech act and inquires into the validity and sincerity of claims."* (Kolb, 1996, p. 16f)

At the same time email threatens classical structures that were erected with the purpose of guaranteeing the truth of claims. In the paper-based world, there are structures such as peer review or editors which aim at ensuring that published material adheres to certain standards. Mullins (1996, p. 276) refers to these structures as "gatekeeping functions." While it has always been possible to circumvent such structures, it is nevertheless true that this was only possible by investing a considerable effort. Therefore we are used to a certain standard of written texts and these have a highly plausible prima facie claim to truth. For email this additional filter does not exist, and it therefore again transcends the division of written and spoken communication with a direct impact on validity claims.

The second example for the effect of IT on validity claims is hypertext. The introduction of hypertext is probably one of the main reasons for the success of the World Wide Web. Clicking on a link and thereby moving to another document, another thought, another thread of discussion is easy even for those who know little of computers. At the same time it seems to appeal to us, maybe because it is closer to our way of thinking than traditional long and linear texts. It seems that hypertext in this respect reflects other social developments which go away from long and strenuous activities toward shorter and more entertaining ones. A good example of this trend is to be found in e-commerce and its approach to customers. Consumers have to deal with a flood of information that they cannot possibly process and most of which is therefore ignored. The emphasis in e-commerce is therefore increasingly on catching the customer's attention, and one can frequently hear talk of attention as the central resource in the information age (cf. Zerdick et al., 2001; Liebl, 1999). While it is not easy to see what exactly the effects of such developments on social relations are, it is clear that they can impact on real discourses and on our evaluation of validity claims.

On the other hand, the use of computers and information technology offers new chances for responsibility ascriptions. New interest groups can form and new objects of responsibility can be identified. While this argument is often used to demonstrate the democratic nature of new technologies, especially the Internet, it is also applicable to an organisational setting. Group collaboration systems, for example, can help increase communication between members of one organisation and thereby stimulate new areas of responsibility. This is often described as the purpose of collaboration systems even if the term responsibility is not used.

While information technology can help identify dimensions of responsibility and the formation of interests, it can also be helpful in conducting responsibility ascriptions. If we continue to employ Habermas' theory of communication to responsibility claims, then one of the conclusions is that real discourses, which can be responsibility discourses, need to approximate ideal discourses in order to produce valid results. From the point of view of reflective responsibility, the validity and viability of ascriptions is important. Therefore real responsibility discourses should be as close to the ideal speech situation as possible. It is possible to employ information technology for these purposes. According to Lyytinen and Hirschheim (1988, p. 24f), information systems can have emancipatory effects. They can make social relationships more symmetrical, thereby reducing organisational power, and they can allow new interpretations of data by redistributing access. Empirical research in systems which have the express purpose of facilitating communication between hierarchies, for example group decision support systems, suggests that some features of computer-mediated communication can live up to these emancipatory promises (cf. Laudon & Laudon, 1999). An important factor here seems to be anonymity. By using anonymous communication in computer-mediated discussions, real-life power differences can be overcome and discussions can be held in a more detached and objective atmosphere. This allows participants to voice their opinions who would otherwise be kept out of the discussion. Since the equality of the speakers and their mutual recognition is a key part of Habermas' ideal speech situation, one can conclude that the use of IT can facilitate discourses and help approximate them to ideal discourses.

There are of course also downsides to responsibility ascriptions by discourses mediated by computers and IT. A first counterargument could use the same starting point as the last one and argue that IT has the opposite effect, that it moves discussions away from ideal discourses. This can happen in several ways. Firstly, IT-mediated discussions require technical access and competencies in the use of technologies. The majority of humanity has neither and is therefore excluded from them. But also in an organisational setting where management could ensure equal access, the ability and willingness to use technologies varies and thereby changes the power that individuals can wield in their social setting. Secondly, technology-mediated discourses also offer the possibility of hidden manipulations of power. Group decisions support systems (GDSSs), for example, tend to have a central mediator who controls the entire communication. This allows her to set the agenda and to rule which contributions are admitted and which ones are not. Similarly, many other technologies allow manipulations of communication of which the participants are not aware.

Another argument against the use of technology in responsibility ascriptions is the formal structure of information systems. It is true, particularly of information systems used in businesses, that they are rather fixed and that they thereby violate some of the ground rules for discourses, the chance to express opinions through argumentation. Also, commercial information systems usually do not aim at testing people's opinions but aim at facilitating action. In this way they can produce particular social relations (cf. Lyytinen & Hirschheim, 1988, p. 24). This happens because information gets objectified in information systems, and therefore discourses and responsibility ascriptions get frozen and objectified too (cf. Ulrich, 2001).

Another problem with the use of information technology in ascribing responsibility is information overload. Even under the best of circumstances, where IT helps identify the dimensions, clarify the rules, and facilitate discourse, it comes up against the limitation of human reason. Humans can only process a limited amount of information, and the information available through technological means manifolds this amount. The old axiom of economics that more of a good is always better therefore is not applicable to information (Kolb, 1996).

Most of these points refer to the effect of the use of computers and information technology on responsibility and discourses in general. They are nevertheless easily applied to business or organisational responsibility ascriptions. Going back to the central idea of this chapter, to the question of what managers can learn from the theory of reflective responsibility with regard to IS, it is easy to see that the aspect of responsibility through IS is quite ambivalent. Managers who want to be responsible, who want to facilitate or realise ascriptions of responsibility, will in many cases have to rely on the medium of ICT for this purpose. This last section has shown that the use of this medium is not neutral, but can improve or degrade the quality and thus the acceptability of responsibility ascriptions. This knowledge is important because it affects the viability of responsibility and therefore also its ethical acceptability.

THE ADVANTAGES OF REFLECTIVE RESPONSIBILITY IN INFORMATION SYSTEMS

The business use of information technology produces ethical and moral problems. For these problems responsibility can and will be ascribed. There is no possibility to opt out. Whether the responsibility is of legal, moral, role, or other nature, whether its goal is punishment or reward, whether it aims at retribution or education, responsibility is inevitable. In the light of this, decision makers will ask themselves how they can deal with the responsibilities that are heading in their direction. The traditional approach of defining responsibilities from an *ex ante* and solipsist viewpoint and hoping that these will be enough has a low probability of success. It will also overburden managers who are necessarily incapable of finding out all of the responsibilities that they will be subjected to. The alternative is to actively search for the participation of the stakeholders in a discursive manner.

We have reiterated the advantages of reflective responsibility several times, and we will try to summarise these advantages now for a last time. Reflective responsibility allows managers (who are at the centre of attention in this chapter, but the argument is of course not limited to managers) to transcend the limits that usually preclude individuals from successfully assuming responsibility in a modern society. This modern society, characterised by risk, uncertainty, and contingency, structured and governed by social and socio-technical systems, does not allow individuals to assume responsibility for important developments because individuals lack the knowledge and the power to influence them. This is true for societal developments, but it goes down to relatively minor decisions in an organisational context. One part of this development is caused by the change from uncertainty to risk, by the fact that the reach of our responsibilities grows with our knowledge while the individual does not have the ability to catch up with all of the knowledge that is available. New social actors such as corporations or NGOs gain in importance, but traditionally it is unclear in how far they can be responsible.

The solution to these problems that we developed in this book is the idea of reflective responsibility. Reflective responsibility emphasises the three features developed from a discussion of responsibility: openness, affinity to action, and a teleological background that aims at the improvement of our circumstances. The methodological trick of reflection, the attempt to apply these three features to the concept of responsibility, has allowed us to draw several conclusions regarding the application of responsibility. We were able to show that the idea of reflective responsibility is related to the stakeholder approach and the discursive approach that we find in contemporary business ethics. Reflexive responsibility was developed as a formal approach which has an ethical basis that relies on the answerability, on communication. It implies an ethical standpoint because it takes the stakeholder seriously.

Acting responsibly in our sense is therefore a moral thing to do, but it is at the same time a smart thing to do in an economic sense. While responsibility discourses do not offer the guarantee of success and may come at a steep price, they will often be the only way in which responsibility can be realised at all. Adhering to the formal structure of including stakeholders in a discourse about discussions will in many cases be the only way in which a manager can act responsibly. The reflective approach is not only moral, but it is also the most promising way of acquiring the necessary knowledge and participation to change things.

Furthermore, we have seen that the responsibility discourse will in most cases have to rely on certain characteristics of the participants and will most likely come to certain results. Responsibility discourses must rely not only on the willingness of the participants to participate, but also on a high level of prudence and good judgment. In the course of the discourse, the normative rules relevant to a specific case will be developed, but at the same time the application of these rules to given facts must be decided. Moral, legal, and other rules will play a part as well as cultural norms and understandings. Responsibility discourses in large multi-national organisations will therefore run into unexpected problems.

Among the results of these discourses, there will have to be clear structures that will allow the ascription of objects to subjects. Since this will happen in an environment of uncertainty, it is clear that part of the solution will consist of institutions that allow the ascription. These will be institutions that can have every form imaginable and will have the task of producing accountability. Accountability in this sense means that the preconditions of an ascription are cleared up. The discourse and resulting institutions will have to clarify, for example, what the temporal reach of a given ascription is, how far side effects will be considered, what sort of subject is admissible, etc.

Finally, reflective responsibility must take its own fallibility into account and keep in mind the modesty that lies at the root of the concept. One of the important features of reflective responsibility that distinguishes it from the traditional approaches is that the combination of consequentialism and the aim of the good life allows it to become active where there is a chance that it will lead to results that improve human life, independent of whether ascriptions are perfect and fully defined. It is this characteristic of reflective responsibility that allows us to overcome the traditional limitations by saying that an ascription that will most likely improve our lot is justified, even if we know that it is fallible and that we may have to retract to it later. During all of our attempts to ascribe responsibility, during the creation of institutions of accountability, during non-optimal discourses, this fact must remain present. The reason why the discursive process of reflective responsibility can produce any acceptable results at all, despite its inability to live up to the standards of discourse theory, is exactly this intellectual modesty.

Let us return for a last time to our central example in this book, to the question of privacy and surveillance. As was demonstrated earlier, the reflective approach allows the CIO, whom we have supposed to be the central subject, to combine different responsibility ascriptions based on the decision to introduce a surveillance system. We have seen that there is a multitude of different arguments that speak for and against such a system. An individual like our CIO would be hard pressed to identify all of the relevant angles and would most likely fail. The result would be that she might be able to live up to some ascriptions, but would be vulnerable to others because of a lack of awareness and preparation. To continue the example, we can now state that the reflective approach allows not only the identification of different subjects, objects, norms, and therefore different ascriptions. It also allows the combination of the different aspects discussed in this chapter, of responsibility because of, for, and through IS. If the process of responsibility ascription starts, which will include the discussion of the different validity claims, of truth, norms, and authenticity, then all of the aspects of responsibility will be covered. This means that not only the different possible subjects, norms, and objects are discussed, but also the temporal aspect, the question of what responsibility for past or future action means, and how the two are connected. In the context of the norms and sanctioning authority, the question of institutions will have to be addressed and institutions of accountability will be discussed to facilitate the ascription. A shared view of the good life, at least some aspects of it, will be necessary to come to any conclusion and the viability of the result requires that the process be open and lead to results. Finally, the fallibility of the process necessitates that it be open, that structures be put into place that allow the revision of results and the modification of ascriptions when the stakeholders' views change.

A CHECKLIST FOR MANAGERIAL RESPONSIBILITY IN INFORMATION SYSTEMS

In this chapter we have discussed three important aspects of responsibility and IS: responsibility because of, for, and through IS. The underlying idea was that management wants to act responsibly and asks how this can be done. It turned out that both of the temporal directions, prospective as well as retrospective, must be considered. Furthermore, the role of technology in the ascription is also of importance.

Given the communicative nature of responsibility, however, it proved to be impossible to deduce easy-to-follow rules that managers must simply adhere to. Responsibility ascriptions are complex social interactions that require many tacit skills such as prudence and judgment. They are not transformable into simple deontologies or codes of conduct. Managers who usually do not have a lot of training in moral philosophy may be disappointed by this, but philosophical ethics, as we have seen earlier, does not usually give clear-cut directions. However, from a point of view of reflective responsibility, it seems too weak an answer to managers wanting to know how to act responsibly if one just tells them to act on their judgment. We will therefore develop a list of aspects that are of relevance and that should be taken into account when acting responsibly. This list should not be misunderstood as a code of ethics that tells managers what to do or how to do it. Whichever definition of ethics one prefers, be it the German or the French as discussed earlier or any of a number of others, it is generally true that it cannot be codified. This is not to completely condemn codes of ethics, but it should be noted that such codes can only have a limited effect.[24] The checklist that we will introduce should rather be understood as something to be used by managers when visualising responsibility. The multitude of aspects discussed so far can easily lead to confusion and to the neglecting of important aspects. The checklist is therefore just a brief summary of the most important points discussed here. Its purpose is to remind people who want to act responsibly what can be of relevance and what aspects they may have to think of. It does not prescribe a certain way to act or any particular outcome. The point is to remind people who are involved in responsibility ascriptions which aspects can be important and thus how the processes can be formed to maximise their acceptability and viability.

The checklist is divided into six points, each of which is again divided further. The points will be demonstrated by questions which indicate what aspect should be the centre of attention for each of them. The attempt to answer the questions for a particular case should go a long way toward describing how responsibility can be discharged.

Clarity of the Notion

Is the idea of the ascription clear and is it comprehensible to all of the parties involved?

Social Construction/Ascription

Is the nature of the responsibility as a social construction recognised? Do the parties involved realise that it is a process of ascription?

Type

What type of responsibility ascription are we looking at? Is it a legal, a moral, a task-oriented ascription or another kind? Are we looking at a reflexive or a transitive ascription?

Norms

What sort or norm is going to be the basis for the ascription? Where does it come from, how is it justified? Is it acceptable to the affected parties?

Dimensions

Which are the dimensions, the central parts of the ascription?

Subject

Who or what is to be held responsible? Is the subject generally recognised as being able to assume responsibility? Is the subject an individual or a collective entity?

Object

What is the object for which responsibility is to be ascribed?

Instance

Who is to decide about the eventual outcome of the ascription? How are differences of opinion between the subject and those who ascribe responsibility to the subject overcome? Who determines the sanctions or rewards? Who enforces the ascription?

Conditions

Are the conditions for an ascription fulfilled? These refer to the subject, the object, and to the relationship between the two.

Freedom

Was the subject free to make the decision or do the action that led to its being linked to the object? Could the subject at least have committed to do what it did?

Causality

Is there a causal connection between subject and object which would make it plausible that the object is ascribed to the subject?

Power

Did the subject have the power to change the outcome?

Knowledge

Was the subject aware or could it have been aware of the object?

Validity

The reflective turn of responsibility demands that ascriptions be valid. The question should therefore be whether the ascription can achieve validity.

Viability

Is the ascription possible as intended? Can a link between subject and object be established? Is this link acceptable?

Openness

Is the process of ascription open and accessible to everybody affected? Are mechanisms in place that can clarify questions?

Consequences

Does the ascription lead to consequences?

Good Life

> Does the ascription live up to the general idea of the good life? Is it plausible that the ascription and the resulting sanctions improve social settings?

Stakeholder/Discourse

> Does the ascription follow a model that allows the participation of everybody concerned, as suggested for example by the stakeholder theory or discourse theory?

Realisation

Does the process of responsibility ascription take its own realisation into account? Does it reflect the openness and communicative orientation?

Prudence

> Is the ascription sufficiently open to allow the consideration of the individual's ability to make prudent judgments?

Accountability

> Are there structures which allow the construction of relationships between subject, object, instance as well as assessment of conditions and outcomes?

Institutions

> Are there other institutions apart from those guaranteeing accountability that are necessary for the identification, ascription, enforcement, and viability of responsibility ascription?

Limits

What are the limits of the ascription? Are there excuses or exemptions? To which point are the conditions fulfilled?

Second-Order Responsibilities

Looking at all of the points mentioned so far, are there discernible responsibilities that result from the original ascription? Are there new institutions that need to be created? Is there responsibility on another level of magnitude that needs to be assumed? Is there a need to form subjects, objects, or instances by developing consciousness or by education? If so, who is responsible for initiating these new responsibility ascriptions?

Chapter VII

Conclusion

The use of computers and information technology in businesses and the economy can lead to normative problems. These moral, ethical, legal, or other problems can be expressed in terms of responsibility. The idea of this book was to analyse what responsibility in relation to business information technology can mean. It was shown that responsibility is a normative term that can be placed between the ideas of ethics and morality. It combines the theoretical and the practical approach that we find in the German tradition, and it can mediate between deontology and teleology in the French tradition. A closer analysis of the literature concerning responsibility showed that there are several aspects that combine the different theories of responsibility. Among them we identified openness, an affinity to action, and teleology.

In the light of these three general meanings of responsibility, the term was applied to itself in order to see whether the notion of responsibility itself can be helpful in dealing with responsibility problems. It turned out that the emphasis on openness, action, and teleology allowed the deduction of several principles that can guide us through the process of ascribing responsibility. Among these was the realisation that responsibility is a social construct whose validity depends partly on its viability. This means that the term and all of its dimensions must be clear but at the same time must leave room for individual interpretations. It must allow for prudence and judgment while still maintaining its communicational nature. The viability of reflexive responsibility, which is a result of its teleology and affinity to action, demands the construction of institutions that support it. This means that accountability must be guaranteed on all different levels of society if responsibility is to play a role. This results in the problem of follow-up responsibilities. Ascribing responsibility to a subject for a particular object will often entail the development of other responsibilities which refer to the conditions of possibility of ascribing responsibility.

This theoretical framework of responsibility was then applied to the business use of computers and information technology. The relationship between responsibility and IS was discussed in three parts—in responsibility because of (past) problems with IS, responsibility for (future) use of IS, and responsibility through the medium of information technology in business. It turned out that the reflective use of the idea of responsibility was helpful and could advise decision makers how to behave in morally problematic situations. The communicative nature of responsibility and the resulting similarity to other ethical theories, such as the stakeholder theory or discourse theory, can guide the process of ascribing responsibility. But even on the individual level, the reflective idea of responsibility can in many cases offer insights into the nature of moral problems, which can be helpful when dealing with normative problems of the use of computers in business. In order to demonstrate this point, the situation of managers "responsible for" IS was chosen. The analysis of decision problems of these managers served to clarify the relevance of reflective responsibility to IS. At the same time the theory lends itself to the analysis of these problems from other angles as well.

Generally, it can be summarised that the reflective turn of the concept of responsibility is useful in that it allows the drawing of practically relevant conclusions. The resulting theory of reflective responsibility is a useful tool for dealing with normative problems that result from the encounter of business interests and modern technological developments.

A last and fitting question for the conclusion of this topic is: Does this text live up to its own expectations, and is it responsible to speak of (reflective) responsibility in IS? Using the same criteria developed throughout the text, this question can be answered in the affirmative. Going back to the three main features—to openness, affinity to action, and teleology—it seems that all three of them are met in some way or another. Openness is the most obvious consequence of this text. As was demonstrated earlier on, the conclusion to be drawn from the reflective use of openness is the clarity of the term. Reflective responsibility can only work if all of the aspects and the social meaning of the ascription are clear. It was the main aim of this text to clarify exactly these aspects, to make it clear what reflective responsibility means. Affinity to action and teleology are met less directly, but it stands to reason that the clarification of the term responsibility will help establish them. If a reader of the text has a better idea of responsibility and therefore can realise a viable ascription, then the affinity to action would be met as well. This also implies some sort of teleology. The writing about these issues is also in part motivated by the idea that clarifying ethical theory will help better the circumstances in concrete situations so that the aspect of teleology is met as well.

The final conclusions to be drawn from the ideas presented here would then concern the other levels of responsibilities. Responsibilities, if taken seriously, result in other responsibilities. The questions resulting from this text about responsibility and IS would now be:

- Which institutions will be necessary to allow responsibility apart from the ones mentioned in the managerial sphere?
- What should the government do?
- What international responsibilities are necessary?
- Which normative discourses must be held?
- Which institutions must be constructed?

Without answers to these questions, the managerial responsibility for IS that was the centre of attention in this text is in danger of failing. Managerial responsibility seen from the viewpoint of a reflective theory, however, does offer a good starting point for these further questions.

References

Albrecht, S. (1996). Moral und Moralphilosophie—Vom Unterschied und seinen Folgen. *Ethik und Sozialwissenschaften, 7*(2/3), Opladen.

Ambrose, P.J. & Johnson, G.J. (1998). A trust-based model of buying behaviour in electronic retailing. *Proceedings of the 1998 Americas Conference of the AIS* (August, 14-16, pp. 263-268), Baltimore, Maryland, USA.

Anderson, R.E., Johnson, D.G., Gotterbarn, D., & Perrolle, J. (1993). Using the new ACM code of ethics in decision making. *Communications of the ACM, 36*(2), 98-106.

Apel, K.-O. (1988). *Diskurs und Verantwortung: Das Problem des Übergangs zur postkonventionellen Moral* (3rd edition, 1997). Frankfurt: Suhrkamp.

Apel, K.-O. (1980). The a priori of the communication community and the foundations of ethics: The problem of a rational foundation of ethics in the scientific age. In K.-O. Apel (Ed.), *Towards a Transformation of Philosophy* (pp. 225-300). London et al.: Routledge & Kegan Paul.

Aristoteles. (1967). *Die nikomachische ethik.* Zürich/München: dtv/Artemis.

Baier, K. (1972). Guilt and responsibility. In P. French (Ed.), *Individual and Collective Responsibility — Massacre at My Lai* (pp. 35-62). Cambridge, MA: Schenkman Publishing Company.

Banse, G. (1996). Herkunft und Anspruch der Risikoforschung. In G. Banse (Ed.), *Risikoforschung zwischen Ddisziplinarität und*

Interdisziplinarität—von der Illusion der Sicherheit zum Umgang mit Unsicherheit. Berlin: Edition Sigma Rainer Bohn Verlag.

Banse, G. (1994). Verantwortung unter Unsicherheit und Ungewißheit. *Ethik und Sozialwissenschaften, 5*(1).

Barlow, J.P. (1995). Coming into the country. In D.G. Johnson & H. Nissenbaum (Eds.), *Computers, Ethics & Social Values* (pp. 15-18). Upper Saddle River, NJ: Prentice-Hall.

Bates, S. (1991[1971]). The responsibility of "random collections." In L. May & S. Hoffman (Eds.), *Collective Responsibility: Five Decades of Debate in Theoretical and Applied Ethics* (pp. 101-108). Savage, MD: Rowman & Littlefield.

Bayertz, K. (ed.). (1995a). *Verantwortung: Prinzip oder Problem?* Darmstadt: Wissenschaftliche Buchgesellschaft.

Bayertz, K. (1995b). Eine kurze Ggeschichte der Herkunft der Verantwortung. In K. Bayertz (Ed.), *Verantwortung: Prinzip oder Problem?* (pp. 3-71). Darmstadt: Wissenschaftliche Buchgesellschaft.

Bayertz, K. (1993). Evolution und Ethik. Größe und Grenzen eines philosophischen Forschungsprogramms. In K. Bayertz (Ed.), *Evolution und Ethik.* Stuttgart.

Bechtel, W. (1985). Attributing responsibility to computer systems. *Metaphilosophy, 16*(4), 296-305.

Beck, U. (ed.). (1998a). *Politik der Globalisierung* (1st edition). Frankfurt: Edition Zweite Moderne, Suhrkamp Verlag.

Beck, U. (1986). *Risikogesellschaft. Auf dem weg in eine andere Moderne.* Frankfurt: Suhrkamp.

Becker, G.S. (1976). *The Economic Approach to Human Behaviour.* Chicago, London: The University of Chicago Press.

Beckmann, J. (1777). *Anleitung zur Technologie oder zur Kenntniss der Handwerke, Fabriken und Manufacturen, vornehmlich derer, die mit der Landwirthschaft, Polizey und Cameralwissenschaft in nächster Verbindung stehen (nebst Beyträgen zur Kunstgeschichte).* Göttingen: Publisher.

Benbasat, I., & Zmud, R.W. (1999). Empirical research in information systems: The practice of relevance. *MIS Quarterly, 23*(1), 3-16.

Bender, C. (1994). Wer verantwortet, der riskiert.... *Ethik und Sozialwissenschaften, 5*(1).

Berger, W. (1994). Der paradoxe Imperativ. *Ethik und Sozialwissenschaften, 5*(1), 137.

Bergmann, B. (1996). Die psychische Tätigkeitsregulation als Rahmen für die Erklärung von Zuverlässigkeitsproblemen menschlicher Tätigkeiten. In G. Banse (Ed.), *Risikoforschung zwischen Disziplinarität und Interdisziplinarität—Von der Illusion der Sicherheit zum Umgang mit Unsicherheit* (p. 83ff). Berlin: Edition Sigma Rainer Bohn Verlag.

Berman, J., & Goldman, J. (1995). A federal right of information privacy: The need for reform. In D.G. Johnson & H. Nissenbaum (Eds.), *Computers, Ethics & Social Values* (pp. 374-393). Upper Saddle River, NJ: Prentice-Hall.

Beu, D., & Buckley, M.R. (2001). The hypothesised relationship between accountability and ethical behaviour. *Journal of Business Ethics, 34,* 57-73.

Bienfait, A. (1999). *Freiheit, Verantwortung, Solidarität: Zur Rekonstruktion des politischen Liberalismus.* 1. Auflage. Frankfurt: Suhrkamp.

Bierhoff, H.W. (1995). Verantwortungsbereitschaft, Verantwortungsabwehr und Verantwortungszuschreibung—sozialpsychologische Perspektiven. In K. Bayertz (Ed.), *Verantwortung: Prinzip oder Problem?* (pp. 217-240). Darmstadt: Wissenschaftliche Buchgesellschaft.

Birnbacher, D. (1995). Grenzen der Verantwortung. In K. Bayertz (Ed.), *Verantwortung: Prinzip oder Problem?* (pp. 143-183). Darmstadt: Wissenschaftliche Buchgesellschaft.

Birnbacher, D. (1995b). *Tun und Unterlassen.* Stuttgart: Reclam.

Birnbacher, D. (1988). *Verantwortung für zukünftige Generationen.* Stuttgart: Reclam.

Birnbacher, D. (1980). Sind wir für die Natur verantwortlich? In D. Birnbacher (Ed.), *Ökologie und Ethik* (p. 111ff). Stuttgart: Reclam.

Bochenski, J.M. (1991). Die Struktur der Verantwortung. In M. Sänger (Ed.), *Arbeitstexte für den Unterricht: Verantwortung* (pp. 22-24). Stuttgart: Reclam.

Böhler, D. (1994). In dubio contra projectum. Mensch und Natur im Spannungsfeld von Verstehen, Konstruieren und Verantworten. In D. Böhler (Ed.), *Ethik für die zukunft. Im diskurs mit Hans Jonas* (pp. 244-176). München: C.H. Beck.

Böhret, C. (1987). Technikfolgen und Verantwortung der Politik. *Das Parlament,* (May).

Boncella, R.J. (2001). Internet privacy—at home and at work. *Communications of the Association for Information Systems, 7.*

Bonß, W. (1995). *Vom Risiko. Unsicherheit und Ungewissheit in der Moderne.* Hamburg: Hamburger Edition.

Borning, A. (1995). Case: Computer system reliability and nuclear war. In D.G. Johnson & H. Nissenbaum (Eds.), *Computers, Ethics & Social Values* (pp. 398-421). Upper Saddle River, NJ: Prentice-Hall.

Bourdieu, P. (1998). *Die feinen Unterschiede—Kritik der gesellschaftlichen Urteilskraft* (10th edition). Frankfurt: Suhrkamp.

Bourdieu, P. (1998b). *Contre-feux—propos pour servir à la résistance contre l'invasion néo-libéral.* Paris: Édition RAISON D'Agir.

Bourdil, P.-Y. (1996). *Le temps.* Paris: Ellipses/Édition Marketing.

Bowie, N.E. (1999). *Business ethics—a Kantian perspective.* Oxford: Blackwell.

Breil, R. (1993). *Grundzüge einer Philosophie der Natur.* Würzburg: Königshausen & Neumann.

Britz, J.J. (1999). Ethical guidelines for meeting the challenges of the Information Age. In L.J. Pourciau (Ed.), *Ethics and Electronic Information in the 21st Century* (pp. 9-28). West Lafayette, IN: Purdue University Press.

Brooks, R.A. (2002). *Flesh and Machines: How Robots will Change Us.* New York: Pantheon.

Broome, J. (1998). Ethics out of economics. In C.-H. Grenholm, & G. Helgesson (Eds.), *Ethics, Economics and Feminism* (pp. 25-39). Uppsala: Uppsala University.

Brown, W.S. (2000). Ontological security, existential anxiety and workplace privacy. *Journal of Business Ethics, 23,* 61-65.

Burschel, C. (1996). *Umweltschutz als sozialer Prozess: Die Organisation des Umweltschutzes und die Implementireung von Umwelttechnik im Betrieb.* Opladen: Westdeutscher Verlag.

Castells, M. (2000). The Information Age: Economy, society, and culture. *Volume I: The Rise of the Network Society* (2nd edition). Oxford: Blackwell.

Cheskin Research and Studio Archetype/Sapient. (1999). *eCommerce Trust Study.* Accessed August 1, 2001 at: www.studioarchetype.com/cheskin/.

Chisholm, R.M. (1997[1964]). *La liberté humaine et le moi.* In M. Neuberg (Ed.), *La responsabilité—questions philosophiques* (pp. 39-54). Paris: Presses Universitaires de France. Original: R.M. Chisholm (1964). *Human freedom and the self.* The Lindley Lecture, University of Kansas, Department of Philosophy.

Collste, G. (2000a). The Internet-doctor. In G. Collste (Ed.), *Ethics in the Age of Information Technology* (pp. 119-129). Linköping: Centre for Applied Ethics.

Collste, G. (2000b). Ethical aspects of decision support systems for diabetes care. In G. Collste (Ed.), *Ethics in the Age of Information Technology* (pp. 181-194). Linköping: Centre for Applied Ethics.

Collste, G. (1998). Should every human being get health care? In C.-H. Grenholm & G. Helgesson (Eds.), *Value Assumptions in Economic Theory* (pp. 81-93). Uppsala: Uppsala University.

Conger, S., & Loch, K.D. (1995). Ethics and computer use. *Communications of the ACM, 38*(12), 31-32.

Cooper, D. (1972). Responsibility and the "system." In P. French (Ed.), *Individual and Collective Responsibility—Massacre at My Lai* (pp. 81-100). Cambridge, MA: Schenkman Publishing Company.

Corbato, F.J. (1995). On building systems that will fail. In D.G. Johnson & H. Nissenbaum (Eds.), *Computers, Ethics & Social Values* (pp. 421-432). Upper Saddle River, NJ: Prentice-Hall.

Culnan, M.J. (1993). "How did they get my name?": An exploratory investigation of consumer attitudes toward secondary information use. *MIS Quarterly, 17*(3), 341-363.

Currie, W. (2000). *The Global Information Society.* Chichester, UK: John Wiley & Sons.

De George, R.T. (1999). *Business Ethics* (5th edition). Upper Saddle River, NJ: Prentice-Hall.

De George, R.T. (1998). Computers, ethics, and business. *Philosophic Exchange 1997-1998,* 45-55.

De George, R.T. (1991). Ethical responsibilities of engineers in large organizations: The Pinto case. In L. May & S. Hoffman (Eds.), *Collective Responsibility: Five Decades of Debate in Theoretical and Applied Ethics* (pp. 151-166). Savage, MD: Rowman & Littlefield.

Dehner, K. (1998). *Lust an Moral. Die natürliche Sehnsucht nach Werten.* Darmstadt: Primus Verlag.

Devall, B. (1997). Die tiefenökologische Bewegung. In D. Birnbacher (Ed.), *Ökophilosophie* (p. 17ff). Stuttgart: Reclam.

Donaldson, T., & Dunfee, T.W. (1999). *Ties that Bind: A Social Contracts Approach to Business Ethics.* Boston, MA: Harvard Business School Press.

Donaldson, T., & Preston, L.E. (1995). The stakeholder theory of the corporation: Concepts, evidence, and implications. *Academy of Management Review, 20*(1), 65-91.

Downy, R.S. (1972). Responsibility and social roles. In P. French (Ed.), *Individual and Collective Responsibility—Massacre at My Lai* (pp. 63-80). Cambridge, MA: Schenkman Publishing Company.

Dreyfus, H.L. (1993). *What Computers Still Can't Do.* Cambridge, MA/ London: MIT Press.

Eckard, initial, & Löffler, initial. (1991). Organisation der Arbeit—Organisation der Profession. In H. Lenk & M. Maring (Eds.), *Technikverantwortung. Güterabwägung—Risikobewertung—Verhaltenskodizes.* Frankfurt/ New York.

Ehrenfeld, D. (1997). Das Naturschutzdilemma. In D. Birnbacher (1997), *Ökophilosophie* (p. 135ff). Stuttgart: Reclam.

Eibl-Eibesfeld, I. (1997). *Der Mensch—das riskierte Wesen zur Naturgeschichte menschlicher Unvernunft* (3rd edition). München/ Zürich: Piper.

Elgesiem, D. (1996). Privacy, respect for persons, and risk. In C. Ess (Ed.), *Philosophical Perspectives on Computer-Mediated Communication* (pp. 45-56). Albany, NY: State University of New York Press.

Encarta World English Dictionary. (1999). London: Bloomsbury Publishing.

Ess, C. (1996). Introduction: Thoughts along the I-way: Philosophy and the emergence of computer-mediated communication. In C. Ess (Ed.), *Philosophical Perspectives on Computer-Mediated Communication* (pp. 1-12). Albany, NY: State University of New York Press.

Ess, C. (1996b). The political computer: Democracy, CMC, and Habermas. In C. Ess (Ed.), *Philosophical Perspectives on Computer-Mediated Communication* (pp. 197-230). Albany, NY: State University of New York Press.

Etchegoyen, A. (1999). *La vraie morale se moque de la morale—être responsable.* Paris: Editions du Seuil.

Etchegoyen, A. (1993). *Le temps des responsables.* Paris: Editions Julliard.

Fain, H. (1972). Some moral infirmities of justice. In P. French (Ed.), *Individual and Collective Responsibility—Massacre at My Lai* (pp. 17-34). Cambridge, MA: Schenkman Publishing Company.

Fauconnet, P. (1928). La responsabilité: Étude de sociologie. In M. Neuberg (Ed.), *La responsabilité—questions philosophiques* (pp. 141-152). Paris: Presses Universitaires de France.

Feinberg, J. (1991[1970]). Collective responsibility. In L. May & S. Hoffman (Eds.), *Collective Responsibility: Five Decades of Debate in Theo-*

retical and Applied Ethics (pp. 53-76). Savage, MD: Rowman & Littlefield.

Feinberg, J. (1980). Die rechte der Tiere und zukünftiger Generationen. In D. Birnbacher (Ed.), *Ökologie und Ethik* (p. 140ff). Stuttgart: Reclam.

Fischer, J.M. (1999). Recent work on moral responsibility. *Ethics, 110*(1), 93-139.

Flynn, T.R. (1984). *Sartre and Marxist Existentialism: The Test Case of Collective Responsibility.* Chicago, London: The University of Chicago Press.

Forester, T., & Morrison, P. (1994). *Computer Ethics—Cautionary Tales and Ethical Dilemmas in Computing* (2nd edition). Cambridge, MA/ London: MIT Press.

Foucault, M. (1975). *Surveiller et punir: Naissance de la prison.* Paris: Gallimard.

French, P.A. (1992). *Responsibility Matters.* Lawrence, KS: University Press of Kansas.

French, P.A. (1979). The corporation as a moral person. *American Philosophical Quarterly, 16*(3), 207-215.

French, P. (ed.). (1972). *Individual and Collective Responsibility—Massacre at My Lai.* Cambridge, MA: Schenkman Publishing Company.

Galliers, R.D., & Baets, W.R.J. (eds.). (1998). *Information Technology and Organizational Transformation: Innovation for the 21st Century.* Chichester et al.: John Wiley & Sons.

Galtung, J. (1998). *Frieden mit friedlichen Mitteln—Friede und Konflikt, Entwicklung und Kultur.* Opladen: Leske + Budrich.

Gauthier, D. (1986). *Morals by Agreement.* Oxford: Clarendon.

Gavison, R. (1995). Privacy and limits of law. In D.G. Johnson & H. Nissenbaum (Eds.), *Computers, Ethics & Social Values* (pp. 332-351). Upper Saddle River, NJ: Prentice-Hall.

Gehlen, A. (1973). *Moral und hypermoral.* Frankfurt.

Gethmann, C.F. (1987). Ethische aspekte des handelns unter risiko. *VGB Kraftwerkstechnik, 67,* 12.

Gethmann-Siefert, A. (ed.). (1996). *Wissenschaft und Technik als Gegenstand philosophischer Reflexion.* Hagen: FernUniversität Hagen.

Gethmann-Siefert, A., & Gethmann, C. (1996). Wissenschaft und Technik als Gegenstand philosophischer Reflexion: Ethische probleme der Technik versus Technikfolgenabschätzung. In Gethmann-Siefert, A. (Ed.), Wissenschaft und Technik als Gegenstand philosophischer Reflexion (pp. I-XXIX). Hagen: FernUniversität Hagen.

Gibson, K. (2000). The moral basis of stakeholder theory. *Journal of Business Ethics, 26*, 245-257.

Giel, K., & Breuninger, R. (eds.). (1992). *Risiko—Bausteine zur Philosophie—Band 6 interdisziplinäre Schriftenreihe des Humboldt-Studienzentrums Universität Ulm.* Ulm: Humboldt-Studienzentrums Universität Ulm.

Goh, F., Atif, Y., & Seng, Q.T. (1999). Design and implementation of an Internet-based shopping model. *Proceedings of the Collaborative Electronic Commerce Technology and Research Conference (ACIS'99).*

Goodin, R. (1998). Social welfare as a collective social responsibility. In D. Schmidtz & R. Goodin (Eds.), *Social Welfare and Individual Responsibility.* Cambridge/New York: Cambridge University Press.

Goodpaster, K.E., & Matthews Jr., J.B. (1982). Can a corporation have a moral conscience? *Harvard Business Review*, (January-February), 132-141.

Grunwald, A. (1996). Ethik der Technik—Systematisierung und Kritik vorliegender Entwürfe. *Ethik und Sozialwissenschaften, 7*(2/3), 191.

Guggenberger, B. (1992). Fehlerfreundliche Strukturen. In K. Giel & R. Breuninger (Eds.), *Risiko—Bausteine zur Philosophie—Band 6 interdisziplinäre Schriftenreihe des Humboldt-Studienzentrums Universität Ulm.* Ulm: Humboldt-Studienzentrums Universität Ulm.

Gumpert, G., & Drucker, S.J. (2000). The demise of privacy in a private world. In R.M. Baird, R. Ramsower, & S.E. Rosenbaum (Eds.), *Cyberethics—Social and Moral Issues in the Computer Age* (pp. 171-187). New York: Prometheus Books.

Habermas, J. (ed.). (1998a). *Faktizität und Geltung: Beiträge zur Diskurstheorie des Rechts und des demokratischen Rechtsstaats.* Frankfurt: Suhrkamp.

Habermas, J. (1998b). Recht und Moral (Tanner Lectures 1986). In J. Habermas (Ed.), *Faktizität und Geltung: Beiträge zur Diskurstheorie des Rechts und des demokratischen Rechtsstaats* (pp. 541-599). Frankfurt: Suhrkamp.

Habermas, J. (1998c). Konzeptionen der Moderne—ein Rückblick auf zwei Traditionen. In J. Habermas (Ed.), *Die postnationale Konstellation—politische Essays.* Frankfurt: Surkamp.

Habermas, J. (1991). *Erläuterungen zur Diskursethik.* Frankfurt: Surkamp.

Habermas, J. (1983). *Moralbewußtsein und kommunikatives Handeln.* Frankfurt: Suhrkamp.

Habermas, J. (1981a). *Theorie des kommunikativen Handelns—Band I.* Frankfurt: Suhrkamp Verlag.

Habermas, J. (1981b). *Theorie des kommunikativen Handelns—Band II.* Frankfurt: Suhrkamp Verlag.

Hager, N. (1990). Vernunft und Verantwortung. *Ethik und Sozialwissenschaften, 1*(1).

Hallam, S. (1998). Misconduct on the Information Highway: Abuse and misuse of the Internet. In R.N. Stichler & R. Hauptman (Eds.), *Ethics, Information and Technology: Readings* (pp. 241-253). Jefferson, NC: MacFarland & Company.

Hank, R. (2000). *Das ende der Gleichheit oder warum der Kapitalismus mehr Wettbewerb braucht.* Frankfurt: S. Fischer Verlag.

Hart, H.L.A. (1968). *Punishment and Responsibility—Essays in the Philosophy of Law.* Oxford: Clarendon Press.

Hartman, L. (2001). Technology and ethics: Privacy in the workplace. *Business and Society Review, 106*(1), 1-27.

Hassemer, W. (1990). Kollektive Verantwortung und moralische Fallen. *Ethik und Sozialwissenschaften, 1*(1), 63.

Hastedt, H. (1994). *Aufklärung und Technik. Grundprobleme einer Ethik der Technik.* Frankfurt.

Hauptman, R. (1999). Ethics, information technology and crisis. In L.J. Pourciau (Ed.), *Ethics and Electronic Information in the 21st Century* (pp. 1-5). West Lafayette, IN: Purdue University Press.

Hausman, D.M., & McPherson, M.S. (1996). *Economic Analysis and Moral Philosophy.* Cambridge et al.: Cambridge University Press.

Held, V. (1991[1970]). Can a random collection of individuals be morally responsible? In L. May & S. Hoffman (Eds.), *Collective Responsibility: Five Decades of Debate in Theoretical and Applied Ethics.* Savage, MD: Rowman & Littlefield.

Held, V. (1972). Moral responsibility and collective action. In P. French (Ed.), *Individual and Collective Responsibility—Massacre at My Lai* (pp. 101-118). Cambridge, MA: Schenkman Publishing Company.

Hegselmann, R. (1991). Wissenschaftsethik und moralische Bildung. In H. Lenk (Ed.), *Wissenschaft und Ethik* (pp. 215-232). Stuttgart: Reclam.

Helgesson, G. (1998). Ethical preconditions in economic theory—a first inventory. In C.-H. Grenholm & G. Helgesson (Eds.), *Ethics, Economics and Feminism* (pp. 51-82). Uppsala: Uppsala University.

Hendry, J. (2001). Economic contracts versus social relationships as a foundation for normative stakeholder theory. *Business Ethics: A European Review, 10*(3), 223-232.

Hengsbach, F. (1993). *Wirtschaftsethik—Aufbruch—Konflikte—Perspektiven (2nd edition).* Freiburg: Herder Verlag.

Himanen, P. (2001). *The Hacker Ethic and the Spirit of the Information Age.* London: Secker & Warburg.

Hoerster, N. (ed.). (1987). *Recht und Moral—Texte zur Rechtsphilosophie.* Stuttgart: Reclam. Höffe, O. (1996). *Immanuel Kant* (4th edition) (p. 506). München: Becksche Reihe Denker.

Höffe, O. (1995). *Moral als Preis der Moderne: Ein Versuch über Wissenschaft, Technik und Umwelt* (3rd edition). Frankfurt: Suhrkamp.

Höffe, O. (1990). Univeralistische Ethik und Urteilskraft: Ein aristotelischer Blick auf Kant. *Zeitschrift für philosophische Forschung, 44,* 537-561.

Hoffman, D.L., Novak, T.P., & Peralta, M. (1999). Building consumer trust online. *Communications of the ACM, 42*(4), 80-87.

Hoffmann-Riem, W. (2001). Wider die Geistespolizei. *Die Zeit Nr. 50* (6.12), 13.

Holzheu, F. (1993). Institutionalisierte Risikowahrnehmung. Eine ökonomische Perspektive. In R. Bayerische (Ed.), *Risiko ist ein Konstrukt. Wahrnehmungen zur Risikowahrnehmung* (pp. 263-292). München: Knesebeck.

Homann, K. (1998). Introduction to Summer. In initial Ludwig (Ed.), *Der unternehmensethische Begriff der "Verantwortung": Eine Grundlegung im Anschluss an Jonas, Kant und Habermas.* Wiesbaden: Deutscher Universitätsverlag.

Homann, K. (1997). Individualisierung: Verfall der Moral? Zum ökonomischen Fundament aller Moral. *Aus Politik und Zeitgeschehen—Beilage zur Wochenzeitung das Parlament—B21/97 16.05.1997.* Bonn: Bundeszentrale für Politische Bildung.

Homann, K., & Blome-Drees, F. (1992). *Wirtschafts—und Unternehmensethik.* Göttingen: Vandenhoek & Ruprecht.

Hubig, C. (1995). Verantwortung und Hochtechnologie. In K. Bayertz (Ed.), *Verantwortung: Prinzip oder Problem?* (pp. 98-139). Darmstadt: Wissenschaftliche Buchgesellschaft.

Hubig, C. (1995b). *Technik—und Wissenschaftsethik.* 2. Auflage Berlin, Heidelberg, New York: Springer Verlag.

Hubig, C. (1994). Unternehmensethik versus Technikethik—doch ein Institutionenproblem? In W. Zimmerli & V.M. Brennecke (Eds.), *Technikverantwortung in der Unternehmenskultur—von theoretischen Konzepten zur praktischen Umsetzung* (p. 155ff). Stuttgart: Schäffer-Poeschel.

Hubig, C. (1993). Technikbewertung auf der Basis einer Institutionenethik. In H. Lenk & G. Ropohl (Eds.), *Technik und Ethik* (2nd edition) (pp. 282-307). Stuttgart: Reclam.

Huff, C., & Martin, C.D. (1995). Computing consequences: A framework for teaching ethical computing. *Communications of the ACM, 38*(12), 75-84.

Hunter, L. (1995). Public image. In D.G. Johnson & H. Nissenbaum (Eds.), *Computers, Ethics & Social Values* (pp. 293-299). Upper Saddle River, NJ: Prentice-Hall.

Ilting, K.-H. (1994). Verantwortung. eine transzendentalphilosophische Grundlegung. In K.-H. Ilting (Ed.), *Grundfragen der praktischen Philosophie* (pp. 176-198). Frankfurt: Suhrkamp.

Ilting, K.-H. (1994b). Wahrheit und Verbindlichkeit In K.-H. Ilting (Ed.), *Grundfragen der praktischen Philosophie* (pp. 66-102). Frankfurt: Suhrkamp.

Introna, L. (2000). Privacy and the computer—why we need privacy in the information society. In R.M. Baird, R. Ramsower, & S.E. Rosenbaum (Eds.), *Cyberethics—Social and Moral Issues in the Computer Age* (pp. 188-199). New York: Prometheus Books.

John Paul II. (1991). *Encyclical Letter Centesimus Annus.* Accessed online January 23, 2001 from: http://www.vatican.va/holy_father/john_paul_ii/encyclicals/documents/hf_jp-ii_enc_01051991_centesimusannus_en.html.

Johnson, D.G. (2001). *Computer Ethics* (3rd edition). Upper Saddle River, NJ: Prentice-Hall.

Johnson, D.G., & Nissenbaum, H. (eds.). (1995). *Computers, Ethics & Social Values.* Upper Saddle River, NJ: Prentice-Hall.

Johnson, D.G., & Mulvey, J.M. (1995). Accountability and computer decision systems. *Communications of the ACM, 38*(12), 58-64.

Jonas, H. (1991). Wissenschaft und Forschungsfreiheit. Ist erlaubt, was machbar ist? In H. Lenk (Ed.), *Wissenschaft und Ethik* (pp. 193-214). Stuttgart: Reclam.

Jonas, H. (1987). *Technik, Medizin und Ethik. Zur Praxis des Prinzips Verantwortung* (2nd edition). Frankfurt: Insel Verlag.

Jonas, H. (1984). *Das Prinzip Verantwortung*. Frankfurt: Suhrkamp.

Judt, T. (1998). *The Burden of Responsibility: Blum, Camus, Aron, and the French Twentieth Century*. Chicago, IL: The University of Chicago Press.

Kafka, P. (1994). Künstliches Gewissen. *Ethik und Sozialwissenschaften, 5*(1).

Kant, I. (1995a). *Kritik der praktischen Vernunft, Grundlegung zur Metaphysik der Sitten*. Frankfurt: Suhrkamp Taschenbuch Wissenschaft.

Kant, I. (1995b). *Kritik der reinen vernunft* (2 tomes). Wiesbaden (Riga): Suhrkamp Verlag Wissenschaft.

Kant, I. (1990). *Die Metaphysik der Sitten*. Stuttgart: Reclam.

Kaufmann, F.-X. (1995). Risiko, Verantwortung und gesellschaftliche Komplexität. In K. Bayertz (Ed.), *Verantwortung: Prinzip oder Problem?* (pp. 72-97). Darmstadt: Wissenschaftliche Buchgesellschaft.

Kaufmann, F.-X. (1992). *Der Ruf nach Verantwortung*. Freiburg im Breisgau: Herder.

Kaufmann, F.-X. (1990). Leistet Verantwortung, was wir ihr zumuten? *Ethik und Sozialwissenschaften, 1*(1).

Kelsen, H. (1987). Hans Kelsen: Die Rechtsordnung als hierarchisches System von Zwangsnormen. In N.Hoerster (Ed.), *Recht und Moral—Texte zur Rechtsphilosophie* (pp. 20-42). Stuttgart: Reclam.

Kemerling, G. (2000). *Kant: The moral order*. Accessed online November 15, 2000 from: http://www.philosophypages.com/hy/5i.htm.

Kettner, M. (1995). Wie ist eine diskursethische Begründung ökologischer Rechts—und Moralnormen möglich?. In J. Nida-Rümelin & D. v. d. Pfordten (Eds.), *Ökologische Ethik und Rechtstheorie* (pp. 301-323). Baden-Baden: Nomos Verlagsgesellschaft.

Kissling, C. (1995). Ethische Verantwortung und rechtliche Haftung. *Chimia, 49*.

Kleinwellfonder, B. (1996). *Der Risikodiskurs*. Opladen: Westdeutscher Verlag.

Kliemt, H. (1990). Statische Sozialfallen und repetetive Spiele. *Ethik und Sozialwissenschaften, 1*(1), 72.

Koehn, D. (2001). Ethical challenges confronting businesses today. *Proceedings of the 11th International Symposium on Ethics, Business and Society: Ethical Challenges in the Age of Globalization. The Message of the Encyclical Centesimus Annus on the 10th Anniversary of its Publication*, Barcelona, Spain, (July 4-6).

Kohlberg, L. (1995). *Die psychologie der Moralentwicklung.* Frankfurt: Suhrkamp.

Kolb, D. (1996). Discourse across links. In C. Ess (Ed.), *Philosophical Perspectives on Computer-Mediated Communication* (pp. 15-26). Albany, NY: State University of New York Press.

Koller, P. (1996). Freiheit als Problem der politischen Philosophie. In K. Bayertz (Ed.), *Politik und Ethik* (pp. 111-138). Stuttgart: Reclam.

Kornwachs, K. (1996). Risiko versus Zuverlässigkeit. In G. Banse (Ed.), *Risikoforschung zwischen Disziplinarität und Interdisziplinarität—von der Illusion der Sicherheit zum Umgang mit Unsicherheit* (p. 73ff). Berlin: Edition Sigma Rainer Bohn Verlag.

Koslowski, P. (2000). The limits of shareholder value. *Journal of Business Ethics, 27,* 137-148.

Krawietz, W. (1995). Theorie der Verantwortung—neu oder alt? Zur normativen Cerantwortungsattribution mit mitteln des Rechts. In K. Bayertz (Ed.), *Verantwortung: Prinzip oder Problem?* (pp. 194-216). Darmstadt: Wissenschaftliche Buchgesellschaft.

Kreikebaum, H. (1996). *Grundlagen der Unternehmensethik.* Stuttgart: Schaeffer-Poeschel.

Kuflik, A. (1995). Moral foundation of intellectual property rights. In D.G. Johnson & H. Nissenbaum (Eds.), *Computers, Ethics & Social Values* (pp. 169-180). Upper Saddle River, NJ: Prentice-Hall.

Kujala, J. (2001). Analysing moral issues in stakeholder relations. *Business Ethics: A European Review, 10*(3), 233-247.

Küng, H. (1997). *Weltethos für Weltpolitik und Weltwirtschaft* (3rd edition). München: Pieper.

Ladd, J. (1995). The quest for a code of professional ethics: An intellectual and moral confusion. In D.G. Johnson & H. Nissenbaum (Eds.), *Computers, Ethics & Social Values* (pp. 580-585). Upper Saddle River, NJ: Prentice-Hall.

Ladd, J. (1992). Bhopal: Moralische Verantwortung, normalen Katastrophen und Bürgertugend. In H. Lenk & M. Maring (Eds.), *Wirtschaft und ethik* (pp. 285-300). Stuttgart: Reclam.

Langford, D. (1999a). Beyond human control—some implications of today's Internet. In L.J. Pourciau (Ed.), *Ethics and Electronic Information in the 21st Century* (pp. 65-75). West Lafayette, IN: Purdue University Press.

Langford, D. (1999b). *Business Computer Ethics.* Harlow et al.: Addison-Wesley.

Laudon, K.C., & Laudon, J.P. (1999). *Essentials of Management Informa- tion Systems* (4th edition). London et al.: Prentice-Hall.

Lenk, H. (1998). *Konkrete Humanität: Vorlesungen über Verantwortung und Menschlichkeit* (stw 1250). Frankfurt: Suhrkamp Verlag.

Lenk, H. (1997). *Einführung in die angewandte Ethik.* Stuttgart, Berlin: Köln.

Lenk, H. (1994). *Macht und Machbarkeit der Technik.* Stuttgart: Reclam.

Lenk, H. (1994b). Hat die bloß individuelle Verantwortung noch eine Zukunft? In W.C. Zimmerli & V.M. Brennecke (Eds.), *Technikverantwortung in der Unternehmenskultur—von theoretischen Konzepten zur praktischen Umsetzung.* Stuttgart: Schäffer-Poeschel.

Lenk, H. (1991a). Komplexe Ebenen der Verantwortung. In M. Sänger (Ed.), *Arbeitstexte für den Unterricht: Verantwortung* (pp. 64-73). Stuttgart: Reclam.

Lenk, H. (ed.). (1991b). *Wissenschaft und Ethik.* Stuttgart: Reclam.

Lenk, H. (1984). Zum Verantwortungsproblem in Wissenschaft und Technik. In E. Ströker (Ed.), *Ethik der wissenschaften.* München: Publisher.

Lenk, H. (1993). Über Verantwortungsbegriffe und das Verantwortungsproblem in der Technik. In H. Lenk & G. Ropohl (Eds.), *Technik und Ethik* (2nd edition) (pp. 112-148). Stuttgart: Reclam.

Lenk, H., & Maring, M. (1996). Untauglichkeit der Verantwortungsethik? *Ethik und Sozialwissenschaften, 7*(2/3), 238.

Lenk, H., & Maring, M. (1996b). Wirtschaftsethik—ein Widerspruch in sich selbst? In H. Lenk et al. (Eds.), *Ethik in der Wirtschaft—Chancen verantwortlichen Handelns* (pp. 1-22). Stuttgart, Berlin, Köln: Verlag W. Kohlhammer.

Lenk, H., & Maring, M. (1995). Wer soll Verantwortung tragen? Probleme der Verantwortungsverteilung in komplexen (soziotechnischen sozioökonomischen) Systemen. In K. Bayertz (Ed.), *Verantwortung: Prinzip oder Problem?* (pp. 241-286). Darmstadt: Wissenschaftliche Buchgesellschaft.

Lenk, H., & Maring, M. (eds.). (1992). *Wirtschaft und Ethik.* Stuttgart: Reclam.

Lenk, H., & Maring, M. (eds.). (1991). *Technikverantwortung. Güterabwägung—Risikobewertung—Verhaltenskodizes.* Frankfurt, New York: Campus.

Lenk, H., & Maring, M. (eds.). (1990). Verantwortung und soziale Fallen. *Ethik und Sozialwissenschaften, 1*(1).

Lenk, H., & Ropohl, G. (eds.). (1993). *Technik und Ethik* (2nd edition). Stuttgart: Reclam.

Lenoir, F. (ed.). (1991). *Le temps de la responsabilité—entretiens sur l'éthique*. Paris: Fayard.

Leveson, N.G., & Turner, C.S. (1995). Case: An investigation of the Tharac-25 accidents. In D.G. Johnson & H. Nissenbaum (Eds.), *Computers, Ethics & Social Values* (pp. 474-514). Upper Saddle River, NJ: Prentice-Hall.

Levinas, E. (1984). Entretien avec Emmanuel Lévinas. In S. Malka (Ed.), *Lire lévinas* (pp. 103-114). Paris: Les Editions du Cerf.

Levinas, E. (1983). *Le temps et l'autre*. Paris: Quadrige/Presses Universitaires de France.

Levy, S. (1995). Battle of the clipper chip. In D.G. Johnson & H. Nissenbaum (Eds.), *Computers, Ethics & Social Values* (pp. 651-664). Upper Saddle River, NJ: Prentice-Hall.

Lewis, H.D. (1991[1948]). Collective responsibility. In L. May & S. Hoffman (Eds.), *Collective Responsibility: Five Decades of Debate in Theoretical and Applied Ethics* (pp. 17-34). Savage, MD: Rowman & Littlefield.

Lewis, H.D. (1972). The non-moral notion of collective responsibility. In P. French (Ed.), *Individual and Collective Responsibility—Massacre at My Lai* (pp. 116-144). Cambridge, MA: Schenkman Publishing Company.

Liebl, F. (1999). "What system have you announced?" Impressionen aus einer Ökonomie der Ankündigung. In F. Liebl (Ed.), *E-conomy—Management und Ökonomie in digitalen Kontexten* (pp. 7-10). Marburg: Metropolis Verlag.

Littlewood, B., & Stringy, L. (1995). The risks of software. In D.G. Johnson & H. Nissenbaum (Eds.), *Computers, Ethics & Social Values* (pp. 432-437). Upper Saddle River, NJ: Prentice-Hall.

Long, R., & Roderick, T. (1999). The irrelevance of responsibility. In E.F. Paul, F.D. Miller, & J. Paul (Eds.), *Responsibility* (pp. 118-145). Cambridge et al.: Cambridge University Press.

Lorenz, K. (1981). *Das sogenannte Böse—zur Naturgeschichte der Aggression* (9th edition). München: Deutscher Taschenbuch Verlag.

Lübbe, H. (1993). Sicherheit. Risikowahrnehmung im Zivilisationsprozess. In R. Bayerische (Ed.), *Risiko ist ein Konstrukt. Wahrnehmungen zur Risikowahrnehmung* (pp. 23-42). München: Knesebeck.

Lübbe, H. (1990). *Der Lebenssinn der Industriegesellschaft—über die moralische Verfassung der wissenschaftlich-technischen Zivilisation.* Berlin et al: Springer Verlag.

Lübbe, W. (1998). *Verantwortung in komplexen Kulturellen Prozessen.* Freiburg, München: Verlag Karl Alber.

Luhmann, N. (1990). *Paradigm lost: Über die ethische Reflexion der Moral.* Frankfurt: Suhrkamp.

Lyotard, J.-F. (1993). *Moralités postmodernes.* Paris: Galilée.

Lyytinen, K., & Hirschheim, R. (1988). Information systems as rational discourse: An application of Habermas' Theory of Communicative Action. *Scandinavian Journal of Management, 4*(1/2), 19-30.

Mai, M. (1996). Über die Operationalisierung ethischer Diskurse oder: Die Löcher im Systemkäse. *Ethik und Sozialwissenschaften, 7*(2/3).

Mai, M. (1994). Das Risiko im Prinzip Demokratie. *Ethik und Sozialwissenschaften, 5*(1).

Makropoulos, M. (1997). *Modernität und Kontingenz.* München: Wilhelm Fink Verlag.

Malka, S. (Ed.). (1984). *Lire lévinas.* Paris: Les Editions du Cerf.

Maring, M. (2001). Verantwortung von Korporationen. In J. Wieland (Ed.), *Die moralische Verantwortung kollektiver Akteure* (pp. 103-145). Heidelberg: Physica-Verlag.

Maring, M. (1989). Modelle korporativer Verantwortung. *Conceptus XXIII,* (58), 25-41.

Maritain, J. (1960). *La philosophie morale—examen historique et critque des grands systèmes.* Pairs: Librarie Gallimard.

Marx, K. (1998). *Das Kapital—Kritik der politischen Ökonomie* (3 Bd, Band 1, MEW Bd 23; 16th edition). Berlin: Dietz Verlag.

Mason, R.O. (1986). Four ethical issues of the Information Age. *MIS Quarterly, 10,* 5-12.

Mason, R.O., Mason, F., & Culnan, M.J. (1995). *Ethics of Information Management.* Thousand Oaks, London, New Delhi: Sage.

May, L. (1992). *Sharing Responsibility.* Chicago, IL: University of Chicago Press.

May, L. (1991). Metaphysical guilt and moral taint. In L. May & S. Hoffman (Eds.), *Collective Responsibility: Five Decades of Debate in Theoretical and Applied Ethics* (pp. 239-254). Savage, MD: Rowman & Littlefield.

May, L., & Hoffman, S. (eds.). (1991). *Collective Responsibility: Five Decades of Debate in Theoretical and Applied Ethics.* Savage, MD: Rowman & Littlefield.

McGary, H. (1991). Morality and collective liability. In L. May & S. Hoffman (Eds.), *Collective Responsibility: Five Decades of Debate in Theoretical and Applied Ethics* (pp. 77-88). Savage, MD: Rowman & Littlefield.

Mendieta, E. (1999). Review essay: Ethics for an age of globalization and exclusion. *Philosophy & Social Criticism, 25*(2), 115-121.

Menniger, K. (1987). Therapie statt Strafe. In N. Hoerster (Ed.), *Recht und Moral—Texte zur Rechtsphilosophie* (pp. 231-147). Stuttgart: Reclam.

Meyer, R. (1999). *Entscheidungstheorie.* Wiesbaden: Gabler.

Meyer, S.S. (1999). Fate, fatalism, and agency in stoicism. In E.F. Paul, F.D. Miller, & J. Paul (Eds.), *Responsibility* (pp. 250-273). Cambridge et al.: Cambridge University Press.

Milberg, S., Burke, S., Smith, H.J., & Kallman, E. (1995). Values, personal information, privacy, and regulatory approaches. *Communications of the ACM, 38*(12), 65-74.

Mill, J.S. (1976). *Der Utilitarismus.* Stuttgart: Reclam Verlag.

Mittelstraß, J. (1997). *Technikfolgenabschätzung und Ethik.* Europäische Akademie Brief Nr. 7. Bad Neuenahr-Ahrweiler.

Mittelstraß, J. (1996). Die Angst und das Wissen—oder was leistet die Technikfolgenabschätzung? In A. Gethmann-Siefert (Ed.), *Wissenschaft und Technik als Gegenstand philosophischer Reflexion* (pp. 1-16). Hagen: FernUniversität Hagen.

Mohr, H. (1995). *Qualitatives Wachstum—Lösung für die Zukunft.* Stuttgart, Wien: Weitbrecht Verlag.

Montaigne, M. (1976). *Essais* (edited by Ralph-Rainer Wuthenow). Frankfurt: Insel Verlag.

Moor, J.H. (2000). Toward a theory of privacy in the Information Age. In R.M. Baird, R. Ramsower, & S.E. Rosenbaum (Eds.), *Cyberethics. Social and Moral Issues in the Computer Age.* Prometheus Books.

Moor, J.H. (1985). What is computer ethics? *Metaphilosophy, 16*(4), 266-275.

Moore, M.S. (1999). Causation and responsibility. In E.F. Paul, F.D. Miller, & J. Paul (Eds.), *Responsibility* (pp. 1-51). Cambridge et al.: Cambridge University Press.

Moran, D. (2000). *Introduction to Phenomenology.* London, New York: Routledge.

Mullins, P. (1996). Sacred text in the sea of texts: The Bible in North American electronic culture. In C. Ess (Ed.), *Philosophical Perspectives on Computer-Mediated Communication* (pp. 271-302). Albany, NY: State University of New York Press.

Murswik, D. (1991). Technische Risiken als Verfassungsrechtliches Problem. In H. Lenk & M. Maring (Eds.), *Technikverantwortung. Güterabwägung—Risikobewertung—Verhaltenskodizes.* Frankfurt, New York: Campus.

Neubauer, B. (ed.). (1998). *Eigenverantwortung: Positionen und Perspektiven.* Waake: Licet Verlag.

Neuberg, M. (ed.). (1997a). *La responsabilité—questions philosophiques.* Paris: Presses Universitaires de France.

Neuberg, M. (1997b). Introduction à "la responsabilité." In M. Neuberg (Ed.), *La responsabilité—questions philosophiques* (pp. 1-24). Paris: Presses Universitaires de France.

Neuberg, M. (1997c). La responsabilité collective. In In M. Neuberg (Ed.), *La responsabilité—questions philosophiques* (pp. 253-273). Paris: Presses Universitaires de France.

Nida-Rümelin, J. (1998). Über den Respekt vor der Eigenverantwortung des Anderen. In B. Neubauer (Ed.), *Eigenverantwortung: Positionen und Perspektiven.* Waake: Licet Verlag.

Nietzsche, F. (1987). Friedrich Nietzsche: Argumente gegen Vergeltung und Abschreckung. In N. Hoerster (Ed.), *Recht und Moral—Texte zur Rechtsphilosophie* (pp. 229-231). Stuttgart: Reclam.

Nissenbaum, H. (1995). Computing and accountability. In D.G. Johnson & H. Nissenbaum (Eds.), *Computers, Ethics & Social Values* (pp. 526-538). Upper Saddle River, NJ: Prentice-Hall.

Nozick, R. (1974). *Anarchy, state, and utopia.* City: Basic Books.

O'Leary, S.D., & Brasher, B.E. (1996). The unknown God of the Internet: Religious communication from the ancient Agora to the virtual forum. In C. Ess (Ed.), *Philosophical Perspectives on Computer-Mediated Communication* (pp. 233-269). Albany, NY: State University of New York Press.

Paul, E.F., Miller, F.D., & Paul, J. (Eds.). (1999). *Responsibility.* Cambridge et al.: Cambridge University Press.

Pennings, J. (1998). Innovations as precursors of organizational performance. In R.D. Galliers, & W.R.J. Baets, Walter R. J. (Eds.), *Information Technology and Organizational Transformation: Innovation for the 21st Century* (pp. 153-178). Chichester et al.: John Wiley & Sons.

Philippe, M.-D. (1991). Entretien avec Marie-Dominique Philippe. In F. Lenoir (Ed.), *Le temps de la responsabilité—entretiens sur l'éthique* (pp. 229-242). Paris: Fayard.

Piccoli, G., Ahmad, R., & Ives, B. (2001). Web-based virtual learning environments: A research framework and a preliminary assessment of effectiveness in basic it skills training. *MIS Quarterly, 25*(4), 401-426.

Picht, G. (1991). Georg Picht: Die Dimension der Verantwortung. In M. Sänger (Ed.), *Arbeitstexte für den Unterricht: Verantwortung* (pp. 28-32). Stuttgart: Reclam.

Pies, I. (2001). Können Unternehmen Verantwortung tragen? Ein ökonomisches Kooperationsangebot an die Philosophische Ethik. In J. Wieland (Ed.), *Die moralische Verantwortung kollektiver Akteure* (pp. 171-199). Heidelberg: Physica-Verlag.

Pietschmann, P. (1992). Zusammenschau, Reflexion und Interpretation. In K. Giel & R. Breuninger (Eds.), *Risiko—Bausteine zur Philosophie—Band 6 interdisziplinäre Schriftenreihe des Humboldt-Studienzentrums Universität Ulm.* Ulm: Humboldt-Studienzentrums Universität Ulm.

Pitt, L. (1999). Strategy in the Digital Age—five new forces. In F. Liebl (Ed.), *E-conomy—Management und Ökonomie in digitalen Kontexten* (pp. 117-124). Marburg: Metropolis Verlag.

Pius XII. (1987). Pius XII: Die Schuldvergeltung als metaphysisches Strafziel. In N. Hoerster (Ed.), *Recht und Moral—Texte zur Rechtsphilosophie* (pp. 218-226). Stuttgart: Reclam.

Popper, K.R. (1992). *Die offene Gesellschaft und ihre Feinde* (parts I and II). München et al.: JCB Mohr.

Posner, R.A. (1995). An economic theory of privacy. In D.G. Johnson & H. Nissenbaum (Eds.), *Computers, Ethics & Social Values* (pp. 358-366). Upper Saddle River, NJ: Prentice-Hall.

Postman, N. (1992). *Technopoly—The Surrender of Culture to Technology.* New York: Vintage Books.

Preuss, L. (1999). Ethical theory in German business ethics research. *Journal of Business Ethics, 18,* 407-419.

Priddat, B.P. (1998). *Moralischer Konsum—13 Lektionen über die Käuflichkeit.* Stuttgart Leipzig: Hirzel Verlag.

Priddat, B.P. (1996). Risiko, Ungewissheit und neues: Epistemologische Probleme ökonomischer Entscheidungsbildung. In G. Banse (Ed.), *Risikoforschung zwischenDdisziplinarität und Interdisziplinarität—von der illusion der Sicherheit zum Umgang mit Unsicherheit.* Berlin: Edition Sigma Rainer Bohn Verlag.

Priddat, B.P. (1994). *Ökonomische Knappheit und moralischer Überschuß: Theoretische Essays zum Verhältnis von Ökonomie und Ethik.* Hamburg: Steuer und Wirtschaftsverlag.

Rachels, J. (1997). Tuer et laisser mourir de faim. In M. Neuberg (Ed.), *La responsabilité—questions philosophiques* (pp. 195-214). Paris: Presses Universitaires de France. Original: Rachels, J. (1979). Killing and starving to death. *Philosophy, 54.*

Rachels, J. (1995). Why privacy is important. In D.G. Johnson & H. Nissenbaum (Eds.), *Computers, Ethics & Social Values* (pp. 351-357). Upper Saddle River, NJ: Prentice-Hall.

Rapp, F. (1994). *Die Dynamik der modernen Welt.* Hamburg: Junius Verlag.

Rapp, F. (1991). Die moderne Technik im Konflikt zwischen Entfaltung und Beschränkung. *Technikverantwortung. Güterabwägung— Risikobewertung—Verhaltenskodizes.* Frankfurt, New York: Campus.

Rayner, S. (1993). Risikowahrnehmung, Technologieakzeptanz und institutionelle Kultur: Fallstudien für einige neue Definitionen. In R. Bayerische (Ed.), *Risiko ist ein Konstrukt. Wahrnehmungen zur Risikowahrnehmung* (pp. 213-244). München: Knesebeck,

Renn, O. (1996). Diskurs als leeres Gefäss. *Ethik und Sozialwissenschaften, 7*(2/3).

Richardson, H.S. (1999). Institutionally divided moral responsibility. In E.F. Paul, F.D. Miller, & J. Paul (Eds.), *Responsibility* (pp. 218-249). Cambridge et al.: Cambridge University Press.

Ricoeur, P. (1995a). Sanction, réhabilitation, pardon. In P. Ricoeur (Ed.), *Le juste.* Paris: Editions Esprit.

Ricoeur, P. (1995b). Avant-propos (Le Juste). In P. Ricoeur (Ed.), *Le juste.* Paris: Editions Esprit.

Ricoeur, P. (1995c). Le concept de responsabilité—essai d'analyse sémantique. In P. Ricoeur (Ed.), *Le juste.* Paris: Editions Esprit.

Ricoeur, P. (1994). Entretien avec Paul Ricoeur. In J.-C. Aeschlimann (Ed.), *Ethique et responsabilité—Paul Ricoeur* (pp. 11-34). Boudry-Neuchâtel: Editions de la Baconnière.

Ricoeur, P. (1991a). *Lectures 1—autour du politique.* Paris: Edition du Seuil.

Ricoeur, P. (1991b). Postface au temps de la responsabilité. In P. Ricoeur (Ed.), *Lectures 1—autour du politique* (pp. 270-293). Paris: Edition du Seuil.

Ricoeur, P. (1991c). La "philosophe politique" d'Eric Weil. In P. Ricoeur (Ed.), *Lectures 1—autour du politique* (pp. 95-114). Paris: Edition du Seuil.

Ricoeur, P. (1990a). *Soi-même comme un autre.* Paris: Edition du Seuil.

Ricoeur, P. (1990b). Ethique et morale. In P. Ricoeur (Ed.), *Lectures 1— autour du politique* (pp. 256-269). Paris: Edition du Seuil.

Ricoeur, P. (1988). Le cercle de la démonstration. In P. Ricoeur (Ed.), *Lectures 1—autour du politique* (pp. 216-230). Paris: Edition du Seuil.

Riedl, R. (2001). Die Folgen des Ursachendenkens. In P. Watzlawik (Ed.), *Die erfundene Wirklichkeit* (13th edition; pp. 67-90). München, Zürich: Piper.

Robison, W.L. (2000). Privacy and appropriation of identity. In G. Collste (Ed.), *Ethics in the Age of Information Technology* (pp. 70-86). Linköping: Centre for Applied Ethics.

Rogerson, S. (1998). *Ethical Aspects of Information Technology—Issues for Senior Executives*. London: Institute of Business Ethics.

Rohbeck, J. (1993). *Technologische Urteilskraft. Zu einer Ethik technischen Handelns*. Frankfurt: Suhrkamp.

Rolf, A. (1998). *Grundlagen der Organisations—und Wirtschaftsinformatik*. Berlin et al: Springer Verlag.

Ropohl, G. (1996). *Ethik und technikbewertung*. Frankfurt: Suhrkamp.

Ropohl, G. (1994a). Ein paar Gewissheiten unter Unsicherheit. *Ethik und Sozialwissenschaften, 5*(1), 185ff.

Ropohl, G. (1994b). Das Risiko im Prinzip Cerantwortung. *Ethik und sozialwissenschaften, 5*(1), 110ff.

Ropohl, G. (1991). Ob man die Ambivalenz des technischen Fortschritts mit einer neuen Ethik meistern kann? In H. Lenk & M. Maring (Eds.), *Technikverantwortung. Güterabwägung—Risikobewertung— Verhaltenskodizes*. Frankfurt, New York: Campus.

Ropohl, G. (1987). Neue Wege, die Technik zu verantworten. In H. Lenk & G. Ropohl (Eds.), *Technik und Ethik* (pp. 149-176). Stuttgart: Reclam.

Rorty, R. (1994). *Hoffnung statt Erkenntnis*. Wien: Passagen Verlag.

Rotenberg, M. (1998). Communications privacy: Implications for network design. In R.N. Stichler & R. Hauptman (Eds.), *Ethics, Information and Technology: Readings* (pp. 152-168). Jefferson, NC: MacFarland & Company.

Rotenberg, M. (1995). Computer virus legislation. In D.G. Johnson & H. Nissenbaum (Eds.), *Computers, Ethics & Social Values* (pp. 135-147). Upper Saddle River, NJ: Prentice-Hall.

Rötzer, F. (1998). Eigenverantwortung in komplexen Systemen und als komplexes System. In B. Neubauer (Ed.), *Eigenverantwortung: Positionen und Perspektiven*. Waake: Licet Verlag.

Rule, J.B. et al. (1995). Preserving individual autonomy in a informationoriented society. In D.G. Johnson & H. Nissenbaum (Eds.), *Computers, Ethics & Social Values* (pp. 314-332). Upper Saddle River, NJ: Prentice-Hall.

Russ, J. (1995). *La pensée éthique contemporaine* (2nd edition). Paris: Presses Universitaires de France.

Rustemeyer, D. (2001). Enttäuschende Theorie. *Zeitschrift für pädagogische Historiographie, 7,* 106-115.

Sachsse, H. (1972). *Technik und Verantwortung. Probleme der Ethik im technischen Zeitalter.* Freiburg: Publisher.

Sänger, M. (ed.). (1991). *Arbeitstexte für den Unterricht: Verantwortung.* Stuttgart: Reclam.

Sartre, J.-P. (1997). Choix, liberté et responsabilité. In M. Neuberg (Ed.), *La responsabilité—questions philosophiques* (pp. 103-108). Paris: Presses Universitaires de France. Original: Sartre, J.P. (1976[1943]). *Extraits de l'être et le néant* (pp. 536-537 and 612-615). Paris, Gallimard.

Scarbrough, H. (1998). Linking strategy and IT-based innovation: The importance of the "management of expertise." In R.D. Galliers & W.R.J. Baets (Eds.), *Information Technology and Organizational Transformation: Innovation for the 21st Century* (pp. 19-36). Chichester et al.: John Wiley & Sons.

Schalk, F. (ed.). (1995). *Französische Moralisten.* Zürich: Diogenes.

Scheuch, E. (1990). Ethische Probleme als Forschungsartefakte. *Ethik und Sozialwissenschaften, 1*(1), 91.

Schiller, D. (1999). *Digital Capitalism: Networking the Global Market System.* Cambridge (MA), London: MIT Press.

Schlick, M. (1930). Quand sommes-nous responsable? In M. Neuberg (Ed.), *La responsabilité—questions philosophiques* (pp. 27-38). Paris: Presses Universitaires de France.

Schmidt, H. (1996). Technikphilosophie exemplarisch: Das Auto. In A. Gethmann-Siefert (Ed.), *Wissenschaft und Technik als Gegenstand philosophischer Reflexion* (pp. 145-159). Hagen: FernUniversität Hagen.

Schmidt, H. (1992). Verantwortung im technischen Zeitalter. *Zeitschrift für Didaktik der Philosophie, 14,* 159-173.

Schmidtz, D. (1998). Taking responsibility. In D. Schmidtz & R. Goodin (Eds.), *Social Welfare and Individual Responsibility.* Cambridge, New York: Cambridge University Press.

Schulman, M. (2000). Littlebrother is watching you. In R.M. Baird, R. Ramsower, & S.E. Rosenbaum (Eds.), *Cyberethics—Social and Moral Issues in the Computer Age* (pp. 155-161). New York: Prometheus Books.

Schwartländer, J. (1991). Johannes Schwartländer: Die Bedeutung und Geschichte des Verantwortungsbegriffs. In M. Sänger (Ed.), *Arbeitstexte für den Unterricht: Verantwortung* (pp. 17-22). Stuttgart: Reclam.

Schwartz, P., & Gibb, B. (1999). *When Good Companies Do Bad Things: Responsibility and Risk in an Age of Globalization.* New York et al.: John Wiley & Sons.

Schweitzer, A. (1991). Albert Schweitzer: Ehrfurcht vor dem Leben. In M. Sänger (Ed.), *Arbeitstexte für den Unterricht: Verantwortung* (pp. 118-122). Stuttgart: Reclam.

Seebass, G. (2001). Kollektive Verantwortung und individuelle Verhaltenskontrolle. In J. Wieland (Ed.), *Die moralische Verantwortung kollektiver Akteure* (pp. 79-99). Heidelberg: Physica-Verlag.

Severson, R.J. (1997). *The Principles of Information Ethics.* Armonk (NY), London: M.E. Sharpe.

Shattuck, J. (1995). Computer matching is a serious threat to individual rights. In D.G. Johnson & H. Nissenbaum (Eds.), *Computers, Ethics & Social Values* (pp. 305-310). Upper Saddle River, NJ: Prentice-Hall.

Sherman, N. (1999): Taking Responsibility for our Emotions. In E.F. Paul, F.D. Miller, & J. Paul (Eds.), *Responsibility* (pp. 294-323). Cambridge et al.: Cambridge University Press.

Sinn, H., & Zimmerli, W.C. (1986). Ist die friedliche Nutzung der Kernenergie moralisch Verantwortbar? *VDI-Dokumentation zu Tschernobyl. Beilage der VDI-Nachrichten, 40*(46), 32-37.

Sipior, J.C., & Ward, B.T. (1995). The ethical and legal quandary of email privacy. *Communications of the ACM, 38*(12), 48-54.

Smiers, J. (2001). La propriété intellectuelle, c'est ie vol! *Le Monde Diplomatique, 570*(Septembre), 3.

Smith, B.C. (1995). Limits of correctness in computers. In D.G. Johnson & H. Nissenbaum (Eds.), *Computers, Ethics & Social Values* (pp. 456-469). Upper Saddle River, NJ: Prentice-Hall.

Snapper, J.W. (1995). Intellectual property protections for computer software. In D.G. Johnson & H. Nissenbaum (Eds.), *Computers, Ethics & Social Values* (pp. 181-190). Upper Saddle River, NJ: Prentice-Hall.

Spaemann, R. (1980). Technische Eingriffe in die Natur als Problem der politischen Ethik. In D. Birnbacher (Ed.), *Ökologie und Ethik* (p. 180ff). Stuttgart: Reclam.

Spaemann, R. (1975). Nebenwirkungen als moralisches Problem. *Philosophisches Jahrbuch, 82,* 323-335.

Spinello, R. (1997). *Case Studies in Information and Computer Ethics.* Upper Saddle River, NJ: Prentice-Hall.

Staddon, J. (1999). On responsibility in science and law. In E.F. Paul, F.D. Miller, & J. Paul (Eds.), *Responsibility* (pp. 146-174). Cambridge et al.: Cambridge University Press.

Stahl, B.C. (2002a). Ethical issues in e-teaching—a theoretical framework. In G. King et al. (Eds.), *Proceedings of INSPIRE VII, Quality in Learning and Delivery Techniques* (March 25-27, pp. 135-148), Limerick, Ireland. The British Computer Society.

Stahl, B.C. (2002b). Information technology, responsibility, and anthropology. In *Proceedings of the 35th Annual Hawaii International Conference on Systems Sciences,* Hawaii (January 7-10).

Stahl, B.C. (2001a). Constructing a brave new IT-world: Will the computer finally become a subject of responsibility? In R. Hackney & D. Dunn (Eds.), *Constructing IS Futures—11th Annual BIT 2001 Conference,* Manchester, UK (October 30-31, 2001).

Stahl, B.C. (2001b). Democracy, responsibility, and information technology. In D. Remenyi & F. Bannister (Eds.), *Proceedings of the European Conference on e-Government* (September 27-28, pp. 429-439), Trinity College, Dublin.

Stahl, B.C. (2001c). Responsibility in the interconnected economy. *Business Ethics: A European Review, 10*(3), 213-222.

Stahl, B.C. (2001d). Who is responsible for globalisation? Business ethics in a modern society. *Estonian Business School Review No. 12* (pp. 19-26). Tallinn: EBS.

Stahl, B.C. (2000). Das kollektive subjekt der verantwortung. *Zeitschrift für Wirtschafts—und Unternehmensethik, 1/2,* 225-236. City: Rainer Hampp Verlag.

Stallman, R. (1995). Why software should be free. In D.G. Johnson & H. Nissenbaum (Eds.), *Computers, Ethics & Social Values* (pp. 190-200). Upper Saddle River, NJ: Prentice-Hall.

Stallman, R. (1995b). Are computer property rights absolute? In D.G. Johnson & H. Nissenbaum (Eds.), *Computers, Ethics & Social Values* (pp. 115-119). Upper Saddle River, NJ: Prentice-Hall.

Starobinski, J. (1986). *Montaigne—Denken und Existenz.* Darmstadt: Wissenschaftliche Buchgesellschaft.

Stead, B.A., & Glibert, J. (2001). Ethical issues in electronic commerce. *Journal of Business Ethics, 34,* 75-85.

Steinmann, H., & Löhr, A. (1994). *Grundlagen der Unternehmensethik* (2nd edition). Stuttgart: Schäffer Poeschel.

Steward, I. (1997). Mathematische Unterhaltungen. *Spektrum der Wissenschaft, 7,* 8.

Stichler, R.N. (1998). Ethics in the information market. In R.N. Stichler & R. Hauptman (Eds.), *Ethics, Information and Technology: Readings* (pp. 169-183). Jefferson, NC: MacFarland & Company.

Stocker, M. (1999). Responsibility and the abuse excuse. In E.F. Paul, F.D. Miller, & J. Paul (Eds.), *Responsibility* (pp. 175-200). Cambridge et al.: Cambridge University Press.

Straub, D.W., & Collins, R.W. (1990). Key information liability issues facing managers: Software piracy, proprietary databases, and individual rights to privacy. *MIS Quarterly, 14,* 143-156.

Strawson, P.F. (1997). Liberté et ressentiment. In M. Neuberg (Ed.), *La responsabilité—questions philosophiques* (pp. 109-140). Paris: Presses Universitaires de France.

Ströker, E. (1996). Verantwortungsethik: Was meint sie, was fordert sie, und was könnte sie leisten in unserer technischen Welt. In A. Gethmann-Siefert (Ed.), *Wissenschaft und Technik als Gegenstand philosophischer Reflexion* (pp. 14-34). Hagen: FernUniversität Hagen.

Summer, L. (1998). *Der unternehmensethische Begriff der "Verantwortung": Eine Grundlegung im Anschluß an Jonas, Kant und Habermas.* Wiesbaden: Deutscher Universitätsverlag.

Tavani, H. (2000). Privacy and security. In D. Langford (Ed.), *Internet Ethics* (pp. 65-89). London: McMillan.

Taylor, C. (1995). *Negative Freiheit? Zur Kritik des Neuzeitlichen individualismus* (2nd edition). Frankfurt: Suhrkamp.

Thompson, P.B. (1985). Risking or being willing: Hamlet and the DC-10. *The Journal of Value Inquiry, 19,* 301-310.

Tribe, L.H. (1980). Was spricht gegen Plastikbäume? In D. Birnbacher (Ed.), *Ökologie und Ethik* (p. 9ff). Stuttgart: Reclam.

Trigeaud, J.-M. (1999). *L'homme coupable—critique d'une philosophie de la responsabilité.* Bordeaux: Editions Bière.

Tugendhat, E. (1990a). Das Euthanasieproblem und die Redefreiheit. In E. Tugendhat (Ed.), *Ethik und Politik.* Frankfurt.

Tugendhat, E. (1990b). Die Hilflosigkeit der Philosophie angesichts der moralischen Herausforderungen unserer Zeit. *Information Philosophie, 2,* 5-15.

Tugendhat, E. (1984). *Probleme der Ethik.* Stuttgart: Reclam.

Turner, J. (1998). The role of information techology in organizational transformation. In R.D. Galliers & W.R.J. Baets (Eds.), *Information Technology and Organizational Transformation: Innovation for the 21st Century* (pp. 245-260). Chichester et al.: John Wiley & Sons.

Ulrich, P. (1998). *Wofür sind unternehmen verantwortlich?* St. Gallen: Institut für Wirtschaftsethik, Uni St. Gallen.

Ulrich, P. (1997). *Integrative Wirtschaftsethik—Grundlagen einer lebensdienlichen Ökonomie.* Bern, Stuttgart, Wien: Haupt.

Ulrich, W. (2001). A philosophical staircase for information systems definition, design, and development. *Journal of Information Technology Theory and Application, 3*(3), 55-84.

van Luijk, H. (1990). Les trois faces de la responsabilité. *Entreprise, la vague éthique* (pp. 40-48), Revue Project No 224.

Vanberg, V. (1990). Die Grenzen von Verantwortung und die Bedeutung von Regeln. *Ethik und Sozialwissenschaften, 1*(1), 93.

van den Daele, W. (1993). Hintergrund der Wahrnehmung von Risiken der Gentechnik: Naturkonzepte und Risikosemantik. In R. Bayerische (Ed.), Risiko ist ein Konstrukt. Wahrnehmungen zur Risikowahrnehmung (pp. 169-190). München: Knesebeck.

van den Hoven, M.J. (1999). Privacy or informational injustice? In L.J. Pourciau (Ed.), *Ethics and Electronic Information in the 21st Century* (pp. 139-150). West Lafayette, IN: Purdue University Press.

Velasquez, M. (1998). *Business Ethics: Concepts and Cases* (4th edition). Upper Saddle River, NJ: Prentice-Hall.

Velasquez, M. (1991). Why corporations are not morally responsible for anything they do. In L. May & S. Hoffman (Eds.), *Collective Responsibility: Five Decades of Debate in Theoretical and Applied Ethics* (pp. 111-131). Savage, MD: Rowman & Littlefield.

Voland, E. (1998). Verantwortlichkeit—Legitimationsprobleme einer gesellschaftlichen Notwendigkeit. In B. Neubauer (Ed.), *Eigenverantwortung: Positionen und Perspektiven.* Waake: Licet Verlag.

von Cube, F. (1995). *Gefährliche Sicherheit—die Verhaltensbiologie des Risikos.* Stuttgart, Leipzig: S. Hirzel.

von Weizsäcker, C.C. (1999). Globalisierung: Garantie für Freiheit und Wohlstand oder Ende der Politik und Abschied vom Staat? Aus ökonomischer Sicht. In H. Von Mangold & C.C. von Weizsäcker (Eds),

Globalisierung—Bedeutung für Staat und Wirtschaft (pp. 9-51). Köln: Wirtschaftsverlag Bachem.

von Weizsäcker, C.F. (1991). Moralische Verantwortung in der Wissenschaft. In H. Lenk (Ed.), *Wissenschaft und Ethik* (pp. 95-98). Stuttgart: Reclam.

von Weizsäcker, C.F. (1964). *Geschichte der Natur.* Göttingen.

Vossenkuhl, W. (1991). Moralische und rechtliche Verantwortung. In M. Sänger (Ed.), *Arbeitstexte für den Unterricht: Verantwortung* (pp. 48-53). Stuttgart: Reclam.

Wallace, R.J. (1996). *Responsibility and the Moral Sentiment.* Cambridge (MA), London: Harvard University Press.

Walther, C. (1992). *Ethik und Technik Grundfragen—Meinungen—Kontroversen.* Berlin, New York: de Gruyter Studienbuch.

Walzer, M. (1994). *Sphären der Gerechtigkeit. Ein Plädoyer für Pluralität und Gleichheit.* Frankfurt, New York: Campus Verlag.

Ward, J., & Peppard, J. (1996). Reconciling the IT/business relationship: A troubled marriage in need of guidance. *Journal of Strategic Information Systems, 5,* 37-65.

Warren, S.D., & Brandeis, L.D. (1890). The right to privacy. *Harvard Law Review, 5,* 193-220.

Watzlawik, P. (ed.), *Die erfundene Wirklichkeit* (13th edition). München, Zürich: Piper.

Watzlawik, P. (2001b). Selbsterfüllende Prophezeiungen. In P. Watzlawik (Ed.), *Die erfundene Wirklichkeit* (13th edition, pp. 91-110). München, Zürich: Piper.

Weber, M. (1992). *Politik als Beruf.* Stuttgart: Reclam.

Weckert, J., & Adeney, D. (1997). *Computer and Information Ethics.* Westport (CT), London: Greenwood Press.

Wehowsky, S. (1999). *Über Verantwortung—von der Kunst seinem Gewissen zu Folgen.* München: C.H. Beck, becksche Reihe 1302.

Weil, É. (1998/1960). *Philosophie morale* (5th edition). Paris: Librairie Philosophique J. Vrin.

Weisband, S.P., & Reining, B.A. (1995). Managing user perceptions of email privacy. *Communications of the ACM, 38*(12), 40-47.

Weizenbaum, J. (1995). On the impact of the computer on society. In D.G. Johnson & H. Nissenbaum (Eds.), *Computers, Ethics & Social Values* (pp. 549-559). Upper Saddle River, NJ: Prentice-Hall.

Weizenbaum, J. (1976). *Computer power and human reason.* San Francisco: W.H. Freeman and Company.

Wellmer, A. (1986). *Ethik und Dialog: Elemente des moralischen Urteils bei Kant und in der Diskursethik.* Frankfurt: Suhrkamp Verlag.

Welty, B., & Becerra-Fernandez, I. (2001). Managing trust and commitment in collaborative supply chain relationships. *Communications of the ACM, 44*(6), 67-73.

Werhane, P. (1985). *Persons, Rights, and Corporations.* Englewood Cliffs, NJ: Prentice-Hall.

Wiedemann, P.M. (1993). Tabu, Sünde, Risiko: Veränderungen der gesellschaftlichen Wahrnehmung von Gefährdungen. In R. Bayerische (Ed.), Risiko ist ein Konstrukt. Wahrnehmungen zur Risikowahrnehmung (pp. 43-68). München: Knesebeck.

Wieland, J. (2001a). Die Tugend Kollektiver Akteure. In J. Wieland, Josef (Ed.), *Die moralische Verantwortung kollektiver Akteure* (pp. 22-40). Heidelberg: Physica-Verlag.

Wieland, J. (2001b). eine Theorie der Governanceethik. *Zeitschrift für Wirtschafts—und Unternehmensethik, 2*(1), 8-33.

Wieland, J. (1999). *Die Ethik der Governance.* Marburg: Metropolis.

Wiesenthal, H. (1990). *Unsicherheit und multiple-self-identität: Eine Spekulation über die Voraussetzungen strategischen Handelns.* Köln: MPIFG Discussion Paper 90/2.

Wild, W. (1991). Dürfen wir heute noch neugierig sein? In H. Lenk & M. Maring (Eds.), *Technikverantwortung. Güterabwägung— Risikobewertung—Verhaltenskodizes.* Frankfurt, New York: Campus.

Wunenburger, J.-J. (1993). *Questions d'éthique* (1st edition). Paris: Presses Universitaires de France.

Wutenow, R.-R. (1976). Selbsterfahrung und Skepsis—die >Essais< von Michel de Montaigne. In M. Montaigne, *Essais* (edited by Ralph-Rainer Wuthenow). Frankfurt: Insel Verlag.

Yoon, S.-H. (1996). Power online: A post-structuralist perspective on computer-mediated communication. In C. Ess (Ed.), *Philosophical perspectives on Computer-Mediated Communication* (pp. 171-196). Albany, NY: State University of New York Press.

Zerdick, A. et al. (2001). *European Communication Councel report: Die Internet-ökonomie: Strategien für die digitale wirtschaft* (3rd edition). Berlin, Heidelberg: Springer.

Zimmerli, W.C. (1994a). Der neueste Angriff auf das Individuum. *Ethik und Sozialwissenschaften, 5*(1), 182.

Zimmerli, W.C. (1994b). Unternehmenskultur—neues Denken in alten Begriffen. Verantwortung, Technologie und Wirtschaft an der Schwelle zum dritten

Jahrtausend. In W.C. Zimmerli & V.M. Brennecke (Eds.), *Technikverantwortung in der Unternehmenskultur—von theoretischen Konzepten zur Praktischen Umsetzung.* Stuttgart: Schäffer-Poeschel.

Zimmerli, W.C. (1991). Verantwortung des Individuums—Basis einer Ethik von Technik und Wirtschaft. In H. Lenk & M. Maring (Eds.), *Technikverantwortung. Güterabwägung—Risikobewertung— Verhaltenskodizes.* Frankfurt, New York.

Zimmerli, W.C. (1987). Wandelt sich die Verantwortung mit dem technischen Wandel? In H. Lenk & G. Ropohl (Eds.), *Technik und Ethik* (pp. 92-111). Stuttgart: Reclam.

Zimmerli, W.C., & Brennecke, V.M. (eds.). (1994). *Technikverantwortung in der Unternehmenskultur—von theoretischen Konzepten zur praktischen Umsetzung.* Stuttgart: Schäffer-Poeschel.

Endnotes

[1]   The distinction of morality (moral) and ethics (ethik) as practice and theory of moral dealings is a defining feature of German moral philosophy. However, there is a problem with the consistency of the use of these two notions. The distinction, as we just introduced it, can be found in many works of modern thinkers of practical philosophy. Unfortunately the use of the terms is ambiguous, and neither Kant nor Habermas use them exactly in the way just explained. In the case of Habermas, the terms even have an inverse meaning, with moral (morality) standing for the universal ethical considerations. The different concepts behind the notions are nevertheless visible, and we will stick to the distinctions because it is widely spread in German philosophy today. It also facilitates the discussion of the value of the notion of responsibility later on.

[2]   Kant's philosophy is, of course, more complex than it appears here. The maxim is not easy to assign either to morality or to ethics, since it has a practical side but also is a theoretical construct. For our purposes it will suffice, however, to demonstrate that the distinction between ethics and morality exists since this distinction leads to problems, which the notion of responsibility is to overcome.

[3]   For a more detailed discussion of the moralists' scepticism of reason, see Rustemeyer (2001).

⁴ The "other" (originally *l'autre, l'Autre, autrui*) is in many cases hard to translate, as it can refer to the other person who is opposite me, the other as person but in an abstract way, and also the other as the genuinely unknown, as for example death in the writing of Levinas (1983).

⁵ The good Kantian would of course argue that Kant demonstrated that suicide is unethical because it is self-contradictory. The autonomous subject cannot will its own non-existence without contradicting itself. However, it is not clear whether the same argument applies to the mere chance of being killed that is part of the risks we are talking about. If we wanted to rule this out on Kantian grounds, then this would lead to the unconvincing result that the Kantian could no longer go shopping because he might be run over by a car.

⁶ Whether they have to maximise profits is a different question to which we will return later on.

⁷ Foucault (1975) gives a good overview of the change in the perception of punishment from a medieval spectacle with the purpose of revenging the breach of the prince's sovereignty to the modern perception of punishment as socially useful, aimed at rehabilitating the perpetrator and deterring future crimes.

⁸ We do not want to go into a discussion whether this argument falls into the trap of the naturalistic fallacy, that is to say whether it draws normative conclusions from factual statements. We would not necessarily deny that this is so, but think that the validity of the argument is not affected by it.

⁹ See, e.g., Neuberg, 1997, Part I; French, 1992, Chapter 4; Fischer, 1999; Wallace, 1996.

¹⁰ May (1992) argues that it is the solution to the problem of collective responsibility to hold people responsible for their attitudes. If someone has racist attitudes and lives in a society where racially motivated crimes occur, then that person would be considered responsible for the crimes even if he did not participate in the racist activities himself. While this is an interesting approach that might allow dealing with some of the most difficult problems of responsibility, it is not visible how this would lead to clear ascriptions and sanctions.

¹¹ Wieland (2001a, p. 23) points out that this argument is in fact tautological. The classical argument against collective responsibility does nothing more than define responsibility in individual terms and then show that a collective cannot fulfil it.

¹² Some staunch defenders of the field of artificial intelligence (AI) such as Brooks (2002) are convinced that we will be able to build computers that

become like humans, that eventually the limits between information systems and humans will vanish. But even outspoken critics of this approach—who think that computers as we know them are fundamentally unable to ever develop understanding or meaning, such as Dreyfus (1993)—are careful not to say that building self-conscious computers is impossible. This is a good indication of how unclear the notion of consciousness still is.

[13]   For a thorough discussion of responsibility, see Birnbacher (1988).

[14]   The analogous question in the case of scepticism would have been: Can we approve of the use of the term scepticism and its results from the point of view of a theory of scepticism? The answer in this case would have been no, or at least not without considerable explanation.

[15]   Reflective responsibility thus rules out an entire class of theories of responsibility. These are the theories that one is responsible for everything just because of one's being. The young Sartre is one example of an author propagating this kind of idea in relation with his existentialism. The phrase "I am responsible for everything" (*Je suis responsable de tout;* Sartre, 1997, p. 107) does not make sense in our sense of the word.

[16]   A related idea can be found in Donaldson and Dunfee's (1999) Integrative Social Contract Theory. There they try to show that efficiency is a hypernorm. That means that the efficient use of resources has a moral quality and that it is even invariant to cultural influences.

[17]   A good example for this problem and also for the difficulties of finding a convincing position is offered by Benbasat and Zmud (1999).

[18]   Even though we support the idea of the rational and intentional creation of institutions, this has to be taken with a grain of salt. One has to agree with Downy (1972, p. 72) when he says that "…some of our institutions can less properly be said to have been built up by judgment and decision than to have grown up by custom: we did not so much create them as find ourselves in possession of them." Just as there is a limit and a fundamental fallibility of responsibility, the same can be said for institutions.

[19]   For a more detailed discussion of this point, see Stahl (2001a).

[20]   For a more detailed discussion of the ethical impacts of IT on democracy, see Stahl (2001b).

[21]   For a more detailed discussion, see Stahl (2001c).

[22]   For a more complete overview of the impact IT has on the ethical aspect of democracy, see Stahl (2001b).

[23]   One sometimes finds references to a fourth claim, to understandability. For our purposes the three above claims are sufficient; since the fourth claim is not reflected in most of the literature, we will just leave it aside.

[24]   For a thorough philosophical critique of the idea of codes of ethics, see Ladd (1995).

Glossary

BIT
Business Information Technology

BPR
Business Process Reengineering/Redesign

CEO
Chief Executive Officer

CIO
Chief Information Officer

EU
European Union

GDSS
Group Decision Support Systems

ICT
Information and Communication Technology

IS
Information Systems

IT

Information Technology

WIPO

World Intellectual Property Organisation

WTO

World Trade Organisation

About the Author

Bernd Carsten Stahl (Dr. rer. pol., Dipl.-Wi.-Ing., M.A., D.E.A.) studied mechanical engineering, business, economics and philosophy in Hamburg, Hagen, Bordeaux and Witten. From 1987-1997 he was an officer of the German Armed Forces. From 2000-2003 he lectured in the Department of MIS and the German Department of University College Dublin, Ireland. Since 2003 he has been working as a senior lecturer in the Faculty of Computer Sciences and Engineering and as a research associate at the Centre for Computing and Social Responsibility of De Montfort University, Leicester, UK. His area of research consists of philosophical, more specifically of normative, questions arising from the use of information and communication technology. The emphasis in this area is on the notion of responsibility. He researches the application of such normative questions in economic organisations, but also education and governmental institutions. His second area of interest consists of epistemological questions in Information Systems research.

Index

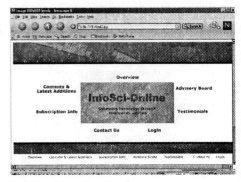